AF668338

BEYOND THE TRAPPINGS OF OFFICE

BEYOND THE TRAPPINGS OF OFFICE

A CIVIL SERVANT'S JOURNEY IN PUNJAB

RAJAN KASHYAP

NIYOGI
BOOKS

Published by
NIYOGI BOOKS
Block D, Building No. 77,
Okhla Industrial Area, Phase-I,
New Delhi-110 020, INDIA
Tel: 91-11-26816301, 26818960
Email: niyogibooks@gmail.com
Website: www.niyogibooksindia.com

Editor: Arkaprabha Biswas, Anwesha Panda
Design: Nadeem Ahmed
Cover Design: Disha Keshav

ISBN: 978-93-91125-58-5
Publication: 2023

Printed at Niyogi Offset Pvt. Ltd., New Delhi, India

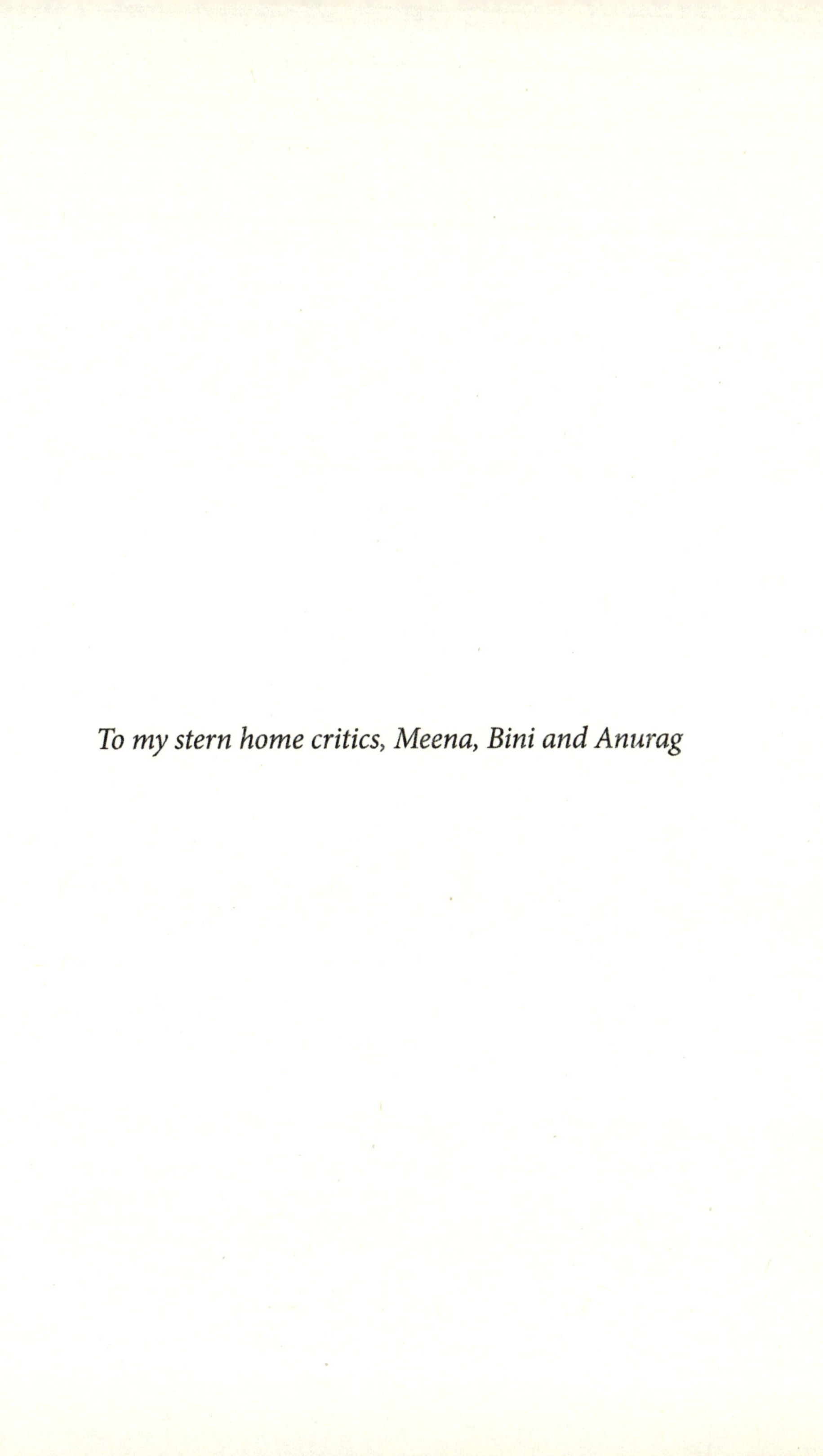

To my stern home critics, Meena, Bini and Anurag

CONTENTS

FOREWORD

'I like the evening in India', the Canadian film-maker James Cameron once wrote, 'the one magic moment when the sun balances on the rim of the world, and the hush descends, and ten thousand civil servants drift homewards on a river of bicycles, brooding on Lord Krishna and the cost of living.' I doubt if Rajan Kashyap ever drifted homewards on a bicycle—since he entered the civil service at a much higher level from the beginning—nor do I think that he was ever too concerned about the cost of living. But he did keep brooding, for years it seems: on life, on relationships, on rights and wrongs, on cares and concerns, on duty, responsibility and governance. And what we have here, in this absorbing, engagingly honest book, is a record of sorts of his broodings. With all his yesterdays walking alongside, he keeps recalling—page after page—how the scroll of his life kept unrolling itself and words written on it revealed themselves: some aglitter in gold, some smudged and stained, others impossible to read. From the very beginning, he picks us up and lets us into his world: from his growing up days when his grandfather worked for a Maharaja, through his long career in the administrative service spanning close to four decades, to the present when he can look back upon life, as if at the street below from a balcony—'gone are the intra-service and interstate rivalries, the race for coveted assignments, the currying of favour with the high and powerful... forgotten is the weight of hierarchy', in his own words—and manage the leisured world of doing good, and playing or managing tennis. But at no point in the telling does one get the feeling that he has broken his contract with the reader: the contract of telling the truth. The world that he inhabited was peopled with events and personalities, gentle concerns and hard challenges, but we can see that he weathered it all with an air of equanimity. Of a very large measure of balance.

The poet Dylan Thomas, speaking of the miscellany of life, talked of 'the eyes and secrets of the dreamers in the streets... the titbits and topsy-turvies, bobs and button-tops, bags and bones, ash and rind and moulted feathers of dreams....' that you have to deal with. If you look at it with care, the life of a civil servant, certainly in our land, and especially at the district level, where the common man, the *riyaaya*, looks up to you for everything, does appear to be a bit like this. And to keep your head in the midst of all this, even when you become the highest-ranked bureaucrat in a state, is not the simplest thing in the world.

Rajan, whom I have had the pleasure of knowing for long, long years, tells it all—the trials and the tribulations, the highs and the lows—with wit and elegance. His warmth for people and places spreads like a leafy shade over everything, overriding all the papers and forms and red tape that form so much a part of the life of a bureaucrat. One sees this everywhere and when it comes to observation, one has only to turn to the vivid description of his visit to Lahore in the later days, to realize how sharp it is, and how humane. But somewhere in all this, one might also detect a vein of detachment, of *virakti* as it might be called. It is as if he is somehow able to withdraw from it all when he wishes. The poet Akbar Allahabadi wove this moving couplet in one of his *ghazals*:

Duniya mein hoon, duniya ka talab-gaar nahin hoon
Baazaar sey guzraa hoon, kharidaar nahin hoon

meaning, roughly:

'True, that I am of this world, and belong to it, but, truly, I seek nothing from it;
I walk through this bazaar every day, but no; buying anything is not on my mind.'

There is something very becalming in the thought.

B.N. Goswamy*
Chandigarh

*B.N. Goswamy, international authority on art history, is Professor Emeritus of Art History at Panjab University, Chandigarh, India. He is a recipient of the Padma Shri (1998) and Padma Bhushan (2008) from the President of India.

INTRODUCTION

In a memoir the writer uses a pen brush to colour the canvas with recall of the events of a lifetime. Related in this book are happenings within the walls of home and workplace, and also outside. Amusing or dramatic, I consider them memorable.

I have recounted a variety of sights and sounds that I encountered during my journey from childhood to the days as a student, as a professional in a position of authority and thereafter. The personages en route were both eminent and commonplace, but colourful nonetheless. I was fortunate to have been at the right spot and at the right time, to interact with diverse personalities, and observe their qualities of head and heart, not to mention their foibles and frailties. As a civil servant, I was perched to have an insider's view of the government and its affairs. The voyage, however, traversed a landscape beyond the pale of officialdom.

In most countries, the civil service is not commonly regarded as glamorous. Nor are civil servants expected, as part of their normal activities, to be involved in matters theatrical or sensational, let alone epochal. A young person searching for a career would scarcely find the handling of official files as exciting an engagement as, say, military service, or scientific pursuit. Nor do government officials aspire to great financial rewards, such as professionals in medicine, law or business might. Bureaucrats, in comparison, are modestly paid. Further, they are perceived usually as staid and faceless. They are expected to merge into the background, even as the political leaders they assist occupy space in the media. In some democracies, bureaucrats are derided as similar to the brushers of noblemen's clothes. Civil servants are even pilloried as hewers of red tape, who design elaborate government regulations that affect the public as well as individuals.

With all this, in India the civil servant is still viewed by the common man with some awe. After all, he has been selected after a rigorous competition from among hundreds of thousands of aspirants. Even if he is not paid as handsomely as his peers in the corporate sector, a bureaucrat is perceived to enjoy more power and authority over men and matters at a young age. The prestige enjoyed by the Indian Administrative Service (IAS) is a continuum of that vested in the erstwhile Indian Civil Service (ICS) that served as an effective instrument of governance—the steel frame of administration as it was called—by the colonial British before India became independent in 1947.

While travelling with me in an official car, my newly married daughter-in-law, herself a business executive, was thrilled when a luxurious Mercedes, belonging no doubt to a top businessman, deferentially gave right of way to our vehicle on the highway. What confounded her was the impact of an official flag, which fluttered atop my humble Ambassador car. It took a while for her to realise that in real life, the position of a civil servant is more complex that the visible emblems of authority suggested. In due course, she was startled to note the nature of tensions that pervade the functioning of government, and especially the need for those in public office to maintain equanimity in the face of frequent conflicts. She was struck with the myriad forms of individual interaction that a job like mine entailed. Some aspects of human nature in action are depicted in these pages.

During my earliest years I found myself akin to a spectator in a detached balcony to the drama of withering of a princely state, where my grandfather worked directly with the Maharaja. I could at that time vaguely perceive the glory of the princedom, and vicariously perceive the human faces behind the famed palace walls. The eclipse of the British crown meant that the Maharaja and his courtiers, including my grandfather, were reduced to commoners almost overnight. The book begins with a retrospective, through the eyes of a young boy, of officialdom in an anachronistic princely state. As a child I found myself concurrently in the milieu of two Indias, conflicting with and complementing each other as the country headed toward independence from British rule. On one side I was part of a large joint family, which was dependent on the goodwill of a benevolent ruler, who was himself propped up by a paramount foreign power. Juxtaposed with this opulence of a princely state was the austere habitat of my relatives on the maternal side in a primitive village. What was valued there was spiritual advancement and simple, traditional living. This side of the family included staunch nationalists in conflict with the Raj.

To the extent that my father was a police officer in his own right; in his person our family retained some semblance of the vanished authority that my grandfather had enjoyed. Even after the close of the Raj, I could watch some spit and polish attached to the uniformed police, which my father headed. The initial chapters describe adventures within an unusual pattern of education, at home in a desolate rural homestead, then in a Christian missionary institution, and later in the rough and tumble of an upcoming public school. The journey through school, college and university was a novel learning experience, which epitomised Mark Twain's refrain, 'I have not let my schooling interfere with my education.' The process of my learning was, perhaps, subtle.

The next stage of the journey, which entailed preparation for and entry into the civil service, was for me an exciting travail in its own right. Recalled from memory are the sights of a new university taking root in the new city of Chandigarh. A youthful existence, marked with harmless escapades, merged seamlessly into the two years of training as an officer of the government.

It was fascinating to be a part of the changing systems of governance in an emerging democracy. Especially lively were my initial years from the age of 24 onwards, where the office enjoined considerable responsibility along with its inbuilt authority. In these pages I have admitted to display of some kind of brashness in behaviour, which naturally ruffled feathers, even as the work itself was satisfying. Subsequently, in the offices of the state and central government, I could observe my peers and superiors in transparent pursuit of power and patronage, which are the factors commonly considered a yardstick for measuring success. At the risk of being labelled sanctimonious, I accept that I could not excel in the art of boss management.

An interregnum in the normal course of my professional career was a short return, a full academic term in fact, to the world of academics in one of the world's reputed centres of learning, the University of Cambridge in the United Kingdom. Acclimatising in a prestigious institution was painful and satisfying in equal measure. Shorn of the trappings and privileges attached to India's elite government service, I was a student again. The challenge now was to balance a household budget with limited resources, and to cope with the rigour of research. It seems unbelievable today that in terms of financial resources, my family, including my wife and two young children who had accompanied me abroad, would have been living at a level close to the poverty line, as I learnt to define it in economic jargon. To have managed to secure a gilt-edged degree was a reward in itself.

The civil service offered me a wide variety of assignments. As the Chief Executive of a gargantuan public undertaking, an important position at the heart of the process of transformation of the agricultural economy, I struggled with the twin obstacles of inefficiency and corruption. If success in the corporate world was limited, it was somewhat disheartening, while handling the government's finances, not to be able to balance the state budget. A dispassionate observer might stare in amazement at the spectacle of conflict between political expediency and pure economic sense. In a narrative like this, it was impossible for me not to drop names, ranging from important political figures at the national and regional level, to legends in social uplift like Mother Teresa. Inevitably, some lesser known personalities dot the pages. I hope I have been objective in depicting the innate stolidity and imperviousness of the bureaucracy in the context of its role in political and economic change.

After I had bid adieu to bureaucracy, there was an unexpected privilege of functioning as a judge for regulating the flow of information in a democratic state. I was bound to delineate the confrontation between the activists for information freedom and the custodians of official record, who tried to block it from public view. Demitting office after four decades at the desk was of course touched with some pangs of parting. Post retirement, there was plenty to do, and gainfully. I could indulge in my passion for sports, and also enjoy working for a worthy social cause in an NGO. This period provided a unique foray as a commoner into Pakistan, a country with an umbilical link with ours. The description of Lahore and Islamabad is less of a travelogue than an unravelling of bonds between two hostile neighbours.

Albert Einstein once commented, 'There are two ways to live your life. One is as though nothing is a miracle. The other is as though everything is a miracle.' Moving back and ahead in time, I think I fall in both categories of persons envisioned by the philosopher. I was probably an ordinary individual amidst events, both substantial and slight. With me, the miracle lay in being born in an exceptional family, and being shaped by myriad influences throughout life. One doesn't choose one's parents, teachers and friends. They are God sent.

In order to place in perspective the mode of governance as it emerged before free India's democracy took root, I studied the systems that developed and obtained in the erstwhile princely state of Kapurthala, where I was born, and where my father and grandfather had worked as civil servants.

These are the recollections of a person who found colour and excitement in the humdrum of life, beyond his vocational calling of scratching files on dusty tables.

Rajan Kashyap
Chandigarh

CRADLED IN THE RAJ

I was born in the small princely state of Kapurthala in the north of present-day India in the year 1943, four years before the country gained independence from British colonial rule. I understood at an early age that my father was a uniformed police officer. I can also vividly recall the image of my paternal grandfather, clad formally in a buttoned up *achhkan,*[1] and a light-coloured turban, leaving home punctually every day for his office in the palace of Maharaja Jagatjit Singh. In due course, I learnt that my grandfather had been endowed with the honorific title of Sardar, and also held the rank of an Honorary Colonel of the state army. Colonel Bharpur Singh (Kashyap) was the head of a large family—there were 11 brothers and a sister, my father being the eldest of the siblings, and the youngest brothers, my uncles, in fact, close to me in age. Three generations of that typical joint family would have greeted me as the first entrant of the fourth generation. My grandfather himself, a sprightly, athletic figure of 54 years, his own mother-in-law, my father aged 26 years, along with his

1 *Achkan:* a traditional long coat, considered as a formal outfit in India.

siblings, were all housed in separate sprawling, disorganised wings built around a large paved courtyard. This was Kashi Bhawan, my ancestral abode, named after my great grandfather Kashi Ram, who had served as a middle-level official, called *Khazanchi* or treasury officer, in the state of Kapurthala.

Our household would have been the envy of the town, for the sheer number of young active boys in a single family. In later years we would boast of a full cricket team of players drawn from the family's ranks to challenge the best one in town. As a teenager, I recall that some older boys mocked at the large size of the family, teasing me with the revelation that I myself was older in years than two of my father's youngest brothers. Notwithstanding, even the younger generation of the city was in some awe of the sporting prowess displayed by the Kashyap brothers, all of whom were gifted sportsmen. Sports came to the siblings as perhaps a genetic inheritance. Bharpur Singh had been a champion tennis player, having won the Punjab State Championship in the year 1920 in Lahore, which was considered as the premier national tennis tournament in those days. From memory some contemporaries recount the unabashed pride of the Maharaja when my grandfather, Bharpur Singh and his partner Nar Singh Das, both players sponsored by him, defeated the favoured top British pair of Dean and Atkinson before a vociferous crowd in Lahore. It was the first time in history that native Indians won a coveted crown of excellence in an elite sport.

During the days of the British Raj, a number of princes were avowed patrons of sports as well as of music and the arts. By nature taciturn, my grandfather recalled that his employment in the palace resulted from a chance encounter with Maharaja Jagatjit Singh. The prince was frequently seen in public, sometimes at official functions, and on other occasions during informal visits to educational institutions. On one impromptu visit to the local school, the Maharaja noticed a boy hitting an old tennis ball with a clumsy wooden club. The royal visitor was struck by the fluency with which the boy was striking the ball against the wall. The boy, Bharpur Singh, then aged 12 or 13 years, was summoned to the palace. Following that princely impulse, began two concurrent careers of Bharpur Singh. As a tennis player, his success earned some recognition for his employer, the princely state. The growing boy developed athletic skills under systematic patronage. Simultaneously the lad joined the prince's household as an employee with vaguely defined responsibilities. In performing his dual functions, Bharpur would obviously have displayed some promise—he rose in later years to work as a secretary to the Maharaja. The Maharaja was obviously pleased to observe that his young protégé was winning prestigious titles, thereby justifying the confidence reposed in him by his mentor. I traced from old records that Bharpur Singh of Kapurthala state of India had indeed played and won some matches at Wimbledon, London, in the All England Tennis Championships in the years 1921 and 1922, and also at the French Open event in Paris during the same years. By an error, some reports in Paris newspapers identified Bharpur Singh as a prince of an Indian state, instead of an employee sponsored by a Maharaja. The Maharaja indulgently allowed his protégé the borrowed feathers.

In today's setting, the career of Bharpur Singh and other state officials could appear to have proceeded on the whims of their mentor. During the Raj, the Maharaja exercised discretion in respect of some recruitment into the state's service, a form of authority inherited from his forefathers. Official documents[2] published by the state between the year 1860 and 1947 are unapologetic about how the prince selected young men from established families in the state, for education and studies, in due course to appoint the same persons in various positions in the government of the state. With respect to the retinue of the household, the prince could exercise a level of freedom. The British colonial masters seem to have acquiesced in this method of recruitment, even as there were institutional safeguards against arbitrary decision-making.

An Unusual Liaison

As I grew up, I was to learn about the circumstances of the marriage of my parents in the year 1942. The episode throws some light on social interaction between families of officials

---

2 These include official Annual Administrative Reports from 1878 to 1947, *The Imperial Gazetteer of India*, 1908 and *Gazetteer of the State of Kapurthala* 1928, *Accounts Code, Kapurthala State* 1937.

working for a princely state and those outside the state, some of whom were participants in the growing struggle against colonial rule. The nuptial liaison was considered not only unusual; from the outset some expected it would fail. The reason was that despite being arranged with mutual consent of the two families, as many marriages still are in India, it brought together a couple with conflicting social, cultural and political views. On one side was my father, then an Assistant Superintendent of Police, a dashing young man of 25 years, brought up in the tradition of the Raj, in a society given to good living, duty bound to uphold the establishment. As a state employee, the police officer was committed to the colonial Government of India in Delhi, backed by a distant London.

On the other hand was my mother, who hailed from a family of freedom fighters, pitted conspicuously against a detested foreign rule. Members of my mother's family had participated in the struggle for freedom organised by well-known leaders. Some had spent time in jail for passive protest inspired by Mahatma Gandhi. As directed by the organised opposition of the nationalists, they stood for *Swaraj* (self-rule) and *Swadeshi* (use of local produce) in preference to British made goods. When I was old enough to understand such matters my mother told me that, when she was as yet a schoolgirl, members of her family had symbolically set fire to cloth imported from England. This must have been around the year 1930, when the freedom movement directed the boycott of foreign goods. Her family hailed from Ludhiana, then a part of British India. Strict vegetarians by conviction, they were fired by nationalist fervour. Her uncle (mother's brother) had been in prison as an activist in the movement for civil disobedience. While in jail, he had declined privileges offered to protesters who were university graduates, preferring to be treated like one of his commoner comrades. With open contempt they dubbed every official in a princely state as a 'toady', a person who had sold his conscience to the British rulers for material gain. Incidentally, the family in Kapurthala flaunted the latest in fashion, their apparel imported from abroad, much to the chagrin of the new bride, my mother.

In Kapurthala it seemed almost heretical that a distinguished family, loyal to the state establishment, should link with an upstart professed nationalist clan, directly inimical to colonial rule. By a quirk of fate, any clash of ideologies, which had appeared imminent, was thankfully averted. It transpired that both my mother and my grandmother (my father's mother) followed the same spiritual faith, which enjoined vegetarianism and abstinence from alcohol, and a form of meditation. My father was often required to drive the two women to their spiritual centre, which was located in Beas, in the district of Amritsar, falling in British India. The spiritual colony was situated just 17 miles away from Kapurthala town. Perforce having to attend some discourses at Beas, the young police officer was attracted by the tenets of the faith, and decided suddenly to join his wife and mother as a follower. My mother maintained a diary, where she recorded noteworthy events in her life. From this record I was to discover, years after both my parents died, that my father had vowed to abjure alcohol, meat and eggs immediately after his marriage. Thus, it was that a common spiritual link had been forged, which bound together my parents for life. A compromise ensued. No debate of political nature took place in the household. It was accepted that as a disciplined police officer, my father had to be loyal to the State and the Crown. This direction was cheerfully accepted by both the partners. In any case the winds of change were soon, in five years' time to be exact, to blow away the Raj, to usher in a free and democratic India. And so compromise cemented the relationship between my parents. A spiritual mooring, which enjoined simple and honest living, would have conditioned my father's long career of 34 years as a police officer. The spiritual link proved to be permanent. After retirement from service, he settled in the colony, to spend the remaining 35 years of his life, cheerfully engaged in honorary social activity.

Career-wise, my father rose to the very highest rank of chief of police to serve as the Inspector General in two different states of India, Himachal Pradesh in the north and Manipur in the extreme east. As he was a uniformed police officer, I myself had a ring-side view of the functioning of the police in India. Indeed, for about 10 years, 1965–1975, my father and I were contemporary officials working in different states, he at a top position in the Indian Police Service, and I at a junior rank in the Indian Administrative Service.

I spent my earliest years in Kapurthala. Later in life—from 1965 to 2003, to be exact—I was a civil servant at various levels in the state of Punjab, India. I was thus witness to the changing façade of administration two decades after princely rule had ended. Being but an infant in 1947, the year of Indian independence, my personal recollection of life under the Raj is naturally hazy and insignificant. This was somewhat compensated by my experience with the government in Punjab, which includes the old princedom of Kapurthala, now a district of the state.

By all accounts, I must have been a pampered child. As the firstborn in a new generation, my status in the family was further enhanced when the family astrologer, by the name of Damodar Das, predicted from the horoscope that the newborn child would prove fortunate for his grandfather. Damodar also prophesied that I would be a high-ranked official in government. It is possible that, in that milieu, attaining an eminent official position was the limit to which citizens of a vassal state could aspire. Now, in the twilight of my life, I quote, somewhat extravagantly, lines attributed to the famous Spanish artist, Picasso, 'My mother said to me, if you are a soldier, you will become a general. If you are a monk, you will become the Pope. Instead, I was a painter, and became Picasso'. If it was the stars that ordained for me the pushing of official files, what they conferred on me in due course was a limited distinction in officialdom.

My grandfather took literally the astrologer's forecast that I, the latest entrant to the ranks, would bring him luck.

He showered me with special attention. In that large close-knit family, I found myself closer to my uncles than to my father. I enjoyed a personal bond with each of them; they indulged me protectively, considering me as their equal, like a younger brother. My own father, on the other hand, was not given to open display of affection; with me, he maintained a somewhat formal relationship. For me he was a figure to admire from a distance, rather than to embrace, literally or figuratively. My mother maintained a diary, which I read after her death. Here she had recorded that, when I was around six years old, I asked her to distinguish between the two words from Sanskrit, '*pyaar*' (love) and '*moha*' (excessive attachment to worldly relations). She tried to explain that Indian tradition extols '*pyaar*' as an elevating emotion, whereas '*moha*' is reviled as one of the five deadly sins. 'In that case,' I seem to have remarked to her in a tone of finality, 'What I have for you is *moha*; for my father my feeling is one of *pyaar*!'

After my father chose his spiritual path, he scrupulously shunned consumption of animal products and alcohol. I suspect his new lifestyle did not go too well with his circle of friends, who might have considered him a wet blanket for declining to share the convivial spirits as he did earlier. My mother had a passion for cooking, and also for music—she was an accomplished singer of Hindustani classical music. The family had little interest in classical music, but her sumptuous creations for the dining table endeared her to the members. To demonstrate that vegetarian dishes could be as delicious as meat-based items; she systematically developed culinary skills. I recall meeting the chef from the Maharaja's palace in our own kitchen. My mother had requested him to share with her his recipes for preparing certain exotic delicacies.

My mother's side of the family comprised her brother Dev Prakash, two sisters and her widowed mother. During the early years of the 20th century, my maternal grandparents had migrated to the town of Mandalay, Burma, then a British colony. On the death of her husband, a doctor, my grandmother was compelled to return, along with her four small children, to her home state of Punjab. Initially they lived in the town of Ludhiana. After his sisters were married, Dev Prakash and my grandmother moved to a rural settlement on the banks of the river Beas, in the district of Amritsar. This was a colony established by a faith known as Radha Soami Satsang. It was the teachings of this very spiritual centre that my father too was to embrace. The faith advocates moral and spiritual development. There are no rituals, nor worship of any deity; the adherents are expected primarily to devote time to daily meditation, even as they pursue their normal vocations for earning their livelihood. Meditation is to be undertaken in the privacy of home; no pilgrimage to any shrine is deemed necessary. The followers belong to many religious denominations; indeed they are encouraged to maintain their original religious belief. Each individual pursues meditation as a personal goal. The Radha Soami faith now has several million followers, who are spread in all parts of India and in many countries abroad. From being a nondescript village in the middle of the 20th century, the colony, called Dera Baba Jaimal Singh (*Dera* in Punjabi means 'abode') after its founder Baba Jaimal Singh, is today a modern and vibrant settlement.

During my early childhood the Dera was an undeveloped village adjoining the west bank of the river in an inhospitable terrain of deep ravines and wild growth of vegetation. The permanent inhabitants were limited to just a few thousand, but a larger number, in thousands, came from the neighbouring area daily to offer voluntary labour for ongoing work in the colony. During monthly '*satsangs*' (spiritual discourses)[3] by Baba Sawan Singh, who was then the head of the institution, as many as two lakh visitors congregated. In his daily discourses at Dera, the spiritual master frequently quoted from the teachings of the Sufi[4] mystics, from the saints of the Bhakti movement[5] in India (12th to 18th century), and also from hymns from the Sikh[6] scriptures. During his discourses Baba Sawan

3 *Satsang* means literally a meeting for the truth.

4 *Sufism* is considered a mystical tradition in Islam. Successive Sufi saints (6th to 18th century) advocate a practical path leading to God, learned from and practiced under the supervision of a spiritual teacher, generally called a *Murshid* or *Pir*.

5 The Bhakti movement, as it came to be known, comprised a number of prominent mystic poets who wrote in many parts of India. They include Kabir, Namadev, Surdas and Tulsi Das.

6 The Sikh faith was led by ten Gurus, from Guru Nanak Dev (1469–1539) to Guru Gobind Singh (1666–1708). The *Adi Granth* is a compilation of the teachings of many mystics, including the Sikh gurus, and includes Sufi poets like Baba Farid (1173–1266).

Singh emphasised that all faiths have an identical belief in the supreme Almighty. His recurring message was one of humanism. The masters who succeeded Baba Sawan Singh have been carrying forward his tradition of *Sant Mat*, which means philosophy of the saints.

As a self-contained institution, Dera functions with the voluntary involvement of its believers in activities of welfare. I recall that even as a child I was encouraged to join inhabitants and visitors in *sewa*, a form of voluntary service. Thousands of men, women and children were engaged in carrying basket loads of earth to reclaim wasteland adjoining the river bank. At that stage of innocence, I was charmed and enthusiastic to accompany my mother and uncle Dev (Prakash) with the multitude.

Located geographically at it was, in the year 1947 the Dera became involuntarily a place of temporary shelter for thousands of people who had been uprooted from home in the wake of the partition of the country. These migrants belonged to the major communities in the region—Hindu, Sikh and Muslim. The colony of Dera Beas adjoins the Grand Trunk Road, the major communication link between the two parts of Punjab that had suddenly been torn asunder. After the announcement of division of India on communal lines, Muslims from the Indian East Punjab province as well as Hindus and Sikhs from the Pakistani West Punjab province faced persecution as minorities in their original homelands. There was a massive cross exodus of panic-stricken families across the newly defined border. The spiritual master at Dera,

Baba Sawan Singh, then 90 years of age, had devoted his entire life to promoting religious harmony and brotherhood. Absolute protection for all persons, no matter what their religious persuasion, was for him an article of faith. The turmoil in the surrounding areas was not allowed to upset harmony in the campus. With his moral stature, the colony remained an island of peace throughout. Dera offered food and shelter to the hapless visitors, many of them destitute, for as long as they wished. My father was then the Superintendent of Police in Kapurthala and was witness to several violent incidents in his own district. He would recoil when narrating the gory sights of suffering and agony endured by the affected families. Among the unfortunate families that had been forced to flee their homes was that of my mother's sister, Dev Kumari. She, along with her husband, Dr G.L. Arora, a university teacher and three young children had been forced to leave Lahore, the town which fell in Pakistan. They stayed for many months in the family home in the Dera, before they moved to the town of Hoshiarpur. At Dera Beas I often had for company these three cousins, all boys, who were about the same age as I.

At Dera, my uncle Dev was as solicitous of my welfare as my other uncles were at Kapurthala. The task he was assigned, which he performed with flair in an honorary capacity, was the welfare of visitors, especially facilitating groups of foreigners, who were followers in the spiritual quest. Uncle Dev was a scholar of the Urdu, Persian and Arabic languages. I would sit at his feet as he recounted numerous tales from his favourite Sufi mystic, Maulana Rumi (1207–1273) of Persia. Even if at that age Rumi's philosophy went miles above my head, the remarkable fables left an indelible mark on my mind. In later years, as I entered college and subsequently when I began to work, I found every discussion with my uncle immensely stimulating. I soon developed a love for Urdu poetry, although I could not write the script. Uncle Dev could skilfully convey the depth of mystic philosophy in simple, chaste language. Before he died at the age of 90, he gifted me his collection of the works of Urdu and Persian mystics. The rare books are a valuable part of my little library.

In retrospect, I am convinced that I was doubly blessed. Even as I inhabited a stately princedom, I was simultaneously a domicile of an elevating world of practical spiritualism, which enjoined humility, dignity of labour and public service. The two worlds of Kapurthala and Beas were just 17 miles apart.

A Princely State

Any narration of the nature and form of governance in the former state of Kapurthala prevailing at the advent of India's independence in 1947 has to describe the 72-year-long reign (1877–1949) of the ruler Maharaja Jagatjit Singh. Copious material from the archives and libraries at Kapurthala and of the Government of Punjab trace the events that brought the state of Kapurthala under the protection of the British through a formal political treaty. Explaining the modicum of autonomy enjoyed by the ruling prince, the documents focus on the development and functioning of the system of administration. They reveal the peculiar relationship of the paramount power with the princely state.

Of some interest is the nature of some interaction that my grandfather and father had with the Maharaja of Kapurthala, and also their personal observations from memory on the facets of administration.

The motivations of administration during the heyday of colonial rule obviously vary from those guiding present-day democratic India, which professes to be an egalitarian welfare state. The compulsions of policy and the nature of accountability would be different too. The social and economic milieu has changed drastically in the last century. The faces of the custodians of state authority are transformed beyond recognition. The British Raj in India was concerned primarily with its self-perpetuation. The pragmatic goal was maintenance of law and order at all costs. Any organized dissent to state (read: colonial) authority was to be pre-empted. Ideals of social equality of the subjects mattered less than the status quo of tranquility in the state concerned. The sovereignty of the paramount power needed to be demonstrated at all times. The cultivated public image was a display of firmness and impartiality, efficiency in the delivery of quality service and an adherence to strict norms of managerial and financial discipline. Kapurthala is a sample of how an unelected head of a non-representative state, holding office at the pleasure of an alien, remote power, could sustain itself for more than a century.

The tenure of Jagatjit Singh (1872–1949), as Raja from 1877 to 1911, and as Maharaja after 1911 coincides with the peak of British power worldwide. Maharaja Jagatjit Singh died in June 1949, as British rule in India ended, signalling in fact the gradual decimation of the empire. The 'reign', if the limited political autonomy can so be titled, of Maharaja Jagatjit Singh, over an unusually long period of 72 years is considered a golden period in the princedom of Kapurthala. Since disparities between the rich and the poor still abounded in India at that stage in history, the consanguinity of the East and West was admittedly limited to the ruling classes among the 'natives' in relation to their rulers from abroad. In Kapurthala, the period is frequently remembered for the visible embellishments of an authoritarian state. Oriental pomp and pageantry was in display against an unlikely backdrop of grand monuments, designed by aesthetes of the West. Caparisoned elephants stood in sharp contrast outside banquet halls and dance floors, where the elite of the Empire mingled with the cream of local gentry.

What exactly was Kapurthala in those days? *The Imperial Gazetteer of India*, 1908, describes it thus in the official terms of the day, 'Native State in the Punjab, under the political control of the Commissioner, Jullundur Division, lying between 31° 9' N and 31° 44' N, and 75° 3' E and 75° 59' E, with an area of 652 square miles. The population in 1901 was 314,341, giving an average density of 499 persons per square mile. The State consists of three detached pieces of territory.' The state was bound by the two rivers the Beas and the Satluj. Such portions of the state of Punjab today are still known by the name of *Doab*, or two rivers. 'About 57 per cent of the population are Mohammedans, 30 per cent Hindus, and only 13 per cent are Sikhs.'[7]

Maharaja Jagatjit Singh was familiar with the Indian classical languages—Persian, Sanskrit, Punjabi (his mother tongue) and Urdu (the language of official revenue records). He was proficient in several European languages, including French and Italian, besides English. The Maharaja was an inveterate traveller abroad, circumnavigating the globe three times. His exposure to foreign ideas and development influenced Maharaja Jagatjit Singh's vision for his state.

His own undoubted aesthetic taste, coupled with his considerable exposure to Western architecture, would have helped to create the important building landmarks of Kapurthala, notably the Jagatjit Palace, the Mall Road, the Kamra Gardens, the Villa Buona Vista, the Shalimar Gardens with the Shahi Samadhs, the State Gurudwara, the Durbar Hall, and the City Hall clock tower. Two unique pieces of architecture constructed by the Maharaja are the Moorish Mosque in Kapurthala, and the chateau in Mussoorie in Uttar Pradesh state (now the state of

---

7 The composition of the communities as a proportion of the population of Kapurthala district as per the Census of 1971 was 61% Sikhs, 38% Hindus.

Uttarakhand), which served as the summer retreat for the princely family.[8]

The Jagatjit Palace, an imposing edifice built in 1906 by a French architect, M. Marcel, was inspired by the palaces of Versailles and Fontainebleau in France. The architecture and interior design draw upon both Indian and French tradition. The great Durbar Hall, meant for ceremonial occasions (the word 'Durbar' means literally a royal public audience) is in the Mughal style, similar to the Agra Fort in India and the Lahore Fort, now in Pakistan. Soon after independence of the country, the palace was transferred to the government. It now houses the Sainik School—an institution for preparing promising young boys for joining the country's armed forces. Brigadier Sukhjit Singh, himself a blue-blooded professional soldier, who was awarded the Mahavir Chakra, the country's second highest award for gallantry during the 1971 war with Pakistan, lives in the villa, an erstwhile hunting lodge built by Maharaja Jagatjit Singh, his grandfather, on the outskirts of Kapurthala town. He has co-authored a book, *Maharaja Jagatjit Singh* (2019)[9] describing the life and times of the Maharaja. Years later, when I worked for the government, I was privileged to enjoy

8 Indian National Trust for Art and Heritage (INTACH), New Delhi and Guru Nanak Dev University, Amritsar, have compiled a list of more than one hundred monuments in Kapurthala, and recommended that these be notified and preserved as 'heritage buildings'. Unfortunately the grand creations of the state are crumbling for want of funds for their maintenance.

9 Brigadier H.H. Sukhjit Singh and Cynthia Meera Frederick, *Prince, Patron and Patriarch: Maharaja Jagatjit Singh of Kapurthala* (New Delhi: Roli Books, 2019).

the hospitality of Brigadier Sukhjit at his royal retreat in Kapurthala, and also at Mussoorie.

In Brigadier Sukhjit Singh's book, Maharaja Jagatjit Singh comes across as a genteel, open-minded ruler who enjoyed considerable goodwill with the population. Parts of the small town of Kapurthala, with a population of about 20,000 at that time, was planned by reputed foreign architects, and was quite modern by the prevalent standards. It boasted of neatly lined streets, access to electric power and water supply for domestic use and an active municipal council. The landmark clock tower has a rare clock, still in working order, which chimes every 15 minutes. I recall that as recently as the year 1997, when I was working as Secretary in the Punjab Government for the department of local bodies, Kapurthala was touted as the only town in the state of Punjab that had round-the-clock metered supply of drinking water for domestic users. The other towns did not measure the consumption by individual users for billing purposes, but relied on rough estimates based on the covered area of individual houses. Overall, the town was accepted as the neatest among all urban settlements in Punjab and best served by the civic local body.

A Prince in Real Life

My grandfather Bharpur Singh, who served at various positions in the household, including secretary, recalled some interesting facets of the Maharaja's personality. Punctual to the minute at all times, the Maharaja often castigated his son and heir for being late for engagements, despite the young man perpetually wearing more than one watch on his person (a harmless quirk in his son that Maharaja Jagatjit was quick to point out). The Maharaja was wont to tour the rural parts of the state and also visited institutions in the town regularly, meeting all who sought an audience. Entering classrooms in schools, the ruler would question the pupils as though on inspection, to observe aspects of the school work. He had a quaint habit of varying his mode of transport; one day it could be the grand horse-driven state carriage, on another a luxury motorcar, and sometimes the prince could be seen riding on horseback to meet his commitments. On rare occasions his carriage might even be drawn by zebras. He was accessible easily to the public, though his staff would have played a role in regulating his visitors. Priding himself as a linguist, the Maharaja was equally at home in the vernacular and foreign languages. He insisted, though, that every conversation be carried out in a single tongue, be it Punjabi, Urdu, English or French. No mixing of languages during any discussion was permitted in his presence. He laid great emphasis on personal interaction, pointing out, in Hindustani, '*mulaqat karamat*'. In other words, face-to-face meetings can perform miracles in persuading associates to one's view. Application of the dictum in real-life situations could well have contributed to the Maharaja's personal rapport with the high and mighty at home and abroad.

Surrounded as the ruler was by several officials in the state's hierarchy, there must have been scope for inevitable palace intrigue among rivals for the Maharaja's proximity. My grandfather recalls regular evening parties on the palace tennis lawns, where friendly tennis matches were played. Members of the officialdom considered the tennis courts a perfect venue to interact personally with His Highness, and other distinguished guests. These sporting ties involved friendly doubles matches. For his partner the Maharaja invariably chose my grandfather, Bharpur Singh, who was the most accomplished player in the company. Understandably, some officials would have been piqued at the display of camaraderie of the prince with his tennis partner. On one rare occasion, Bharpur Singh missed the evening tennis engagement, which was considered an unpardonable lapse in protocol, and did not proffer even an apology for his absence from the evening sports. Summoned next morning to explain his (mis)conduct, Bharpur stiffly declared to the Boss, 'Sir, you have ordered my retirement from your service. Retired persons have no place in the palace'. When His Highness questioned further, it transpired that an official order had indeed been issued, whereby the services of Bharpur stood terminated, and that he was deemed retired from service. The Maharaja was taken aback, for he could not recall having taken any decision to relieve his trusted adviser from his assignment. 'The *ahalkar*s (senior officials) might have obtained my signatures without informing me!', he confessed in child-like innocence. Needless to say, the very next day the palace administration rescinded the dubious orders. Bharpur Singh found himself back in favour (in fact he had never lost the confidence of his boss at all!). Not only this, the Maharaja ordered that since his tennis partner had been sinned against, he should be compensated by way of grant of a special increment for his dedicated performance in service!

The little anecdote is a sample of the danger of undue influence by officials working for even an enlightened ruler. As part of his office work, the Maharaja would have been required to append his signatures on numerous official papers. Some schemer could have slipped in a vital page among other innocuous documents. The Maharaja would, of course, have had trustworthy lieutenants manning the bureaucracy. Also, there would be institutional checks and safeguards to check waywardness in the office.

For the common population of the state, then, the Maharaja was a liberal, generous prince, accessible to the common man. The opulence of the palace was perceived as the continuance of a centuries-old tradition of inherited glory. Public events, such as weddings of members of the family of the house of Kapurthala or banquets for visiting dignitaries and the highest representatives of the British crown were designed as spectacles, where the public could vicariously enjoy the interaction of their own Maharaja with the potent foreign power. The impression with the public was that their Maharaja could stand on his feet before a supreme colonial power. The Maharaja himself maintained regal bearing and decorum at all times; indeed he was seen as perpetually on stage for the public to observe. It was a strange relationship; the Maharaja as a picture-perfect prince, who could be seen from afar, and at the same time a fatherly figure whom they could approach with their little problems. Most submissions were passed on for disposal to the bureaucracy. Norms of administrative action were laid down, and adhered to by the officials. To some extent, the elected ministers in today's democratic polity behave similarly. As long as the man in the street received a fair deal from authority, he was not concerned with the lavish style of living of the inmates of the palace. On their part, the British cultivated Maharaja Jagatjit Singh as they did no other prince of similar stature, and in fact built up his public image.

After the princely states of the region formally integrated with the state of Punjab, the enlarged state did not need to look beyond the personnel from Kapurthala and Patiala to find specialists in protocol and hospitality. With their grounding in the palaces of the maharajas they were an ideal choice for appointments demanding finesse and style in public relations. These are the core components of the public face of governance. Within the integrated state of Punjab, it was for decades a given that the heads of the departments of hospitality and public relations would be drawn from the cadres of the original princedoms. If nothing else, the princes supplied expertise for conduct of this important affair of state.

Such then was the face of authority that prevailed in that little princely state when democracy dawned in India. Kapurthala state was surrounded by districts of

Punjab directly ruled by the British authority, but there was free movement between the two areas. My parents hailed from areas subject to administrative control of two different authorities. They professed that in regard to local administration and public services, citizens across the open borders between Kapurthala and British India found little difference in the form of administration.

The Prince on a Bicycle

"Bring out the new Raleigh, that gleaming steed,
Selected with much care from New Bond Street:
It's packed in cargo, with my daily needs
Marked P&O London in baggage neat."

Quoth joyous aide, "Your Highness is too kind,"
Dutifully bowing full ankle low:
"A lovely sight would my children find
Of me on top, imported bike below."

The poor man was cut with a withering glance.
"Some goodies you'll have, my trusted fellow.
But this state bike is for ceremony, not jaunts;
It's to reach my subjects to say Hello!"

Subdued, ADC barely could mumble,
"A spectacle grand it surely will be;

But the royal carriages, the Rolls," he fumbled;
"Will these the street folk no longer see?"

"Forever we keep the subjects in mind:
They'll view me from close in flesh and blood;
This machine moves, but leaves no dust behind.
I love to be loved, sans the heavy rod."

"I shall pedal to reach the heart of the town,"
Declared Maharaja so smart and young:
Perturbed, his Minister jumped double step down,
Determined to foil the strange royal plunge.

"Horses, cycles," Prince declared, "are much the same.
My mind is clear. Don't I gallop and hunt?
Even foreign guests did some lessons gain,
When I led the chase from the very front."

Gingerly gripping new reins of tough steel;
Chief stable groom intoned, "Ready to mount!"
The Prince sportingly clad from tip to heel
For rare state event: three-two-one. The count!

Smooth was the flag off to clap and to cheer,
Rider in full stream along with the breeze:
A pilot in lead, two horsemen at rear;
Caravan in colour, grand as you please.

Cold Street[10] all clear, but Bazaar was a crowd
Of carriages, tongas, of many a hue:
Prince waved, throng hailed, in chorus so loud.
But why did the bike stall? I have ne'er a cue.

Lo and behold! The flying cyclist grounded,
Arms flailing with sweetmeats, a dainty spread:
Startled Kapur halwai,[11] his faint voice sounded;
"Grateful, Highness for this visit," he said.

"Savour this fine barfi. Honoured I'm sure:
Esteem has truly crowned my humble shop?
I'm happy though to deliver at palace door;
For this regal sight all citizens must stop."

Striving in vain to dignity retain,
The Maharaja now mopped his forehead wet:
"Climbing the bike is easy as rain,
The art of dismount is not mastered yet."

A happy venture it was in the end,
Though Sovereign lay flat in unflattering pose:
To common pitch had he deigned to descend.
"Great Prince so human!" The call in town rose.

---

10 Cold street (*thandi sarak*): The road from Kapurthala palace to the city bazaar, also called Mall Road.

11 *Halwai,* meaning a seller of Indian sweetmeats. Kapur's business is now run by his inheritors.

GROWING UP

A Haunted Mansion

My first academic lessons began at the age of five, in what I then considered was a haunted house. The year was 1948. The venue of this early schooling, which was to last for three years, was a ramshackle homestead called Haleem Manzil, situated in a dusty backward village named Bassi Pathanan.[1]

The derelict mansion, surrounded by wild undergrowth over land measuring some four or five acres, had belonged to a Muslim family, the descendants of one Haleem Ali, after whom the property was named. Just a few months earlier the owners had hastily deserted their ancestral property, choosing to migrate, along with many others of their community, from the Indian, eastern part of Punjab, to the west, in the new Pakistan. The government had taken possession, and allotted the property for use as offices and for housing.

---

1 Literally, Bassi of the Pathans. The word 'pathanan' differentiated it from other settlements bearing the same name Bassi. Haleem's family was among the Pathans, who had so recently departed from the village. The Pathan tribes constitute a major part of the population of present-day Afghanistan and North West Frontier Province of Pakistan.

Compared to the relatively modern, indeed elegant setting of princely Kapurthala, my home town, Bassi Pathanan was a little rustic settlement of about 2000 souls. Although the headquarters of an administrative district, called Fatehgarh Sahib, the residents of the primitive village did not even have basic civic facilities, such as supply of electricity or running water for domestic use. In the process of reorganising the official machinery, the government had transferred my father, who was Superintendent of Police in Kapurthala, to work in Bassi in the same position. One wing of Haleem Manzil served as his office; his family lodgings were on the first floor. The ground floor was the residence of his colleague, the district and sessions judge, who as head of the judiciary, was charged with delivery of justice.

My own introduction to the building that was to be both school and home was eerie. It was early evening when a dark, sprawling '*haveli*',[2] its four minarets silhouetted against the setting sun, greeted me and my parents. A watchman carrying a sickly oil lantern received us at the entrance. The first figure I observed in the lobby was that of an enormous stuffed tiger, the gleam of its green eyes reflecting

---

2 '*Haveli*' is the Urdu term used for a large farmhouse, belonging to a member of the landed gentry. A typical *haveli* would consist of numerous sets of apartments for lodging individual groups belonging to an extended family, all residing together harmoniously. While the living portion was built around large courtyards, adjacent agricultural land yielded income to the owner. *Haveli*s were the norm for wealthy farmers, called '*zamindars*', who established them in remote rural areas, and even in small semi-urban settlements called '*kasba*', or glorified villages. The tradition of opulent '*havelis*' continues in Punjab, long after the size of land holdings of the farming community has diminished.

fearsomely in the dim light of the hand-held lamp. Gingerly treading past this unexpected apparition, I climbed up a dingy winding staircase, to our dwelling on the first floor. My father had taken charge of the new assignment a few weeks before we, his family, joined him. He had arranged to install some makeshift furnishings in the living rooms. The interiors of the new lodgings were pleasant enough. On the mantelpiece of the living room a brass lamp fired by kerosene oil flickering gloomily, provided just enough light for us to make out the shadowy form of chairs in the background. The silence was broken by the wailing of peacocks running wild in the surrounding land. Pigeons fluttered past us as they returned home at dusk to roost.

It being summer, every one perforce slept in the open, our family on a large terrace. In the absence of electric power, there was no fan to cool the ambience within the bedrooms. Mosquitoes buzzed by in plentiful number, but we were protected from the onslaught of the pesky insects by mosquito nets, which were held aloft by bamboo poles. One had to tuck the bottom of the net under the mattress, so the little pests did not creep in. My first night under the stars was a new experience. I was charmed by the sight of so many glow worms perched on top of the netting. To lessen the obvious shock on a young mind exposed suddenly to an alien environment, my mother began to speak about the stars overhead. Before she could begin to name the major constellations that were visible, I was fast asleep. It was the early morning sun that woke me at daybreak. At Bassi, all activities were determined by the hours of natural daylight. To wake up at dawn, and turn in to sleep just after sunset, was the routine.

In the light of day, our rooms looked quite bright and cheerful. I was taken in by a number of curios, consisting of intricately designed pottery, displayed on the mantelpiece. This was obviously a glass menagerie left behind by the previous occupants. I still remember that the flooring was a delicate design of marble tiles. (Many years later when I nostalgically revisited the old house, I was astonished to see that the grand flooring had disappeared, apparently uprooted and purloined by vandals). I quickly forgot the somber reception that the old *haveli* had accorded us the previous evening. Within the campus everything was novel, especially for a young boy from a more sophisticated, urban setting. The first few days were spent in becoming familiar with the new setting.

The move to Bassi was to prove fortuitous in laying the foundation of my primary education. Bassi at that time did have a government school, but any thought of beginning my education in a backward village school was dismissed out of hand, since a viable alternative presented itself. It transpired that my mother was a trained teacher, having acquired degrees of Bachelor of Arts (BA) and Bachelor of Teaching (BT)[3] from the renowned Kinnaird College for Women in

---

3 The degree is now called Bachelor of Education. BEd is an essential academic qualification for school teachers.

Lahore.[4] It was decided that during the period that my father worked in Bassi, my academic grounding would be at home. The family also decided that my father's younger brother Inderjit, who was just two years older in age to me, should also move to Bassi, along with me, and we would both study at home for the time being. That Inderjit and I were the guinea pigs for my mother to test and apply her teaching skills dawned upon me years later. In any case we perceived the stay in Bassi as a voyage of discovery, interrupted by the imbibing of bookish knowledge during the mornings.

Inside the *Haveli* and Outside it

For me and Inderjit, virtual brothers and comrades, the days in Bassi were one long, continuous adventure. We needed to walk but a few steps from the inside of our room to enter an unexplored world of squirrels and birds, of untrammelled paths that covered our clothes with mud, of dried-out streams that would teem with frogs and toads and other rodents when the rains came. It was nature in the raw. We could search the untended garden for nests of birds whose names we never knew. Climbing up and down prickly trees that scratched our legs, running after peacocks, hoping to grab at least a tail feather to carry home as a trophy, these were the little pleasures that we indulged day after day. The tall elephant grass, called '*sarkanda*' in Punjabi, was ideal for

4 In pre-Independent India, Lahore, the capital of Punjab, was the elite centre for cultural, educational and social activity for all of north India. Like others from prominent families, both my parents earned their graduate degrees from colleges in the Punjab University, Lahore.

school boys to play hide and seek. Within the shrubbery were some bamboo stalks and grasses of indeterminate species. We innovated freely, making bows and arrows out of the scraps of waste vegetation. We found that some bamboo stems could be easily split to create a frame for paper kites. To be found in abundance was acacia (*kikar*), a hardy desert tree, many mango trees and some varieties of cactus. Our favourites were trees bearing hard berries called '*ber*'. We could pick the fruit directly from the branches, just by scampering up the thorny trunk of that humble tree, and bring a goodly number of the *ber*s triumphantly home. Near the boundary wall grew many a wood apple (*bel*) tree. The *bel* had medicinal property, my mother told me, but I found the luscious core unpalatable. I did, however, enjoy the sherbet, a sweet drink made at home from the same clumsy-looking fruit.

Going back almost seven decades in memory, I can recreate an idyllic world. Our repeated strolls in our private jungle were surely a form of communion with nature. In my imagination, the shrubbery and wild undergrowth transformed itself into a deep forest inhabited by wild denizens. Be that as it may, many excursions saw us return with tattered clothes, bruised knees and scruffy faces. My mother's consequent admonishments fell on deaf ears. She took pains to spruce us up as best she could, so that the boys were presentable before the head of the household, my father, returned from work. On our part we contritely assured her of our total and serious application in class on the succeeding day.

The *haveli*, or manor, or estate, as you might call it, was served by a number of workers, all living in outhouses in the campus with their families. The senior officers, such as the deputy commissioner, the superintendent of police and the district judge were temporary residents of such campuses in various parts of the state. They were bound to leave the precincts on transfer from the assignment after a limited tenure of three or four years. The ancillary workers of various categories were a permanent fixture with the *haveli*. Apart from the official security guards attached with the head of district police, there was a washer-man (*dhobi*), a cook, two or three sanitation workers, some gardeners, a cattle minder for milch cattle and even a water-carrier (called a *jhoor* or *mashaki*). The *jhoor*'s duties were to fetch water for the family of the officers from a dedicated well in the campus. He was also required to splash on the floor water from a large leather bag (called a *mashak*) that he carried on his back. The surface of the terrace where our family slept was made of clay coated with cow dung, incidentally the same material that was used for clay tennis courts. The evening watering cooled the surface considerably.

Office hours in summer were from seven in the morning to half past one in the afternoon. Adjusting to the extreme summer heat, almost everyone enjoyed a two-hour siesta. The exception was my father himself, who would be moving in the villages as he toured even in the afternoon. At the door entrance a makeshift desert cooler was created consisting of a thatched screen made of *khus* (a form of selected dry vetiver grass), which was kept moist by repeated watering. Hanging from the ceiling of our siesta room was a large furling cloth, to serve as a fan. While the Sahib and family would enjoy the relative coolness inside, a worker would be tasked with pulling, from outside the room, the strange fan attached with a pulley-mounted rope. This system of air conditioning was commonly used in many households. When I worked in the districts of Punjab many years later, I found that a few of those antique fans still hanging from the ceiling in some government rest houses. I directed that the unique contraptions be preserved as relics of the old world. I doubt if my orders were implemented.

In today's changed setting, the system of deployment of labour described above appears socially unjust and anachronistic. In that day and age, however, it was accepted that each person attached with the household of the representatives of government was carrying out the duty assigned to him. The worker was paid for his task; his family was provided housing free of cost, and he could consume any produce of the land. Inderjit and I mixed freely and played with the children of the staff. We had great fun playing games like hopscotch (*chhatapu* it was called), marbles and *gulli danda*[5] with the children of our age. These little games helped to while away the tedium. The roughly hewn toys cost nothing, and broke any societal barriers between the children of workers and those of the elite.

---

5 A primitibe village sport. The *danda* (wooden stick) is used to hit a *gulli* (peg) as in golf.

I learnt from some boys, the sons of staff members, the art of making and flying a kite. The string attached to the kite could be toughened by applying a mixture of ground glass and kneaded wheat flour. A length of string, which could measure hundreds of feet, is wound around a spindle, and released as the kite soars with the breeze. Kite flying was great fun; even more exciting were battles between competing kite flyers, each attempting to cut down the rival's. This could be a dangerous pastime too, for the glass-treated string could cut the hand of the person manipulating the flight of the bird. It was while pursuing the pastime that I chanced on a peculiar tradition regarding the season assigned for kite flying. I pause here with an aside. In some princely towns like Kapurthala, and here in Bassi, kites were flown during the summer season, that is, from March to September, whereas in most parts of India, kiting was a winter sport. I never could fathom the reason for the difference. The season of spring, commences in March. In Kapurthala the start of the spring season began with a kite flying festival, which the Maharaja himself initiated enthusiastically. In other parts of India, the advent of spring saw the conclusion of kite-flying activity.

Viewed from a distance in time, the days of my early childhood were fun filled; even studying books did not appear a chore. What excited greatest curiosity in me were the forlorn dusty towers designed as minarets that bounded the building of Haleem Manzil. What could be inside, I wondered. My companions, the children living in the outhouses, scared me with stories that the towers were haunted by the ghost of the founder, Haleem Ali, who was distressed that his successors had been evicted from his manor. 'Don't you hear strange howling sounds coming from the minaret next to the terrace where you sleep?' one boy would question with great seriousness. Another would claim that his own father had encountered a ghost emerging from one tower. Armed with the little rationality that my mother's lessons had imparted to my thinking, I determined to ferret out the truth for myself. One afternoon, both Inderjit and I decided to enter the precincts of one of the chambers. It was the monsoon season, but that day there happened to be a let up in the torrential rain. It was unbearably hot. The entrance to the minaret was littered with the remains of birds, including pigeons and bats that had been devoured by dogs or cats. The inside of the tower was suffocating. Cobwebs hung low overhead. It was all filthy and reeking with a foul stench. It seemed that no human being had set foot in the minaret for months. I wondered why the staff in the campus had neglected this portion of the property. As we stumbled in the darkness, I inadvertently touched a dark nest suspended from the ceiling with a stick. Immediately all hell broke loose. We found a swarm of angry bees hovering right over our heads. In a matter of moments, I must have been stung by dozens of the frenzied creatures. As we rushed out screaming, some attendants rushed to our rescue. I recall that my head was dipped in a bucket of water. My face was swollen from multiple stings. That night I was feverish. No doctor was called, for there was none in the vicinity, but painful home remedies advised by a knowledgeable worker were efficacious. It took two days for the fever to vanish, and for my face to resume its normal shape. It wasn't the ghost of Haleem, I was reassured, just a swarm of honey bees that I had accidently disturbed. Incidentally, my passport still mentions the mark on my forehead as a distinguishing mark, a legacy of that encounter. Perhaps an irascible queen bee had done the damage! That day a lesson of nature was learnt. Honey bees are apt to be roused most during the rainy season, the local experts averred. We also learnt that it was the yellow wasp that we needed to beware of; that hornet is vicious and more poisonous than the honey bee, which is basically a docile creature, busy making honey as ordered by the queen bee. Following the episode, a standard operating procedure for maintenance of the minarets and belfries was followed. And the house and its towers were not haunted after all! This was proved for all to see.

One other little incident during my stay in Bassi remains etched in my memory, one that profoundly impacted me for life. One evening, as we sat in our balcony, I saw the cook of our neighbour on the first floor, carrying a full-grown chicken. I thought at first that he was going to play with the bird, but then he brought out a huge knife. Right in front of my eyes, he placed the screeching chicken on a cemented plate, and slaughtered the poor bird with a single flashing blow. Just 10 yards from where I stood, I could see the body of the headless chicken jumping on its legs, while the neck of the stricken bird was on its own separate journey, moving up and down like the living creature it was. For what appeared many minutes of time, both portions of the chicken, the body and the neck, kept bobbing in a grotesque, coordinated, hyperactive motion. My stomach churned at the gruesome scene that I had witnessed. The very day I resolved that I would never eat meat or eggs.

A School at Home

What about the process of schooling that we underwent at Bassi? Not having attended any school earlier, there was no way I could adjudge the quality and methods employed for class work by my mother, our single guide. Inderjit, who had been to a primary school prior to coming to Bassi, opined as a pupil that in comparison with the teachers who had instructed him in his previous institution, the teacher here made lessons interesting. I recall that my mother was innovative, often applying personal observation to drive home a point. We were taught basic concepts in geography by relating to the changing seasons and the movement of the sun and moon. Likewise, she insisted that we put in writing our observations during our frolic in the jungle. Lessons in history included knowledge of the story of struggle for Indian independence. Among current events, we were introduced to the happenings in the Second World War, which had ended just three years earlier. I knew at age six that the span of the wheels of my father's official vehicle, the jeep, was exactly one meter. Imagine the kinds of trivia that excited us! I learnt at that age that the German dictator Adolf Hitler used the railway network in Germany, which was then meter gauge, that is, one meter in breadth, to transport jeeps by removing the rubber tyres, and placing the vehicles on their rims directly on the rails. I think in retrospect that my mother used the opportunity of one-to-one interaction with us pupils to apply in practice concepts she had learnt for her teaching degree. She often mentioned that she had learnt the Montessori system of elementary education, which followed a child-centric educational approach, emphasizing scientific observations of children.

My mother's style of teaching combined the traditional and the modern. To begin with, we were taught to write on a wooden board, called a *takhti*, which had to be coated every day with a cake of yellow-coloured material, called *gachni*. The pen was made from slender shoots from the shrubbery, called *kaana* in Punjabi (sacron is the botanical name). The end of the shoot had to be cut and sharpened to the shape of a nib with a broad point. The method would have originated several hundred years earlier. The home-made pen would be dipped in jet black ink. We were first taught to draw straight lines. Both English and Hindi letters were to be written in bold strokes between two lines parallel to one another. It was like an exercise in calligraphy. Indeed, the idea was to develop a neat and legible hand. We were taught to shape the letters with the movement of the forearm, and not merely with the wrist. When both sides of the wooden board were used up the board was washed clean, and recoated with the yellow paste for reuse on the subsequent day. Likewise, rough writing work did not entail consumption of paper. Old fashioned slates sufficed for writing with a form of chalk. The slate would be wiped clean, and readied to reuse like a blackboard. All in all, it was a highly environmentally friendly and economical use of writing material.

With the fundamental guidance on shaping the letters, my handwriting became quite legible, but it was not characterised as pretty. This was the period when the country was flush with enthusiasm and nationalist fervour. My mother used to read to us extracts from Mahatma Gandhi's autobiography. I latched on to a passage where the Mahatma lamented that his handwriting was untidy. I thought, if such a great man could get by with a less than perfect hand, there was hope for me too to manage in life without calligraphic skills. In the event, by the dint of diligence, my handwriting was eventually passable, if not beautiful.

In less than three years we had picked up the basics of science, arithmetic, history and geography, besides the English and Hindi language. My mother confessed that while she could teach arithmetic, she was unfamiliar with algebra and geometry. At that time the high school examination of matriculation required both boys and girls to learn arithmetic as a compulsory subject. Additionally, boys had to learn algebra and geometry as part of the syllabus for mathematics, but girls had the option of substituting algebra and geometry with learning household skills. A strange chauvinistic concept of the time! There could be good-humoured banter between my parents. As a bright student, my mother had sailed through all her exams comfortably. She would tease that in comparison with her demonstrated academic attainment, my father had had to struggle with studies.

In her assignment as our teacher, my mother must surely have done something right and well. This was attested when, some two years later, Inderjit and I were considered for admission in a boarding school in Mussoorie. The teachers there found that we were ahead of our peers in the respective age groups. I found myself placed in a class much ahead of children of my age. Throughout my career I continued to benefit from this unplanned head start, age wise, as I was promoted from every class to the next. Thus, I completed high school at the age of 14, my graduate degree at age 18 and my Master's before I had turned 20. I was in fact a teacher at the university when I turned 20. When I joined the Indian Administrative Service, I was the youngest of all entrants in my batch. I consequently served in the Indian Administrative Service for a period of 38 years, which is some kind of a record. An unexpected consequence of not having been at a formal school in the initial years!

Off to the Hills

My tuition at home lasted almost three years. In April 1951, Inderjit and I were sent to a boarding school called Vincent Hill, located in the hills of Mussoorie. It was felt that we should move out of our sheltered, remote existence to better adjust to the real world. Not even eight years of age then, I was most reluctant to move to a hostel. It was the first time in life that I was to part from my parents. I was persuaded by logic to comply with their considered decision. It had been ingrained from early childhood that one must strive to attain one's potential. Copious tears were shed by all three generations of the joint family—my grandparents, my parents and I, as Inderjit and I were packed off to a new life. As part of upbringing, I had also been taught that any show of emotion was 'unmanly'. I put on, unsuccessfully as it turned out, a brave face as I prepared for the inevitable. There was some excitement in arranging the items in the list of clothing and bedding, etc., prescribed, but overall there was trepidation at the imminent parting from home and family.

Vincent Hill in Mussoorie was selected for us for two main reasons. One, the institution was run by a sect of Christian missionaries from the USA, called the Seventh Day Adventists, who were by conviction vegetarians and abjured the consumption of alcohol and drugs, just like my parents. There was thus no problem in adjustment to diet in the boarding house. Two, Mussoorie was the place where my grandfather was located during the summer months, when his employer, the Maharaja of Kapurthala, moved, bag and baggage, to his palace in the same town. At Mussoorie, his virtual summer capital, the Maharaja avoided the intense heat and dust of the plains. As boarders at school, we stayed in the hostel, but once a month, we were allowed to spend a weekend at home. During the period that we were in the hostel, at Mussoorie, and later in another school in Patiala, my father, naturally, had to be at work at the stations of his posting.

As it transpired, both Inderjit and I adjusted quickly to the new setting, which comprised well-appointed classrooms and living dormitories on a hill side, as well as a fine chapel for church service and prayers. The boys and girls at VHC (it was called Vincent Hill School and College, although it was a high school) were from several nations, the majority being Americans. The Seventh Day Adventists had strong ethical moorings in the Christian faith. They were conservative, even Puritan in their adherence to the tenets of 'Love, Faith, Hope and Charity'. Flowing from the Biblical postulate that the Lord created the world in six days and rested on the seventh day, Saturday was reserved exclusively for prayer and meditation, and we were expected to desist even from study and any form of labour on Saturdays. On one occasion I was quite surprised when a friend enjoined me to not even polish my shoes on Sabbath, which was Saturday.

We happily attended chapel services on Saturday along with our fellow students; there was no attempt whatever at converting us to the Christian faith. The teachers even questioned us on our personal religious convictions, and were happy to speak about the Indian concept of transmigration of soul and the law of *karma*. The staff respected our ingrained spiritual belief, viz. that all living things, including animals, have a soul. That man, being the top of the creation, must realize that killing an animal for food creates a load of *karma*. That any *karma* (actions or deeds done deliberately), including consumption of animal products, would have to be atoned.

I found no problem in adjusting to the curriculum; my teacher, Miss Poole was surprised that I could, at that early age, solve sums involving multiplication and division of fractions, and that I was fluent in the English language. While the academic lessons were more or less along the lines that we were familiar with, what struck us particularly was an emphasis on moral education (Bible Studies was a subject in the curriculum), and inculcation of dignity of labour in the daily routine. No task, whether carrying baggage, or cleaning toilets, was considered lowly. I recall a little incident during my early days at VHC. A senior asked me to do some small chore for him. Fearing this was an incident of ragging, for which public schools, especially in England, were notorious, I carried out the task with some apprehension. Imagine my reaction when the senior boy paid me a small amount for my labour. It was an open and frank system. Another practice that we found unusual was for the students not to address their teachers with deference as 'Sir' or 'Madam', but to use their names, Miss Poole, Mr Shorter, etc. There was also total equality in treatment of the sexes; no activity was the exclusive prerogative of a male or female. Boys were taught cooking and even knitting (I received appreciation for knitting a brown sweater in a simple design, and that unexpected skill surprises my wife even today). Girls could fly kites and play football. There were frequent nature walks, which I enjoyed immensely. The boys bathed in community bathrooms; to be unclothed before others was a new practice for me, but was considered by all as a common matter of course.

The academic term lasted nine months, March to November, with a winter recess of three months, December, January and February. The school was strict in regard to avoidance in indulgence, even in regard to entertainment and music; cinema was taboo, music was taught—I still remember many little ditties and hymns that I learnt at VHC—but pianists were barred from playing jazz, which was considered as erotic and demeaning. Overall, the school inculcated in the inmates a happy mix of traditional Christian values and modern American customs, with due deference to the mores of conservative Indian society that some Indian children brought with them. Inderjit and I felt completely at home during our two years at Mussoorie. Today I feel that the ambience created and observed at VHC was to some extent artificial and anachronistic. Mussoorie has many boarding schools, mostly run like public schools in England. Among schools with an American orientation, the best known is called Woodstock. There the atmosphere is what one would expect in a typical campus in the USA, but vastly different from the Puritan upbringing that VHC offered. Amazingly, with its core value and ethical norms, Vincent Hill was closer to the traditional Indian schools than contemporary public schools in India.

An Indian Public School

In the year 1953, following a two-year stint in Mussoorie in the hills, Inderjit and I were placed in an entirely different kind of institution, the Yadavindra Public School (YPS) in the city of Patiala, which was the largest of the eight princely states of Punjab. I can say with confidence that the six years (1953 to 1959), served as the true foundation of my academic learning, and also of my overall preparation for life as an adult. The campus of YPS, spread over some 20 acres of land just outside the old city, was bequeathed as an estate owned by the Maharaja of Patiala to an autonomous non-profit trust. This trust was managed by a board of governors of the school, comprising of eminent personages, who modelled the institution on the lines of established public schools in England. As an alumnus, many years into my professional career, I had the privilege of being on the board for a number of years.

YPS always had playing grounds aplenty for all games. The *coup de grace* was a central arena with a standard 400-meter Olympic-size cinder running track, as well as a coal-tarred bicycle track, the best in Punjab at that time. In the year 1957, the stadium was the venue for the National Games. I remember clearly that this was the month of November, when my final examination for Senior Cambridge commenced. To keep us away from the hustle and bustle of the games, the Maharaja of Patiala graciously offered the premises of his palace, Moti Bagh, for our batch to write our papers. Indeed, Maharaja Yadavindra Singh met our batch personally to wish us success in the crucial examination. The Maharaja was an imposing personality, his elegant 6' 3" frame towering over us all. On formal occasions, as when he had functioned as *rajpramukh* or the Governor of the state of PEPSU (Patiala and East Punjab States Union, 1948–56) he wore the splendid regalia of the house of Patiala; a life-size portrait of him so accoutered graced the school assembly hall. At the palace he greeted us, attired in a high-necked, buttoned-up long coat, truly a regal figure, every inch a prince. We had learnt that in the years before Independence, he was the chairman of the Chamber of Princes, representing all the 565 princely states. Maharaja Yadavindra Singh had in fact been the first among all the princes to sign the instrument of accession to the newly independent India. His decision persuaded the princes of the other states to similarly cast their lot with India. In due course, the national government assigned him the position of India's Ambassador to the Hague, in the Netherlands, where he performed his duties with finesse and distinction.

I had thus a unique privilege, that of writing my examination in a palace. I cannot certify, though, that the royal ambience and the comfort of a plush leather chair, aided my performance in any manner.

The stadium building itself included a large number of rooms overlooking the central field. These were ideal for use as classrooms. In its ready-made premises the school quickly took root. When I joined there were about 150 students, all boys then, who stayed in two hostels named Dhani Ram

House (so called after the name of the first headmaster) and Mohindra House (named after a scion of the House of Patiala). Later, as the strength of students increased, a third hostel, named the Headmaster's House, came up. Regular inter-house matches in various sports disciplines were passionately cheered by us partisans. We were lodged in dormitories with facilities that could at best be termed basic, and not at all lavish. As a sample, outside each dormitory was a large earthen pitcher of water, from which the inmates could quench their thirst. During summer the boys slept in the open, each bed protected by a mosquito net. A healthy environment it surely was. Evening prayers were compulsory; the boys could choose to join a group where hymns from the Sikh scriptures were recited, or to one where they sang *bhajans* from Hindu saints. Inderjit and I chose the Sikh group, which seemed closer to our faith at home. As at my previous school in Mussoorie, moral studies were important at YPS.

Rough Discipline and Awesome Leadership

A feature that vitally defines the character of a school is the personality of the head master. A pen portrait of the head could describe the role that the school played in moulding its pupils, and charting their future. After all, as the 19th century English writer Herbert Spencer put it, 'Education has for its object the formation of character'.

Lieutenant Colonel F.A. von Goldstein was the name of the Headmaster, a German Jew, who had fought for the

Allies in the Second World War. Here I picture him still—an ageless form, military in bearing, sitting sternly behind the headmaster's table. It was an exceedingly small office, so narrow that visitors would barely have room enough to keep their knees from knocking against the desk. But for young minds—I was less than 10 years old when I entered school—the headmaster's office had an aura of other-worldliness. In my six years at Yadavindra Public School (YPS), I never once entered those hallowed precincts. The privilege of egress was limited to boys who displayed either extraordinary talents or unpardonable misbehaviour. I fell in neither category, but I do remember some two or three pupils several years older than myself, who boasted of having received 'special treatment' in the headmaster's office on account of having committed some misdemeanours. These offenders became instant heroes. For weeks they would roam around the corridors with an exaggerated swagger, surrounded by envious young hero-worshippers.

Stories grew, fanned by some young recalcitrants, that the headmaster maintained a special leather cane in excellent working condition to enforce discipline. Rarely was the rod used, but such was its reputation, that a mere threat of 'six-of-the best' (six blows of the cane as a corporal punishment) was adequate to assure good conduct of the pupils. It was rumoured among us that for the stick to retain its gloss, it had either to be polished regularly, or to be put to sustained proper use. As for the torture chamber itself, first-hand accounts of the internal environment were difficult to obtain. So much so, that even the décor and furnishings of the office were a matter of conjecture. Not that the HM maintained any deliberate secrecy. The door of his office was kept invariably open, and you could peep in, if you were so inclined. And yet I do not recall that any, even among the deified youths who had experienced those rude disciplinary measures, dared to venture close to that room. Indeed, we all slunk past, making a careful and circuitous detour. The bolder among us would glance with studied casualness over their shoulder as they passed by the study. We, lesser mortals, would be conveyed such snippets of information as that HM's table was covered with a billiard-green table cloth, that there was a pen-stand with four pens (a rarity in those days), that there lay an open file with many report cards (profusely marked in red ink, our spy would have us believe). Our vivid imagination would be fired on hearing that in the far corner stood a hat and umbrella stand displaying that dreaded leather-cane. And a tin of imported polish!

If this teacher of old inspired awe, it was certainly not an account of his appearance. Short and balding, but trim as a professional athlete, he was meticulous in attention to his own turnout, as he was in his insistence on neatness among his wards. He would occasionally order a check of trimness of the boys' finger-nails just before a meal, and defaulters were denied entry into the dining-hall. Unpolished shoes, tousled hair and dirty trousers earned disapprobation, as did any lack of punctuality or loudness in speech.

In the tradition of English public schools, sports were given the pride of place among all activities. There were perhaps 12 groups (teams) of about 15 boys each, each placement being determined by the level of proficiency. Sports being compulsory, and every group being announced on the notice board, any school boy missing a sports period was unheard of. Since I myself did not at that time excel in games, it was my lasting lament that obtaining exemption from a games period was far more difficult than leave from studies. In true public-school tradition, Mr Goldstein joined enthusiastically in all these activities. It amazed me that in all my years at school, he played hockey and football in Group 1–2, that is, with the champions. Considering that YPS had the strongest hockey team among all the top public schools in the country, this was no mean achievement.

This was a time of transition, from the first few years after India's independence, when outstanding academic performance was not an essential pre-requisite to join the services and the professions, to the current world of cut-throat competition where excellence is judged by marks secured in examinations. Excessive diligence in respect of books was not encouraged. So much so that some bright young scholars who markedly aspired to high grades, found their efforts frowned upon by their fellow pupils. Mr G's emphasis was on the basics. Excellence in sports, team spirit, and the development of latent human qualities—that is what he seems to have promoted. Perhaps he felt that he was tasked with the foundation of character building, that a boy's innate qualities would develop as he cruised along in life.

This same emphasis on the development of a boy's personality, as a whole, could be perceived in G's approach to teaching. He taught English and history. Himself an Anglo-German Jew, who had fought along with the Allies in the recent World War, he spoke the Queen's English with just that much of an Indian accent to be fully understood in Patiala. 'There are only three ways of learning English,' he used to say. 'Read, read, and read!' And he would add immediately, 'But there are three other ways of doing it'. We would be all ears. 'Write, write and write!' And so he made us do. An essay had to be written every week in class, which he would check and mark with the highest care. He welcomed originality, in thought as in style. He even conducted a limerick contest in class. The very next day, he himself wrote a limerick on every student in the class. We were all in the last year of Senior Cambridge then, and I still remember how embarrassed some of us were to find our waywardness described in print in the school magazine. For all his bonhomie Mr G would never compromise on discipline. Many a time was an inattentive pupil hit on the nose by a well-aimed piece of chalk. There was an occasion when a drowsy back bencher received the black-board duster straight on his right ear. Sniggers all round, but nary a grin on Mr G's poker face!

In those days, a 'credit' in the English language paper was obligatory for any student aspiring to a first or even a second class. Thanks to our grounding at the hands of G, credits we all obtained. The catch was that in true YPS style ('brawn not brain') many of us missed similar credits in the so-called scoring subjects—mathematics, physics and the like. The end result was that there were more failures than passes in our group. No matter, G reassured us, fall back on good old Panjab University for the Matriculation examination. This was a second line of defence. Those who flopped in the Senior Cambridge examination in November–December could, and actually did, sail through Panjab Matriculation in the following March. The honours board of the school lists names of the boys who rose to the highest ranks in the armed forces, and in the professions, demonstrating G's maxim of that a healthy mind in a healthy body will shape success in life.

I think Mr G understood clearly that his system of teaching English, while attuned to Cambridge requirements, did not assure comparable recognition in Indian under graduate examinations, which emphasize standardized output, rather than originality of thought and expression. It came as no surprise to him, although it was to us, when distinction holders barely scraped through in later intermediate and graduation in Indian universities. The levelling off came, I think, at master's level, when the Chaucer and Shakespeare, imbibed during adolescence, began suddenly and unexpectedly to flower.

What was Lt. Col. F.A. von Goldstein's contribution to YPS, and to education? The question is irreverent. Goldstein was not the headmaster of YPS. He was YPS itself. He had no family, or at least not one that any had heard of. He lived and breathed for the school. I don't recall his ever being on leave, or visiting friends and relatives, or holidaying abroad. He was always here. How carefully he followed every pupil's welfare I realized when my wife received this letter from the old HM on the occasion of our marriage. It simply said, 'You have married one of the good products of YPS.'[6]

Around the year 1956 YPS decided to enlist students in what was then called the Intermediate course, which corresponds to senior secondary or Class 11–12 of today. Intermediate classes were then offered both at college, and in a school like YPS. Most high school boys feel that they have been subject to years of regimentation. They are at an age where they resent any attempt of authority (read: teachers) to spoon-feed them with knowledge. They crave a release from the established bonds of school discipline. I found that most of my class fellows decided to join colleges for the intermediate course. I was among a few who opted to continue with the intermediate course at YPS, that is, at school, rather than move to college. This proved a strategically astute move.

The inbuilt discipline of YPS enabled me to excel at the intermediate level. I recall that we were subject to personal attention of dedicated teachers in the subjects of mathematics, physics and chemistry, besides the headmaster's own guidance as a teacher of English language and literature. All courses were systematically revised many times over. Class

---

6 These reminiscences have been published previously in 'A teacher of old', *The Tribune*, 05 Sept. 2007, https://www.tribuneindia.com/2007/20070905/edit.htm#5.

tests every other day ensured utmost readiness for facing the final examination. Study in the dormitory ended at precisely 9:40 pm as in school. I developed a habit of studying mainly during the daytime. During my academic career I had to take numerous examinations, all of which required sustained and rigorous study and preparation. Carrying forward the habits from school, I never once burnt the midnight oil, even as I saw most of my peers slog around the clock. Even when readying for the IAS qualifying exam, I did my toil during the day time. I find that by 10 pm the mind becomes groggy, the attention begins to wander, and there is no recourse but to throw away the books for the tired eyelids to close.

The final exam for the intermediate course turned out to be just another routine day at the office. The result: I succeeded effortlessly, being placed in the merit list of top candidates. The performance was strong enough to earn me admission in any technical institution in the country. It is another matter that I declined the courses in engineering and technology, and decided instead to go for a graduate degree of Bachelor of Arts in a government college at Chandigarh, which had become the new capital of the state of Punjab. I chose to study Mathematics and English, seemingly disparate subjects, as my teachers at YPS had reported in their assessment (I still have that historical evidence in my papers, which I flaunt before my grandchildren) that they observed 'my aptitude' for these disciplines. Mr R.L. Chitkara, my brilliant Mathematics teacher, who inspired me to secure almost full marks in the intermediate exam, was disappointed that I could not live up to his expectations in performing at higher levels. The fault for such under achievement was entirely mine. Overall it was my teachers and my years at YPS that inculcated in me a habit of systematic tension free study that became second nature to me.

My years of formal schooling, then, were mainly in boarding schools situated at places way from the places where my father worked as police superintendent. The stations where he worked were Bassi, Narnaul in the desert district of Mahendergarh and the state headquarters Patiala. As a policeman's son, I was a spectator of the functioning of the administration of the day. Years later, as a civil servant myself, I could embellish my limited view of yesteryear with my personal experience of men and situations. The attempt of any writer should be, in the words of the English poet-critic Matthew Arnold, 'to see life steadily, and to see it whole.' The milieu of administration in which I grew up was important in shaping my development in life. It thus appears relevant to this narrative.

Administration Viewed through Young Eyes

The district of Fatehgarh Sahib,[7] named after a son of Guru Gobind Singh, the tenth Sikh Guru, was situated about

---

7 In Sikh history, in the year 1704, the Nawab of Sirhind, under orders of the bigoted Mughal Emperor Aurangzeb, had ordered that two of the sons of the great Guru, Fateh Singh and Zoravar Singh, then boys aged seven and nine years, be walled up alive. At the site of the cruel event, 2 miles away from Bassi, stands a famous Gurudwara (Sikh temple), which is highly revered by the faithful. The wall where the grisly crime was committed is a part of the shrine.

100 miles south of Kapurthala, our original home. With the coming of Independence, almost all the princely states of colonial India had acceded to the Union of India. The tiny state of Kapurthala, where my father was working as Superintendent of Police, was merged into the Patiala and East Punjab States Union (PEPSU), a conglomeration of 8 small states in the region that became part of India. The original Punjab state of British India, into which PEPSU was eventually to integrate, was split between India and Pakistan, both named Punjab, as separate provinces in the two nations.

Ensconced as the family had been in the comforts that Kapurthala town offered, Bharpur Singh, my paternal grandfather was mightily upset that his eldest son, my father, would have to move to what was perceived as a remote, unsafe rural area. In the new state of PEPSU, spanning districts from its 8 erstwhile states Kapurthala stood reduced to an inconsequential little dot. It was the first time I heard the word 'transfer', which in fact was the process of relocation of officials from one part of the state to another, a common feature of administration. I recall the whole family according a tearful farewell to my father as he departed from Kapurthala, as if the young police officer was being exiled from civilization to a wild and barbaric region. True it was that the new district comprised primitive, poverty-stricken villages, poor in communication and in infrastructural facilities. There was no cause, though, as I concluded years later, for a police superintendent, which position my father enjoyed, to feel himself impaired by the shift to a new appointment.

In the traditional male dominated household my father took little interest in our welfare, leaving our upbringing as a task for the housemistress, as he dubbed his better half. Indeed, both Inderjit and I held my father in some awe. Seldom, if ever, was he demonstrative in affection toward either of us; rather he preferred to keep some distance between himself and us. He was an imposing figure, athletic in build, having been a champion fast bowler in cricket, a fine tennis and badminton player, and also an excellent shooter and horseman. His work required him to tour the villages in his charge extensively. This he did in his sturdy four-wheel drive vehicle that could traverse the uneven dirt footpaths masquerading as link roads in the villages. On his return from tour there would be an elaborate ritual of dusting off the accumulated mud and dirt. The first round of dusting was by his official orderly, an all-purpose attendant charged with the duty. Thereafter, at the second stage of dust removal, my father would use another cotton duster to flick away any remnants of soil from his person. He was fastidious to the extent that no dust would be carried into the house, and the ritual was invariably performed in the verandah. We could of course hear the noise of the brushing off as it were. The sahib was now ready for a bath, which had been prepared in advance by the water carrier.

We woke and slept as the creatures of nature. Dinner was laid just before sunset. In summer days there used to be just an hour between my father's return from work and our scheduled supper time, but as a proper officer, my father would be formally dressed even for the repast with family, down to shoes and stockings. He had a quaint habit, which he followed until his death at the age of 98, of never taking off his shoes throughout the day, no matter if there were no formal guest to entertain. I suspect that the aura of ever being on duty rubbed off on the uniformed police force that he commanded. It was a tradition from British times. The police manual mandates that every Monday morning a general parade is to be held, which the Superintendent of Police personally inspects. Meant to infuse discipline and smartness in turn out, the commanding officer is expected to wear a more elaborate uniform, beginning with stiff stockings and brown boots. From the stroke of dawn, around 4:30 am in summer and 5:30 am in winter my father would ready himself for the event, assisted by his orderly, who was needed to tie up khaki bandages, called '*pattis*', from ankle to knee, and then touch up the other effects of the elaborate ceremonial regalia. I recall that never during his postings as SP in several districts, come rain or shine, did my father miss out his Monday parade inspection. He never boasted about his strict adherence to the manual in letter and spirit; he considered it an essential part of his duties. Likewise, he visited every single police station in his jurisdiction at least twice every year, attending in great detail to the items listed in the inspection manual. I observed the same fastidiousness and meticulous attention to detail throughout his career as a policeman.

In villages like Bassi Pathanan there were hardly any members of the gentry with whom senior civil and police officers could socialize. Some families did not even join the officers at such remote stations, preferring to remain in other more hospitable towns with which they had ties. Also, differences, in age and social background, precluded the formation of close social links between families. My father being totally immersed in his official duties, my mother would surely have welcomed the opportunity of gainful engagement as a tutor to two young boys. I suspect that the arrangement at Bassi allowed both parents to enjoy their independent space in what was an insulated environment. Could it be that my parents had us two boys to thank for providing gainful diversion to the life partners? A reasonable conjecture!

I was curious to know how exactly the superiors of my father evaluated his performance in service. Inevitably my own image of my father, tinged with hero worship, was apt to be coloured. It was in the year 1979 when I was working in in the Ministry of Home Affairs, New Delhi, that I chanced to see the official confidential record of performance of all IPS officers in the country. It was a matter of personal gratification to observe accolades in the annual confidential reports consistently heaped on my father by his superiors over his 33-year-long career in a number of states. From the record it is obvious that he was regarded as a good and effective police officer. The irony strikes me now. Here was a son studying the report card of performance of his own father!

This chapter seeks to present, through the eyes of a growing boy, a perspective of the working of police administration at a critical time in India's history. The state of PEPSU functioned as a unit of governance from the year 1948 to 1956, when PEPSU was merged with the state of Punjab. Led by the Maharaja of Patiala, the princes of the states of Punjab were the first to accede to the Union of India. This would have persuaded their peers elsewhere in the country to do likewise. It was no surprise that the Government of India, headed by the powerful Home Minister Sardar Vallabhbhai Patel, decided to confer the title of Rajpramukh of PEPSU (Governor of the state) on Maharaja Yadavindra Singh of Patiala. This obviously smoothened the transition of the princes from the enjoyment of deemed autonomy in their erstwhile domain to a commoner's existence in the new democracy.

My father recalled that in the early years of independent India, many parts of PEPSU faced numerous incidents of dacoity and robbery, so much so that the Home Minister Sardar Patel feared a possible breakdown of law and order. For a short period of a few months, PEPSU was placed under direct rule of the Government of India (the President's Rule). My father often lauded the no-nonsense approach of the administration at the time, especially the clear directions of the adviser to the Rajpramukh (the Governor of PEPSU). Mr M.R. Bhide was an officer of the ICS. He would call a joint meeting of all Deputy Commissioners and Superintendents of Police to read out what is termed as 'the riot act'. The substance of directions to the field officers was to bring back the rule of law and re-establish the authority of the government. In any crisis situation, unity of command is of the essence. It is recorded that the carte blanche given to the district officers helped them to restore normalcy in PEPSU within a few months. Many dreaded criminals were eliminated, and gangs that invited dread were broken up. Mr M.R. Bhide built for himself the image of a tough administrator, on the lines of Sardar Patel himself.

Closest coordination between the deputy commissioner, the overall head of district administration, and the superintendent of police, the chief of the district police, was a cornerstone of British administration in India. For the administration, maintenance of law and order at all cost was the top priority. The tradition has continued to a large extent in democratic India, even as the responsibilities of civil administration have multiplied to encompass programmes for economic development, social uplift and crisis management. I found frequent occasions when the DC and SP toured the field areas jointly. In the process of interaction some differences in approach among strong personalities are bound to crop up; both DC and SP are enjoined to present an image of a harmonious administration. This face of administration was assiduously cultivated during the years that my father worked as SP.

If Bassi was a remote, poorly served village, my father's next assignment, at Narnaul, was virtual displacement from the proverbial frying pan to be cast into the fire. As with Bassi, there were no civic services then at Narnaul either. Furthermore, the district of Mahendergarh, of which

Narnaul was headquarters, happened to be located in the midst of a desert, with little communication by road or rail to the rest of the state. There being no road connectivity, one had to travel overnight from Delhi by a dilapidated meter gauge train to reach the district headquarters, which was in fact surrounded by districts of the neighbouring Rajasthan state. Being at boarding school, I did not have to bear the inhospitable conditions of extreme heat, when the temperature rose to 120°F (48 °C) and fell to almost freezing point, 0°C in winter. The district faced annual drought conditions, leading to famine, which was exacerbated by periodic attacks by swarms of locusts, which denuded any standing agricultural crops. Dust storms were the order of the day. On a short visit home in 1953, in all innocence, I enquired from my father if he could estimate the number of ships that would need to be deployed if all the sand in the dunes around Narnaul were to be moved out.

We were relieved that my father's stint at Narnaul, the most backward of all districts in the state, lasted just two years. Being relocated in Patiala, the most prosperous and refined city in the region, seemed to be a heaven-sent miracle. For me personally, it was a relief to be at home after several years in hostels. I could now attend school as a day boarder, as the status was described, which meant being at school for study and games all day, to return home to sleep at night.

It was at that stage of life, when I was around 12 years of age, that I began to realize the value of money, and also the privation that my parents endured in order to provide quality education to me. On my persistent questioning, my father disclosed that of his monthly salary of Rs 500, as much as Rs 135, almost one third of his carry-home pay, went towards my school fees. His salary was the sole source of income. He did not have the luxury of any inherited resources that could supplement his means. As such, existence was virtually hand to mouth. My education, however, was considered top priority; so the household was continuously penny pinching to be able to balance the budget.

After a secluded existence, lasting six years, in remote rural settlements at Bassi and Narnaul, my father found himself working in the most prosperous city in the region. Patiala boasted of style and substance. It was the hub of political and social activity. Even as my father occupied a prestigious position in the official hierarchy, which required a certain expenditure on socializing and hospitality, at no time were we able to splurge on luxuries. Being close to each other in age, at school my uncle Inderjit and I were considered brothers. Inderjit shortly left YPS for another school in Ludhiana, and then to join the National Defence Academy as an army cadet. Inderjit rose to the rank of a Major General in the Indian army, which is no small achievement. By the time my father came to Patiala the family included my two brothers, who were eight and eleven years younger than me. This would have necessitated additional expenses. During the four-year period that I was cycling daily to school, there was not a single occasion that we could afford to dine out in a restaurant. Any guests were entertained only at home, a less expensive proposition. Out of such comparative adversity was born a habit of thrift. It would appear somewhat unusual today, but at age 12, as the eldest of three brothers, I began to think of financial discipline at home. I gathered that the financial compensation even for officers in the Indian Police Service, one of the country's highly regarded civil services, was barely enough to sustain a middle-class existence.

I recall that in the year 1956 my father was inducted from the police service of the group of princely states called PEPSU into the Indian Police Service, which was an important step up in his career. This was part of the plan of the Government of India to strengthen the national cadres of the IAS and IPS with lateral entrance of high quality and experienced officers from state services. IPS and IAS were dubbed as All India Services, controlled by the Government of India, which could assign them to serve in any part of the country. My father's entry into the cadre of IPS did not change the status of his posting in Patiala, but meant an increase in his salary by some 200 rupees per month. My pocket money at that time was two rupees per month. My mother recommended that with more money flowing in, the quantum of my pocket money be doubled. I demurred. Not at the meagerness of the raise, but because I felt that her suggestion as inequitable. Backing up my own proposition empirically, I had calculated that if my allowance were to be enhanced in direct proportion to increased inflow of income in the household, I deserved a revised pocket allowance of exactly two rupees and fourteen and a half annas, slightly less than the revised amount proposed to be paid to me. (The metric system of decimal coinage had not yet been adopted. One rupee equalled sixteen annas, as per the traditional system in India). The little incident reflects not parsimony, nor a wanton display of mathematical skill on my part, but an acceptance that every penny earned must be spent wisely. In recognition of my mathematical application, my stipend was magnanimously increased to five rupees per month, which meant for me a jump of 250 per cent. Such austerity could have motivated me to work to my ability to justify the sacrifice that my parents had made for me. It was a time for frugality all around.

When my youngest brother Robby was about three years old, my parents decided to commit what was to my young mind a monumental folly. Without taking me into confidence they decided to allow him to be adopted by my mother's brother Dev Prakash and his wife, who had no children of their own. As I returned from school one afternoon, I was astounded to see the boy sitting cheerfully atop a trunk, which contained a load of his clothes. An attendant nursemaid was all ready to travel with him to the city of Ludhiana, some 70 miles away, where my Uncle Dev and his wife Damyanti would receive the child as their own. To tell the truth, I was shocked beyond measure. My dismay was not on account of the family by passing me in an important matter, but at what I considered an insensitive step. 'How could anyone dream of parting with their own flesh and blood so casually?' This impassioned protestation must have stirred both parents. Perhaps they too would have been emotionally charged at that critical moment of parting. As it was, the decision was hastily reversed. The trunk containing the boy's belongings was quickly unpacked. Three persons were immediately disappointed at this unexpected change of plans. These were Uncle Dev and his wife, the adoptive parents in waiting, and surprisingly, the young object of competing affection himself. At the age of three all that the child understood was that he had been deprived of an eagerly anticipated journey to visit his uncle. This was the first time that I had succeeded in vetoing the well laid plans of my elders. But for my timely intervention, how differently might several lives have turned out for several persons in the narrative! I was then 14 years of age.

A Fruition of Talents

It was at Patiala that I discovered a new facet in the personality of both my parents. This was a hitherto unsuspected charm and stage presence that came to the fore in company. Official functions and events they would attend as an obligation, but they had also had a group of friends, which met by turn at different homes. At these parties, the members displayed their poetic and musical talent, especially in the recitation of select Urdu poetry. At that time Urdu was a vibrant language in the region, an urbane medium for great literature. After all, the great Mirza Ghalib, who is regarded as the foremost Urdu poet in the world, had been alive barely 80 years earlier, and in his wake many distinguished poets had enriched the world of letters.

While the entertainment was mainly volunteered by the amateur members of the group itself, occasionally some professional performers of repute would be invited to add lustre to the party. From childhood the menfolk knew Urdu as their first language, which was then the official language in the region. Strangely, most of the ladies, including my mother, were grounded in Hindi and Punjabi. They understood the vocabulary of Urdu well enough, but could not read or write the Persian script. In regard to the subtle nuances of the language, my mother would need to consult her Urdu-proficient husband, who enjoyed poetry, but confessed that he had no ear for music. The husband–wife team was popular in every such '*mehfil*' (a gathering for entertainment). As a gifted singer my mother would render the verses in traditional ragas of Hindustani music. I was able to enjoy many a '*mushaira*' (an assembly for poetry recitation) at home. In other homes, guests were, as a matter of course, treated to alcoholic beverages. Then, as now, many reputed poets professed that liquor inspires them to write, and also stimulates audiences to applaud any recital. The company at Patiala accepted, though, that my parents, being teetotalers by conviction, would not serve alcoholic drinks. It was testimony to the stage presence and skill of my mother, abetted by my father, that the musical sessions at our home were keenly anticipated by the guests, even though no stimulants were offered, nor any meat-based dishes for the table.

The evenings were enlivened by the rendition of *ghazal*s, a popular genre of romantic poetry comprising couplets, which, ideally, are sung to tune, with or without accompanying instruments. Many distinguished poets imbue their love songs with a spiritual interpretation. Literary critics agree that it is a mystic component that characterizes the poetry of Mirza Ghalib, as well as that of several other reputed composers, with its universal appeal. On one plane, a *ghazal* celebrates a human emotion, love, that is often unrequited by the beloved. On another, the very same verse evokes a passionate spiritual longing for a bond with God. In highlighting the spiritual aspect, my mother created a niche for herself. Throughout life, she was immensely popular with social groups as an articulate guest speaker. She would embellish her exposition with music and poetry. In her later years, she would often say that she had no worldly goods to bequeath. During her lifetime, she averred, she had managed to accumulate just three categories of possessions. Her three sons and their wives should consider those as her legacy. The items were: her compilation of cooking recipes, her selections of choice *ghazal*s and her anthologies of hymns from the scriptures. From birth, both my brothers were highly gifted. Yajan (nick-named Robby), the youngest, had inherited my mother's musical talent. He received training in vocal classical music, and could hold spellbound audiences by his brilliant performance on stage. He did not take up music as a profession, but built a career in journalism. He had a natural talent for sports and games too, obviously a genetic inheritance from our father. The middle brother, Sajan, displayed exceptional dramatic talent as a stage actor, and in his student days performed in many productions in the Panjab University. Professor Balwant Gargi, an internationally regarded dramatic icon, who was chairman of the Department of Theatre in the university, offered Sajan a career in drama, but the young man declined. He adopted law as a profession.

Compared to my brothers, my ingrained talent was modest, although I did have a lasting passion for both music and sporting activities. I managed to cultivate these interests in my own way. In the 1950s, radio was the medium for common people to access music; only the elite could afford a mechanically operated gramophone, which used a tiny sharp needle to pick up the sound from the grooves of the records. Film music broadcast on radio was popular. In terms of presentation, the stations of the state-run All India Radio could not compete with Radio Ceylon, which packaged music from Hindi films, and relayed these via a powerful short-wave transmitter from Colombo. My favourite programme was a hit parade of popular Hindi songs, ranked as per a weekly popularity chart. This was called the *Binaca Geet Mala*, Binaca toothpaste being the sponsor. Since we had no radio at home then, it was for me a ritual to cycle to the home of a friend (Ranjan Kapoor his name was) every Wednesday at 8 pm. Ranjan and I shared a harmless little pleasure in suspense of which song would top the weekly pops. Incidentally Ranjan Kapoor went into business of professional advertising, and rose to be the head of the Asia operations of Ogilvy and Mather, one of the world's foremost advertising agencies. With an abiding interest in music over many decades, I have managed to preserve in perfect condition hundreds of old lacquer-coated as well as vinyl long-playing gramophone records, spools and tapes, compact discs (CDs) and numerous modern pen drives of recorded music. The collection includes the original gadgets for reproducing the sounds and airs of Hindustani as well as Western music, both light and classical. In the age of digital technology, the unfeeling family has banished to the store some prized items, such as a gramophone that might be from the era of the inventor Thomas Alva Edison. Sadly, the family dismisses my priceless collection as a clutter of ancient relics. A veritable exhibition could easily display the stages of development of music and its technology for reproduction over several generations. Admittedly, the music lovers, likely to appreciate the archives, might comprise a 'fit audience though few' among lovers of music.

A PATH CHARTS ITSELF

Most members of my generation enrolled in a graduate course with little or no idea of where study was likely to lead them. When the country became independent, it was only poorly developed, economically. Agricultural productivity was low. There was little organized industrial activity or commerce, and hardly any opportunity for employment in the private sector, except for low-skill jobs in small family enterprises. By the year 1959, when I had completed my schooling, job opportunities were mainly in the government sectors. A few boys were selected to join the armed forces, where their career progressed as per a set pattern. Some bright students, mostly boys, who secured admission in medical colleges or engineering institutions, would go on to become government doctors or engineers.

I and some class fellows fell into a third category, that is, of persons who did not as yet know their own mind for pursuing a professional career. Having secured reasonable results, a good first class in the Intermediate (Class 12) examination, I had declined to go for a technical degree in engineering or medicine. No career counsel being available, I entered the Government College in the new city of Chandigarh as what could best be considered a default option. At school my teachers had asserted that I had some aptitude for mathematics and could write well in the English language. It was comforting to believe them. I therefore chose to study mathematics, with an honours course in English literature, hoping vaguely that the selected studies might qualify me for a career in teaching. At that time in society teachers were highly respected; education then was highly regarded as 'a noble profession'. In monetary terms, a junior lecturer in the University began with a starting salary of Rs 350 per month, as compared to the Rs 400 per month drawn by a raw civil servant in the IAS. Most of my classmates in the new college aspired similarly to become college lecturers or school teachers, or to join at junior levels as government officials. Some were to use graduation as a step to the profession of law. A degree in law authorized the holder to practice at the bar, and could even lead to a position in the judiciary.

Carefree at College

My ambitions, then, at that stage of life were ill defined. For most students the days at college were a time to enjoy freedom, a period of carefree ebullience—a breath of fresh air after years of supervised discipline at school. Some were seen to plod half-heartedly towards a distant professional career. I was among a minority that enjoyed the study of literature for its own sake. I was fortunate that I could approach learning with some abandon. I had joined the BA course when I was not yet 16 years of age, and the MA at 18. At that stage I had no desperate compulsion to define and aim for long-term ambitious goals. I relished reading for its own sake, and did not view knowledge as a vehicle for high intellectual attainment. Perhaps the absence of a challenging target lurking on the horizon would have helped me to absorb the contents of books with a degree of effortlessness. If a person remains relaxed, and oblivious to the consequences, he can perform better in crucial situations than someone stressed and tension-ridden along the way. Obviously success in life demands visualization of a final goal, but the challenge must not overwhelm one to the extent of impairing concentration, and ability to perform. A delicate balance needs to be maintained. An analogy from sports is apposite. At a certain stage of his journey to excellence, a tennis champion, or a skater, is able to attain a level of focus where the movements become fluid, automatic; he has psyched himself to enter what he terms the 'zone'. In that zone the champion plays with absolute focus of mind, a stage that the critics deem is inspiration. Similarly, any recipe for academic success must include mental strength as an essential ingredient.

It had been my lasting regret that while at school I could not excel at sport, as I suffered from bouts of an undiagnosed energy-sapping, low-grade fever. The moment I joined college that physical shortcoming miraculously vanished, and I found myself doing well at games. At college and in the university, I was captain of the basketball team, and also a member of the winning tennis team in the inter-college competition. At that time private colleges provided special facilities, such as diet, to sportsmen, and at times even exempted players from attending classes. The policy aimed to pamper sportsmen who could build the image of the college for excellence. Students displaying all-round quality, that is, at academics as well as sport, were almost unheard of. Government colleges such as mine in Chandigarh had extensive playgrounds and facilities for all games, but provided no institutional support for building excellence in sports disciplines. It was left to the initiative of the players themselves to organize themselves into a team, and to participate in competitions. Thus, I and my fellow players created our college team on our own, with no special support or sponsorship from the college authorities. I recall embarrassing moments during basketball matches, where the players of our team did not even possess uniform apparel. In the absence of any numbers on our shirts, the referee was forced to identify each player by the colour of the shorts that he wore, much to the amusement of the spectators. On one occasion, when we travelled to play matches in a nearby town, Khanna, we were put up in a cattle shed for the night. I remember that I spent a sleepless November night tossing on wheat straw spread over the floor. Early morning, we had to visit the open fields for our ablutions, as there were not even rudimentary sanitary facilities on offer. I joked that a sportsman's life was literally a bed of straw. Such roughing-up endured in early youth might have served to keep my feet on the ground in later life, when I occupied a position of authority.

Back those days, I also worked on physical fitness fiendishly, if unscientifically, as I had no professional guidance. While on the tennis courts of Panjab University (I was then 18 years old), I had an unexpected encounter with Milkha Singh, who was India's national champion sprinter. In the year 1961, Milkha Singh was fresh with his haul of gold medals at the Asian Games and the Commonwealth Games. At the age of 31, he had made a world record in the 400-metre race in the Rome Olympic Games of 1960. I had heard of Milkha's exploits on the track. It was with awe that I watched the champion from the adjacent tennis lawns as he used to run on the track continuously for four or five hours every afternoon. We would be sweating and exhausted after two sets of tennis, but the Flying Sikh, as he was named during a race in Pakistan, seemed to go tirelessly on and on. On one occasion, he stepped up from the adjacent track, and enquired ever so humbly if he could try his hand at tennis. I was quite overwhelmed to meet the celebrity in real life. Even as he admitted that he was touching a tennis racquet for the very first time in his life, he managed to get the ball across the net comfortably. To retrieve the ball from distant corners of the court seemed to him child's play. Years later, when he had joined the Punjab Government as a sports director, I came to know him as a colleague. He remembered his training days at the University grounds, although naturally, he could hardly have placed me as a student player in the distant past. In later years, we met at social occasions too. I recall that at one dinner party he was persuaded to sing for the assembled guests. He had a surprisingly good singing voice. I can still remember that Milkha rendered in tune a doleful number from the film *Mela*, originally sung by Mohammed Rafi. The sad verse goes:

'*Yeh zindagi ke mele duniyan me kum na honge/ Afsos hum na honge.*' (These celebrations of joy in the world will not wane, but I will sadly not be there to enjoy them.)

Himself an internationally acclaimed sportsman, Milkha lamented that Indian sports had not produced world-class athletes. He often publicly declared that he dreamed of a day when an Indian athlete would win an individual gold medal in the Olympics. That dream was fulfilled some two generations later, by a young Indian javelin thrower named Neeraj Chopra at the Olympic Games at Tokyo in August 2021. Milkha was not there to savour the fulfilment of his dream—the great athlete had died just prior to the event. Neeraj dedicated his gold medal to none other than him, who had been his inspiration. In my condolences to Milkha Singh's son Jeev, I recounted the irony in the words of the poignant lyric. For me it was a privilege to have had Milkha Singh as a friend.

While I did play matches at university level, I must admit that at college I did not exert myself at study as I should have done. That I still managed to secure a first-class honours degree was partly the result of the grounding that I had received at school. The momentum built at school helped to carry me through, on the analogy of the moment of inertia of a moving body, as defined in physics. Once at the university, however, I immersed myself in books. From pure enjoyment of reading to result-oriented study was a crucial step forward.

I went through the studies for the graduate (Honours) degree and the Master's degree without much fuss. It was after completing the Master's that I began to work diligently for the civil services examination of the Union Public Service Commission. For taking the examination you had to be aged between 21 years and 24 years, and to be a graduate. Since I had completed my MA at the age of 20 years, I found that I could wait a full year and three months before I became eligible to sit for the test. This was an ample interregnum, and allowed me valuable time to ready myself for the tough task ahead. I was also lucky that, on account of good performance in MA, the University selected me as a teacher. I had topped the list, albeit securing a good second class, a first class in English being then a rarity. I could thus teach, and at the same time study for the professional test. In fact, I moved seamlessly from student to teacher in the very same Department of English, immediately after my result for MA was declared. This was indeed a happy placement for me; the quality academic environment in Panjab University was ideal to develop skills to face the examination. At that time, of the 30,000 candidates competing in the UPSC exam, just 125 were finally chosen to join the IAS, 20 the Indian Foreign service, 70 the Indian Police Service, besides about 300 being placed in other Central Services.[1] It was a stiff competition for all aspirants, requiring sustained and systematic preparation over more than a year.

At home as a House Guest

I had the benefit of spending these crucial years staying at home in Chandigarh, two years with my parents, as my father happened to be then working as a police officer in the city, and the remaining four years with an aunt and uncle who taught and worked in the university. It was common practice then for students to park themselves at the home of hospitable relatives for their entire academic career. In a milieu where families willingly offered to support youngsters related to them, it was taken for granted that I would stay with my mother's sister, along with her four sons, my first cousins, and another house guest of my age, who was the son of friends of the family. The house was akin to a boys' hostel. All six boys were treated on par, our bicycles neatly lining the garage, each receiving an identical monthly pocket allowance of Rs 20, to meet minor needs. In that carefree atmosphere, we were not bothered to consider the difficulty that my aunt would have had in running the household, from the management, and the financial angle.

I observed that many teachers at the university at that time were similarly supporting students who stayed at home

---

1 The number of aspirants for the civil services now touches the mark of 300,000, a ten-fold increase, even as the number of vacancies in the various services has remained almost the same as was the case half a century earlier.

with them. These long-term student-house guests included some boys and girls who were not even related to the family. This was a wonderful tradition among the educationists of the time. The motivation for my hosts, who put me up for four years, was totally altruistic. Over his teaching career as a professor of Zoology, my uncle, Professor GL Arora had virtually adopted from a young age, several deserving and needy students, to build them up as teachers in their own right. During my stay with the Aroras at Chandigarh, several of these foster children, now established in their respective professions, would often visit their mentors, Professor and Mrs Arora, at what they considered their own home. The only return the Aroras would have secured in nurturing talent was the satisfaction to observe their protégés succeeding in life. I found myself a part of this fine *gurukul*[2] tradition of India, where teachers devoted their time, energy and resources to develop human capital. I think my aunt and uncle were as proud of my achievements as they were of those of their biological sons, my cousins, who rose to be civil servants, teachers and fighter pilots in the Indian Air Force.

Professor Arora was himself an outstanding teacher and guide for his students of Entomology, his specialized discipline in the life sciences. Originally a lecturer at the University at Lahore, he was an eminent teacher in the new

2 The system of *Gurukul*, meaning literally, family of the guru, or teacher, was in vogue in ancient India, and is extolled in the Hindu scriptures. Students were placed under the tutelage of a revered teacher, with whom they lived as a member of the family in the ashram, to receive academic training, as well as grounding in ethics and philosophy.

university at Chandigarh. He had a passion for accuracy in expression. Mercurial in temperament, I would sometimes hear him shout at his researchers, who, incidentally he allowed to visit him at home. 'Take away this bullshit!' he would bluntly admonish a PhD student, throwing a painstakingly drafted document in her face. Seeing the poor girl reduced to tears at the humiliation, Mrs Arora would have to intervene to console the young scholar. As the professor regained composure, he would proceed to devote hours to provide a critique for the benefit of the researcher. Despite his outbursts, Dr Arora was famed as the most popular teacher in his department. And Mrs Arora was ever at hand, a standing and valuable ally for students facing the professor's wrath. The student was considered a part of the tutor's own family, in which capacity she was treated at par with the professor's children. In the person of teachers like Dr Arora, one witnessed the ancient *gurukul* system still alive in its current avatar!

An amazingly healthy, open atmosphere prevailed in the Arora household. In a subtle manner the environment must have aided academic enterprise among the six young men, including myself, all aged between 14 and 20 years in age, who were privy to it. I recall that when I disclosed to my parents that I was enjoying my stay with my aunt, they were pleasantly surprised. Parents and guardians are seldom fully satisfied with the devotion of their wards to their studies. There would certainly have been occasions when I was remiss in application to the books. I must say that that never during my stay with them did the Aroras upbraid me or nag me. A lesson here in motivation was for parents to stay out of the way of the younger generation, and allow the innate talent of youth to blossom.

During the time I was reading for the MA, I would sometimes travel home by bus for the weekend to Ambala, a district town just 30 miles away from Chandigarh, where my father was the Superintendent of Police. In those days youngsters frequently took advantage of the official position held by their parents. I too exploited my connection with the police in a small manner. Chandigarh city was then a part of Ambala district. As I travelled from Chandigarh to Ambala by bus, I allowed myself the privilege of parking my humble bicycle within the Chandigarh central police station in Sector 17, which adjoined the bus stand from where I embarked on my short journey. The police inspector in charge would have been happy to accommodate my petty demand for use of the police station as a parking lot. After all, he was obliging the son of his superior. My friends were astonished at the impunity with which I could enter the police station, normally a bastion dreaded by youngsters.

A Campus for Exploration

None of us six inmates at the Aroras lived in profligacy; all that our meager allowance (fixed at 20 rupees monthly for each boy) allowed was an occasional visit to the cinema, a ticket for which cost one rupee and a half. No one could afford to eat out in restaurants: at best we could sometimes enjoy samosas or cutlets on the roadside. Within the campus proper was a solitary open air tea shop, where some of us assembled under a banyan tree to gossip and lampoon our teachers. A harmless pastime at no cost! Books could be borrowed from the well-stocked University library; purchase of the volumes was beyond our means. To access rare books you had to spend hours in the reference section, taking down copious notes in long hand. In a way, the huge effort involved in transcribing notes would have allowed some part of the contents to be stored in memory, thus aiding comprehension. Today's generation of students can conveniently photocopy extracts from any reference book for subsequent use, and even use the web to augment vital information, but perhaps this instant access to knowledge might not enable them to absorb features of material that came to us by tedious physical reproduction of passages. I still have my handwritten notes from my university days, my lament being that my own children did not take advantage of my labour undertaken a generation before.

By definition, a university is a community of teachers and scholars. With its expansive campus in a sparkling new planned city, Panjab University attracted distinguished teachers in many disciplines, as well as serious and not-so-serious scholars. The original home of Punjab University was Lahore, the capital of Punjab before the state was divided between India and Pakistan at the time of partition of the country in 1947. Following the disruption caused by Partition, the university had been temporarily located in the small town of Hoshiarpur in Punjab. The sprawling campus of the University of Panjab (spelt as Panjab to differentiate it from the parent Punjab University in Lahore) is integral to the city of Chandigarh of le Corbusier, the French-Swiss architect who conceived, planned and designed the capital city. The university at Chandigarh drew academicians of international repute. Professors like the geologist M.R. Sahni, the Hindi litterateur Hazari Prasad Dwivedi, the botanist A.C. Joshi who was the Vice Chancellor, and the chemist R.C. Paul were names we looked up to in silent reverence. The English department boasted of stalwarts like Raj Kumar, Ish Kumar, A.G. George, Jagdish Chander, R.K. Kaul and the novelist Krishna Baldev Vaid. I recall many visiting scholars too, a few from abroad, who added colour and spice to the faculty. Surely some academic flavour would have descended on the new entrants like us. The famous academic faculty swore by the Gandhian ideals of simple living and high thinking. Among all the teachers, just a few owned even two-wheelers; possession of a car was for all a distant dream. Everyone rode bicycles, which were parked in extensive sheds attached with each teaching department. I remember that Professor Hazari Prasad Dwivedi, the first owner of a car in the campus suffered a freak accident in his brand-new vehicle. Not used to his automobile, he lost a finger of his hand that had become stuck in the car door.

The university campus was not merely books and study. As becoming an institution of higher learning, there was considerable interaction across departments and age groups. There was room too for sport, recreation, socializing and such activities for those so inclined. The school and college that I attended had been almost exclusively for boys. Before entering the university, I had hardly any occasion for interaction with girls of my age. One viewed the fair sex from afar, or in the make-believe world of cinema and literature. In that conservative society there were unwritten conventions that obviated excessive familiarity between members of the sexes. There were more girls than boys in the Department of English, as also in most other departments. Like me, the students were mainly from middle class families. Some girls, who had received education in convent schools, that is institutions run by adherents to Christianity, were Westernized in behaviour and appearance. English for this group was first language, akin to mother tongue. In the English department, their group elicited some awe, on account of their fluency in speech. Verbal articulation by itself did not assure high marks, though. This was realized when students outside the group of fluent English speakers scored higher in the final examinations.

It is likely that at the outset the boys might have been awkward in speech and behaviour, and the girls shy and withdrawn. At university the invisible barriers quickly broke down. There was healthy participation in activities such as discussions, debates, seminars and drama. Some musical evenings at the homes of friends brought forth unexpected in-house musical talents. These were mostly group activities. Romantic liaisons were inevitable. Some affairs became cause célèbre, the talk of the campus. At that time there were five independent hostels for boys, and just one for the girls. Additional girls' hostels came up in the early 1960s. The departments of law, commerce and engineering had mainly male students, while the girls outnumbered boys in the humanities and languages. In the science departments, boys and girls were about equal in number. The female students staying in the hostel were closely supervised. Outside teaching hours they were not allowed to move outside the hostel door; they required special permission to receive male visitors. The girls' hostel was akin to a fortress, closed for ingress to the public, and restricted for exit of the inmates. Our group of friends named it Fort William, after the headquarters of the Indian army in Calcutta.[3] The name stuck, until another hostel for girls, code-named Fort George, came up. Some boyfriends, masquerading as cousins, did manage to evade the eagle eye of the authority; I suspect that the obstacles in the way of courting couples would have fanned many emotions, and occasioned enterprise. My aunt Dev Kumari Arora, with whom I was staying at home, happened to be the warden. As the commandant, the vigilance she exercised was a source of reassurance to the parents of her wards.

If the parents of girls welcomed the enforcement of extraordinary discipline over the inmates, the girls themselves chafed at what they felt was the unfairness

3 Until the year 1911, the heavily fortified Fort William served as the seat of the British colonial power. Fort William continues as the Headquarters of the Eastern Command of the Indian army.

of the dispensation. The reasoning, of course, was why should different standards of freedom and conduct apply to students on the basis of sex? If boys were permitted to move out of the hostel at odd hours, why should not girls? On one momentous occasion the simmering discontent came to a head when a male guest (read: boyfriend) of a female student was unceremoniously turned away from the hostel lobby by a warder in charge. It happened that the female concerned was a student leader in her own right. And the 'cousin' was well connected with some member of the syndicate (the governing body) of the university. The girl inmates went on strike with a list of demands, beginning with easing of the restrictions. My aunt was under great stress. She stood her ground, insisting that she was bound to enforce the rules as framed. A minority of girls, along with a majority of their parents would have supported Mrs Arora, the warden, but these were silent, unorganized groups. Meanwhile the demand for girls' freedom was gathering pace. The university authorities decided that discretion was the better part of valour. The warden was replaced; Mrs Arora was transferred to an innocuous position in the library. Peace was restored.

This little episode created some anxious moments in the Arora household. I appreciated entirely the bold and conservative approach of the warden. My endorsement, which was not really of any consequence, was not merely on account of Mrs Arora being an affectionate and respected elder in our family. In any case my aunt was suitably reassigned a less onerous job, which she enjoyed doing.

At that time one little society that attracted me and my friends was called TKT, Talk over a Cup of Tea. We met every Tuesday, if I remember correctly, in a hall in the Department of Psychology. The members included young teachers, and also students of both sexes from departments across the campus. There would be distinguished guest speakers and lively discussions on a variety of topics, and some hilarity in games such as dumb charades. Some members made spontaneous presentation of original creative works of art or poetry. Although not high-brow per se, TKT had some variety in intellectual content. The members used it as a fine occasion to mix freely; some as a time to flirt. As several from amongst the group were successful in the prestigious UPSC examination, it encouraged the younger lot to try for the test as well. I recall that TKT was the forum where I met the formidably gifted Professor B.N. Goswamy, later to be honoured by the Government of India with the Padma Shri and Padma Bhushan. Dr Goswamy was originally a historian. After a brilliant academic career, he joined the IAS. His passion was the study of art. He had the unique distinction of resigning from the IAS to pursue his vocation as an art historian. Indeed, he is acclaimed as one of the leading art critics of the world.

Karuna, Dr Goswamy's wife, who was several years younger than her husband, was my contemporary as a student. Brijendra and Karuna Goswamy made an elegant and imposing couple. In society they came to be esteemed as an epitome of learning and sophistication. I proudly recall an occasion when I was called upon by Karuna to help transport the very first motor vehicle that her husband had acquired. This was a motor scooter. It transpired that the professor was bringing the two-wheeler from Delhi to Chandigarh in the brake van of the night train. Since Dr Goswamy could not drive, on one chilly winter morning I accompanied Karuna to the railway station, armed with a bottle of petrol. The vehicle was duly fuelled, and driven to their home. The trifling event has remained etched in memory. It exhibited the style and simple living of an intellectual icon of the country. Karuna acknowledged, smilingly, that I was superior to her vastly distinguished husband in one important skill: I had learnt to handle a scooter before he could do so.

It was during the days at the university that some six or eight of us close friends, all young men in our early 20s, constituted ourselves into an informal club, called the Dodos, after an extinct flightless bird in some islands of the Indian Ocean. The one rule for the Dodos was that they must be unmarried, for it was a bachelors' club. We were all at the threshold of a career. Some were aiming to sit for an examination for entry into any of the civil services, others hoping to join the nascent corporate sector, or planning for a teaching career. The activities consisted of watching films, playing tennis, dabbling as stage actors in amateur productions, and occasional parties, to which the more adventurous members would invite girls too. Our favourite haunt was the Indian Coffee House, so preferred because the fare there was affordable, being within our limited means. Our parents did not really expect that any members of the loose gang would actually amount to much in real life. They were surprised, pleasantly, no doubt, when we all managed to take some little steps to move out of the category of the 'educated but unemployed youth'. Ajit Kumar and Bhagirath Dwivedi were the first Dodos to qualify for the IAS. Ajit, the most successful as a career administrator, rose in due course to the position of Finance and Defence Secretary in the Government of India, and married a batchmate Kamlesh from the Indian Foreign Service. Bhagirath, unfortunately, was not allowed to join the service, as he was deemed by the medical board as being too short-sighted. Within the group Bhagirath was regarded as a powerful stage actor, but his myopia was beyond the permissible limit of minus 8 diopters. The adversity did not deter his success in the private sector, as he joined a multinational pharmaceutical company as a senior executive in Bombay. He was to marry a celebrated author Sharada Joshi. Likewise, Satish Bedi, who was then fresh from a degree from the University of Cambridge in the UK, was for us the perfect ladies' man, hugely popular with the belles. He was picked up by the petroleum company Burmah Shell, and reached the top in the corporate sector. Sandeep Bhandari and Harish Avasthi were selected for the central cadres of the Indian Railways and Information and Broadcasting respectively. Narinder Arora, who was my cousin, joined the Life Insurance Corporation of India as an administrator. Sadly, Narinder died in a bus accident at the early age of 27. My own distinction within the undistinguished group was that I was the first to be expelled from the Dodo club. It happened that although the youngest in the group, I was the first to be married; so I was summarily disqualified by the bachelors. The telegrams that my friends sent at the wedding were not to congratulate me, but to commiserate as I was no longer one of them. It is another matter that the original club gradually dissipated, when the members, one after another, took the matrimonial plunge. In course of time, the Dodo club amended its regulations, readmitted the founding players, and we reunited. The headquarters of the club shifted to Bombay, where the majority of the original group was based. Whenever I visited Bombay, it was an occasion for the Dodos to reassemble at an evening party, and relive old times.

Teaching and Learning

When I decided to try my luck in the examination for the civil services, it was to Dr Goswamy that I turned for guidance in the modern era of Indian History. He might not remember now, but it was he who suggested that I may rely on a single book, *The Making of Modern India*, by Shripad R. Sharma to educate myself. History being a new subject for me, I followed his advice, in letter and spirit, and based my preparation on the book he had advised.

I wish I had elicited similar guidance from experts in planning my strategy for the professional entrance test for civil servants. The UPSC examination at that time required candidates to take three compulsory papers: General Knowledge, General English and Essay. You could select any three additional subjects of your choice in what was called the lower level, and another two of the higher level, making a total of eight papers to prepare for. In making my choice of papers I blundered badly. Armed with my evaluation of aptitude from school, I opted for a paper in Pure Mathematics. I soon realized that no matter what one's innate understanding, mathematics requires continuous and skilled guidance. A wizard such as my own batch mate S.A.T. Rizvi, from the cadre of Uttar Pradesh state, could score almost cent percent in all three papers offered in Mathematics, which brought him the distinction of topping the list in our batch. In contrast, all that I carried was a vague perception that Mathematics could be a scoring subject. Determined to persist with my choice, I decided to seek a guide. He was Professor S.P. Arora, a well-meaning teacher, but not one who could bluntly tell me that, with my limited study of the abstruse subject, I was barking up the wrong tree. I was in a peculiar situation of taking tuition in one subject (Maths for which I paid Rs 80 per month) while at the same time I was teaching English (earning Rs 350 per month). My obsession with the subject was overpowering, so much so that I devoted most of the period of study in attempting painful solutions and complex formulations. In the process I neglected my other papers in History, a new subject for me at that level. In a childish move at dramatic effect, I assigned a separate corner in my study to different subjects selected for study. Notes for English, History, General Studies and Mathematics were accumulated separately in the four corners of the study. I moved melodramatically from one corner to the next, even as for months the floor beneath remained unclean and unswept.

How far these subterfuges helped me in psyching myself for performance is a matter of conjecture. The test in Pure Mathematics, though, turned out to be a fiasco. The syllabus for the paper included 13 sub-groups of different topics. I had prepared for just five of those, confident that I would manage the answers. When I opened the question paper, I was dismayed to find that the examiner had (perversely, to my mind) left out most of the topics that I had focused on. Most of the question paper itself was beyond my comprehension. Consequently, I scored just 19 per cent in what I had hoped would be a high-scoring paper. Surprisingly in the two papers in history, an unfamiliar subject, I did well. Expectedly, I performed to potential in the papers linked with English, which in fact was my specialization. In the end result, my scores in the other papers enabled me to make up for the dismal shortfall in Pure Mathematics. This was for me a rude awakening. As with the admonishment of Calpurnia, the wife of Julius Caesar in Shakespeare's famous play of the same name, I found that my 'wisdom (was) consumed in confidence'. The lesson that I learnt was that one must seek counsel in making important decisions. Depending on your own judgment based on gut feeling can be disastrous.

I enjoyed my foray into teaching, which began the very day I turned 20. I remember that I presented my very first pay packet to my grandmother, who accepted it hesitantly with tears in her eyes. As the junior most in the faculty, I was to teach English to science students working for what was called an Honours School degree in the respective disciplines of physics, botany, zoology, geology or chemistry. I found myself taking lessons over 17 hours a week, which was the prescribed work load. The task was straightforward enough. It consisted of training the class to write concisely, with grammatical and factual accuracy. Skill in usage of the language equips scientists to communicate better, so was the reasoning. Some books of short stories, one-act plays and poems were the prescribed reading.

On this first assignment as a teacher, I faced two unexpected challenges. Firstly, to establish my credentials as a teacher with students, who were almost as old as me. Secondly, to ensure that my wards took the subject itself with due seriousness. From the very outset I realized that my students considered that learning the English language was inconsequential for them; their concern was with the main discipline of science that they were pursuing. The budding scientists considered English at best a fun subject, which they had perforce to clear as ordained. The solution that I devised made a virtue of a necessity. I assured my wards that, being close to them in age, I would treat them as my equals. I also used innovation to make the sessions interesting, within the parameters of the course content, of course. I linked references in passages in the text with stories and myths from works of literature and even the scriptures. The class became interested in stories from Homer's ancient Greek epic describing the war of Troy, as in the story of Ahilya in the *Ramayana*. While taking up a story of the science fiction writer H.G. Wells, I narrated other stories of Wells. The method, which enlarged the ambit of the young students beyond the texts prescribed, helped me in building rapport with my audience. I took my pupils into the prophetic *Brave New World* of Aldous Huxley, knowing that scientific minds would be excited at the idea of propagation of the human race through technique of artificial insemination in the laboratory. Every little idiom in the English language has as its origin some myth or fable. I traced all such origins. It was understood that when Helen of Troy selected Paris as a paramour by presenting him an apple, he became the apple of Helen's eye, which provoked other suitors, leading eventually to the Trojan War. I was pleasantly surprised when some of my female students requested me to suggest some books of science fiction. On occasions, contrary to protocol, I encouraged the boys and girls to present little items of song and dance in the classroom, taking care to see that the entertainment was sheltered from prying eyes.

Overall, my teaching stint of two academic years was immensely satisfying. Finding young boys and girls attending classes not merely to learn some texts, but to enjoy the classics and even Shakespeare, gave me a sense of achievement. When, at the end of my second year of teaching, the class learned that I had been selected to join the IAS, some students came to seek my autograph. I was nonplussed; I was certain that such honour was due for celebrities, not for a fresh teacher like me. I wondered if this could be a sample of flattery for a parting teacher. One student insisted that I should write something in her book. All that I could think of at the spur of the moment was to quote George Bernard Shaw, 'He who can, does; he who cannot, teaches.' The girl was visibly upset that my note had vilified my own profession, that of a teacher. For years thereafter, I was gratified to receive greetings from some of my former pupils on the occasion of the annual Teachers' Day on 5 September.

Competing for Service

Balancing my commitments as a teacher with the pursuit of a highly competitive examination was not easy. During the academic session my lectures took priority. Vacation time was dedicated to study for the crucial test. Immersed in books and notes, for several months before the test I did not step out of the house at all. At the end of my first year of teaching, I was technically confirmed as a University Tutor, which earned me a handsome increment of Rs 20 per month, in addition to my starting salary of Rs 350 per month. I had requested the University authorities to grant me two months of leave for the critical test. This demand was declined, so I had to be content in taking short leave of absence for each day that my papers were scheduled. I could not risk resigning my teaching post, as success in the gruelling test was uncertain; if I failed, my secure job would be lost, leaving me unemployed. For ease of the aspirants, the UPSC conducts its examinations at centres located in different towns in various states. Candidates from the state of Punjab were at that time required to travel by bus to Patiala city, a distance of about 40 miles from Chandigarh city, for appearing the test. Most papers were scheduled in the late afternoon. On some occasions, I would complete my teaching work in the morning, and thereafter travel to Patiala, to return home late in the evening for the grind of the coming day. In retrospect, I believe that that onerous schedule helped rather than disturbed my concentration.

When the results of the written test were declared in the month of December 1964, I was among the candidates who qualified for the next stage of the selection process, that is, the personality test by an elite panel of intellectuals. Knowing that my marks in one of the important papers were expected to be poor, this preliminary result was a pleasant surprise. I was now to face a group of formidable experts who would determine, on the basis of a half-hour interaction, if I was cut out to be an administrator. In those days there were some professional institutions, located mainly in the metropolitan cities, which prepared you for the personality test. I found that most candidates enrolled in such study circles, where they were taught skills in discussion, face-to-face interaction, and such matters as deportment and confidence building. The study circles also provided aspirants with appropriate reading material on topics anticipated to figure in the final trial.

I studied the guidelines of the UPSC on the personality test. These stated clearly that this final appraisal was not to test the knowledge per se of candidates, but to adjudge their overall suitability for the chosen service. I had disdain, illogical perhaps, for using any external support to mould character at short notice. I was convinced that no techniques, however systematically evolved, could be expected to alter a personality overnight. It was even possible that the props suggested by specialized coaching institutions could impair the spontaneity of the respondents. I airily dismissed the need for personality development techniques, and decided to go virtually unprepared for the important event. It transpired that this iconoclastic approach assisted my performance before the august interviewers. True, I did not know the answers to some questions posed to me, but when I confessed inability to answer, it was taken as a measure of aplomb, rather than a display of ignorance.

The board began with a leading question. Noting that I had been a proficient sportsman, the Chairman enquired why I did not join the Indian Police Service rather than the IAS. My unrehearsed reply, which could well have doomed me, was that my father, himself a serving police officer had advised me against joining his service. The obvious follow up question by a member was, 'So, do you always go to your father for advice, or can you take decisions on your own?' This was a trap. Perhaps by luck, I responded, 'Sir, I accept his advice, when it suits me.' This off-the-cuff reply was unexpected, and disarmed the Board. The members had a hearty laugh, and put me at total ease. Some questions on sports I answered satisfactorily, but I missed a great opportunity to establish my credentials. To a question on the composition of the Indian hockey team that had won the recent Olympics in Tokyo I needlessly boasted that I could name all eleven members, thereby closing a topic on which I was at home. Their questions on English literature I handled comfortably, but when the discussion wandered to Mathematics, I preempted any grilling by stating simply that after my poor show in the Mathematics paper I wished to forget that subject, rather than discuss it further. This reply too would have won me some points. One of the members made a tricky observation that public schools were an unfair advantage for well-off students. My reply was that if the Government valued the quality of public schools, the solution lay in raising the standards in government schools, rather than castigate the elite schools.

On reviewing the personality test I felt vindicated in the approach I adopted, viz. to let the Board judge me as I was, rather than my presenting them a tailor-made version of my personality. The end result of my struggle with the civil services examination was positive, but for my lasting remorse lingered lingered that with a better strategy I could have done better. I remember that the UPSC had allotted me the roll number 13. That ominous number did not prove unlucky. Fate had been kind to me.

FREEDOM AND JOLLITY

My career as a civil servant began with two years of training. The first year was spent in the National Academy of Administration (NAA), a training institute at Mussoorie, in today's state of Uttarakhand.[1] The second year of the training period was in the state of Punjab. At Mussoorie, the trainees are termed probationers; in their states they are referred to as Assistant Commissioners under training. In Punjab a young trainee officer might sometimes be addressed by the public as *chhota* DC, in other words 'little Deputy Commissioner', or the 'DC in the making'. In most states in India, the Deputy Commissioner in a district is the face of authority of the state.

In this initial period the young recruits are expected to learn skills relevant to administration, to orient to the functioning of government, and to acclimatize to the working

---

1 The academy is now called Lal Bahadur Shastri National Academy of Administration. The new entrants now have a short opening spell of four months at Mussoorie, followed by a full year in the states, and return to Mussoorie for the final eight months of training. Since the stint in the states now falls between two periods at Mussoorie, the arrangement is imaginatively called the sandwich pattern of training.

systems. Training aims to motivate young administrators to think and act positively and to instil in them a spirit of service and dedication to the duty.

I must admit that these lofty ideals were not uppermost in the minds of most probationers entering the portals of the academy in its pristine environment in the beautiful hills. First and foremost, the service was perceived as a secure career. While selection was taken as recognition of merit, entry into the service was viewed as a reward for many years of hard work and toil. Nestled in the picturesque hills, the academy seemed a perfect place to enjoy the beginning of life as a professional, to make friends and to ready oneself for being part of the machinery for governance. There would no doubt be study of new subjects in the academy, this I accepted, but after the grind of preparatory work for the entrance examination, I myself was not perturbed with any possible challenge that academics might hold. I looked forward expectantly to life at the academy and beyond.

Mussoorie was one of the hill stations established by the British in the middle of the 19th century. It was primarily a retreat for military and civil officers from the summer heat of the plains. The British also set up in the Mussoorie hills a number of schools for the facility of the officers' children. At the time of independence of the country, Mussoorie had a permanent population of just 20,000. For tourists, it was ideally located, being situated just 20 miles away from the foothill town of Dehra Dun. A steep winding road connects Mussoorie with Dehra Dun, which continues to be a convenient rail head for travellers. After the British departed, the government had showed rare foresight in acquiring an entire hillside in the small town, including a hotel named Charleville. The hotel, and the hillside over which it stands, became the campus for the academy. The academy is located just two miles from the heart of Mussoorie town. I was particularly excited that my finishing school (NAA) should be in the very same hill town where I had begun my school education at the age of seven. It was a peculiar coincidence that I would cherish for days to come.

Training for Life[2]

When I reported for duty at NAA, the prevailing atmosphere was one of unhurried ease, of general relaxation. On paper, there was an elaborate regime, beginning with early-morning sessions for physical fitness and horse riding, mandatory for all probationers, and a series of regular, uninterrupted lectures in the subjects of law, public administration, economics, history and sociology, which, the management fondly believed, was equipping us to face the real world. The training began with a four-month 'Foundation Course', which was common for entrants from the IAS, the Indian Foreign Service, the Indian Police Service and other Central Services. Our group of around 400, from these different services, fell mainly in the age between twenty-two and twenty-five years, largely male, with just a sprinkling of

---

2 The author has drawn on some notes he offered to the Academy for an in-house publication in the year 2015.

female officers that added a different, joyous sensibility, not to mention a wholesome spirit. A substantial proportion of the entrants had joined the respective services straight after college or university, that is, their minds were uncluttered with experience born of employment. Fresh in public service, we could be pardoned for imagining that the stay in Mussoorie would be an extended holiday in the salubrious climate of the hills.

At the academy, we developed life-long friendships, which cut across the services that we were assigned, and also transcended the states where we were to serve during the forthcoming career. There were some romantic liaisons, such as between my close friends Swatantar Kumar Alok, who was allotted to the state of Himachal Pradesh, and C.P. Sujaya from Kerala. On '(com)passionate grounds', as we termed it, the government allowed Sujaya to change her state cadre to that of her husband, so it was convenient for both to serve together for a major part of their career in Simla, the capital of Himachal Pradesh. Another romance, among batchmates Virendra Singh Jafa, IAS and Jyoti Rathod, IFS was equally successful, but the government played spoilsport, and did not allow Jyoti to change her service from IFS to IAS, which might have enabled the young couple to be together while serving the government. It transpired that Jyoti had initially been denied appointment in the IFS, and offered IAS instead. Her appeal for joining the Indian Foreign Service was, unfortunately, as it transpired, accepted. In the meantime, she had decided to marry Jafa, and requested to be restored in the earlier service IAS. The vacillation probably irked the government, as being unbecoming of a civil servant. The only resolution possible was for Jyoti to exit the IFS to be with her husband in the state of Assam. A significant victory of the heart prevailing over government service!

Another warm friendship that began at Mussoorie, and has continued over half a century, was with Sarabjit Singh, an IPS officer from my own Punjab cadre. In the academy at Mussoorie, Sarabjit was nick named Sabre Jet by some fellow probationers who could not pronounce the name. The foundation course of 1965 had in its backdrop India's war with Pakistan, which saw dogfights between India's Russian-made MIG fighter aircraft and Pakistan's US-built Sabre Jet fighters. The name Sabre Jet stuck, and followed him in his career. I recall that one of my first visitors at Ropar, where I served as Deputy Commissioner, was Sabre and his wife, both travelling on a monstrous 7.5 horse power BSA-make motorcycle. It happened that they had eloped. I was delighted to be the first port of call of the adventurous couple. Sarabjit was the youngest among the IPS officers of the batch. He had been a champion weightlifter, who did not mind flaunting his rippling muscles. He boasted that he could out drink any rival probationer, and still remain sober as a monk. This was not entirely true. On one occasion, after he had been engaged in a sensational bout of the bottle the previous evening, I reminded him of a faux pas he had committed in the presence of ladies. Sheepishly, he admitted that he could not recall the event. At the academy he cultivated a façade that he was all brawn, little brain. In reality, Sarabjit was hugely talented, played the harmonica like a professional, and was the all-India topper in the Indian Police Service, no small reflection of his intellectual station. During his three years as Director General of Police, Punjab, he distinguished himself as a fearless and brilliant policeman. Our friendship has straddled many decades.

The Academy Director, I learnt years later (I gained access to some files when I was to serve in the Department of Personnel), had written accurately of many of his wards in their confidential reports, that they showed 'limited application to training.' Truly, many probationers had little patience with the lectures and assignments that constituted the agenda. Many had convinced themselves that attending classes was of nominal value for their career advancement, so they applied themselves assiduously to activities that they found more stimulating, such as playing cards or partying in town. These ebullient youngsters, who would now be in the twilight of their lives, are today quite safe from retrospective official censure for past misconduct. I hesitate, though, to name the culprits who brazenly missed lectures to attend to the business of playing bridge and even *teen patti*, a rudimentary form of gambling at cards. Ironically, Room no. 10, the preferred venue for this social activity, nicknamed the 'gambling den', happened to be located exactly on top of the main lecture theatre.

Several fun-loving groups sprung up. They partook wantonly of life's little pleasures. Loud and extrovert, they contemptuously referred to their more serious-minded colleagues as Keen Type Probationers (KTP), a sobriquet that has remained a part of academy jargon. There were a few daredevils who would travel, without official permission, from Mussoorie to Delhi for romantic reasons. The goings on included late-night binges at BDS (Bhai Dhyan Singh, who ran a restaurant near Library Point, a landmark in town with a license for serving liquor), where efforts were made to convert the abstemious into 'swingers'. The law breakers seriously believed that their behaviour reflected officer-like qualities; the KTPs on their part, indulgently tolerated the colourful habits of their more outgoing colleagues as harmless foibles. Expectedly, the various trainees who interacted in these group activities cut across barriers of state and service. Lifelong friendships were built in the Academy among many mischief-makers hailing from various states, and allotted to different All India and Central Services. The pranks committed at that stage in life created a rare bonhomie. Such, then, was the atmosphere of laissez faire that prevailed when I joined NAA in July 1965.

Advent of High Seriousness

One month after our training began, a senior officer of the Indian Civil Service, Mr M.G. Pimputkar was appointed the Director of the academy. This event was to prove a turning point for the milieu at the academy. The new director's reputation in official circles, of being a firm, no-nonsense man, preceded him. Anecdotes concerning Mr Pimputkar's strictness and of his dedication to duty, were legion. We had heard that, on one occasion when he was late in reaching office, he had reprimanded himself in writing for the lapse. This served as a unique warning for potential offenders. There was even an instance, so the story went, where he refused to intervene when his wife was charged with a minor traffic offence when driving. The majority view among the probationers of the 1965 batch was that Mr Pimputkar had been detailed specifically to enforce discipline on a spoilt force of raw recruits. Would we prove the guinea pigs for Mr Pimputkar's reform process? We waited with bated breath to find the answer.

With the advent of Mr Pimputkar, the change at NAA was swift. It was also electrifying. Attendance at every academic lecture was suddenly enforced with iron rigidity. The director could be noticed sitting in the last row of a lecture room, keeping an obtrusive eye on the proceedings. You never knew when and where the director or his hounds, would turn up. The administration ensured that all activities received focused attention of every individual probationer.

'A busy mind in an active body!' was the central theme of the new approach. No malingering to avoid riding lessons, not even excuse of sickness, was tolerated. Nawal Singh, our horse-riding instructor from the army, revelled in newly discovered authority. He could bark out loud orders to timid trainees to mount, dismount, and mount again without stirrups. 'Kick the b—horse,' he would scream. 'Don't fondle him.' If a raw rider tumbled unceremoniously from his spirited steed, Nawal showed no empathy, only ridicule. His full-throated guffaw on such occasions hit the downcast amateur horsemen like an inquisitor's whiplash. Mr Pimputkar himself was an avid horseman. Almost every day he would join the probationers in their travails. Horse-riding was not meant to be a sport. Field officers needed basic riding skills for touring remote rural areas of uneven terrain, which could not be traversed by automobiles. You needed passable performance to clear the riding test.

Every trainee was assigned classes for Riding (R) and Physical Training (PT) classes on alternate days. If you imagined that the day for PT would offer relief from the torture of riding, you were quickly disillusioned. Mr Pimputkar had discovered a book of physical fitness exercises adopted by the Canadian Air Force for their flying officers. The regime consisted of just five exercises, but with increasing number of repetitions, to be completed in exactly eleven minutes. I was keen on sports, but my sporting ability turned out to be a liability for me personally. I happened to catch the eye of Mr Gaekwad, the PT instructor, who was considered Mr Pimputkar's right-hand man. He cornered me to convey the director's orders that I would perform the duties of a demonstrator of the gruelling 11-minute drill. This meant that I had to work with Mr Gaekwad before the actual PT class, to attain some proficiency and serve as a model for the other pupils. It was no consolation for us to learn that the Director himself did all the drills regularly as per the level stipulated for his age group. I presume that the officers of the Canadian Air Force who completed the excruciating exercises successfully would have become super fit athletes. For mere mortals in the civil service, who had reached the summit of the training academy by dint of excelling in reading and writing, these were tough days. All sports and riding activities were conducted in a venue called Happy Valley, located a few hundred yards lower than the main buildings. Given the agony that they endured, some of my friends felt that the valley of their exertions was anything but happy.

As it transpired, the rigorous physical conditioning at Mussoorie stood us in good stead when, in due course, we were attached with units of the Indian army for a two-week assignment. The Commanding Officer of my battalion expressed open surprise that the civil officers attached with him could cope with the rigours ordained by the army for their short-term guests. Be that as it may, over the years I have managed to continue some of the drills learnt at Mussoorie as my early morning routine. Obviously, the predilections of Mr Pimputkar, a fitness fiend, rubbed off on some trainees.

The aches and bruises contracted in the riding ground and the PT arena had little time to subside, for you had to rush and ready yourself for academic classes. The laggards were often compelled to miss breakfast, for unpunctuality was a non-compoundable offence. The academic schedule was full and packed. The intellectuals among us were expectant that, if they could not excel outdoors, they would be at home in the classroom. Alas! There was no such luck for the weary. Undoubtedly by design, the scheduled class work did not comprise merely learned lectures by experts. The sessions were interactive. During law class, for example, Professor A.M. Pathak, a former District Judge, assigned us such tasks as writing depositions of imaginary witnesses in a murder trial. I recall an incident when, using my little knowledge of English, I cooked up a fancy story of a romantic liaison gone sour as leading to the crime. Mr Pathak tore my paper to shreds. 'It's not literary flourishes that I want. Focus on the legal issues. And read the Indian Evidence Act.' For other subjects too the emphasis was on practical application of tenets and principles, and not on theory. A smattering of facts and opinion was not accepted by our teachers, whether on sociological issues or matters of public administration. Economics not being my forte, I sought instruction from fellow probationer T.S. Vijayraghavan, acknowledged as a guru in the discipline. Whether such assistance helped in clearing the final exam is open to debate. Such instances merely underline the high seriousness that the regime inculcated among the inadequate minds of that generation.

The Director himself, along with Mr J.C. Aggarwal, Joint Director, and Mr R.P. Khosla, Deputy Director, constituted the faculty from the field of practical administration, to be joined later by Mr C.S. Shastri, designated Supervisor of Studies. With his penchant for enforcement of rules, we expected Mr Pimputkar to be a receptacle of anecdotes from his years as a career administrator. But, displaying innate humility, he resolutely refused to divulge any dramatic personal experiences from the field or the Secretariat. Surprisingly, then, his sessions verged on theory, as did those of Mr Aggarwal. Mr R.P. Khosla, on the other hand, was more forthcoming. He did relate some interesting tidbits from his days as Collector of a district in Uttar Pradesh, and generated lively discussion. These sessions on practical administration encouraged original thinking and presentation. I suspect that the faculty was discreetly gauging our potential from our performance in these sessions, and recording their assessment in dossiers.

Later during our stay in Mussoorie, a senior officer of the Indian Audit and Accounts Service, Mr Kenghe joined the faculty. It was Mr Kenghe who introduced us to the fundamental financial rules that obfuscate government functioning. I reacted with shock when Mr Kenghe stated that it required government's advance approval for an officer of the government to accept any gift of a value exceeding Rs 20, even if the donor were his own brother. Certain exercises on the entitlements of earned leave, in conjunction with medical leave and extraordinary leave left many of us confounded. 'Government might not be such fun after all!' could well have been a common reaction.

Financially, life was uncomplicated. When we entered the academy on 5 July 1965, our salary was exactly Rs 400 per month, of which Rs 200 was deducted towards mess charges, which everyone accepted without demur. It was after a few months that we noticed a substantial increase of Rs 40 per month in emoluments. We were told that this was dearness allowance (the first time that anyone among us had heard of the concept), to cover the rising cost of living on account of inflation. True to financial principles, half of the increase in the monthly emoluments, Rs 20, went toward the mess bill. The pocket money amounting to Rs 200 every month seemed to be adequate to meet the cost even of such vital accessories as a buttoned-up black coat, riding breeches and entertainment in town.

Spirited Travel

September 1965 saw the outbreak of war with Pakistan. Away from action in our hill resort, the only direct impact felt in the academy turned out to be denial of dinner every Monday, in line with Prime Minister Lal Bahadur Shastri's commitment to austerity. Despite healthy appetites clamouring for nourishment, the probationers accepted the privation unreservedly. Incidentally, just before embarking on *Bharat Darshan* (a two-month-long extended study tour of the country) the entire IAS 1965 batch of 125 probationers were allowed to call on Mr Lal Bhadur Shastri in New Delhi. The Prime Minister was to travel the very next day to Tashkent to finalise a treaty with Pakistan. One of my brash batchmates had the temerity to question the PM on what he intended to say to General Ayub Khan, then President of Pakistan, when they met. Mr Shastri disarmed us by stating openly that he would decide in the interest of the country. It was to be one of Mr Shastri's last public meetings, for he died in Tashkent immediately after signing a significant accord.

Mr Pimputkar was a multi-faceted personality. Along with his introduction of military-style regimentation, he displayed rare social graces. During the training period he made it a point to invite all probationers, in separate groups, for tea or dinner at his residence. He might scowl at a trainee walking in the campus without a tie and jacket—indeed a few were turned out of class for neglecting the dress code—but at home Mr and Mrs Pimputkar were gracious hosts, who could let down their hair, and allowed similar liberty to their young guests. Amazingly, these informal gatherings were an occasion for song and dance, in which both hosts and guests participated enthusiastically. Such was my experience at the party that I was privileged to attend at the Director's house. Mr Aggarwal and Mr Khosla maintained the fine tradition. I was bowled over when Mrs R.P. Khosla whom I was meeting for the first time ever, called me by my first name at her get together.

Bharat Darshan, literally meaning 'viewing India', was a welcome two-month break from the feverish academy activities. Divided into six separate groups, we lived out of temporary homes in the form of first-class railway bogeys (no air conditioning was available then). Our rail carriage (I still recall its distinctive number 789), housed 22 probationers and an officer in charge, Professor D.C. Tiwari, whose role was to keep unruly elements in check, and to attend to the general welfare of the travelling party. Our group had *darshan* of the states of western and southern parts of India. Our carriage was attached, as per schedule, with various express trains to travel between the cities. Our bogey was usually parked in the yards of major rail junctions, requiring us to march across the railway tracks to access the waiting rooms on the platform. Such treks were in themselves a minor adventure. Daytime was spent in 'educational' visits to such spots as the oil fields near Baroda, or 'cultural tourism' in the Ellora caves off Auragabad, or the mangroves in the Kerala backwaters. Three days in Ooty, a hill station in the state of Tamil Nadu, were pure fun. In Madras, we purchased T-shirts that had just landed at the docks from abroad. A batch mate from Odisha, R.M. Senapati, who, like me, was wearing clothes made of synthetic material for the first time in life, proudly announced that he had acquired a shirt of 'smuggled terylene.' He had purchased the imported item in a bazaar in Bombay. Just like the sheltered Indian economy of the time, many probationers then had been shrouded in innocence.

In retrospect, it was not the lack of creature comforts that oppressed our team of tourists. Two other inconveniences presented a greater challenge. One was the issue of our meals, which lacked both variety and quantity. The dining cars in trains were nowhere as well stocked or handsomely served as they are today. In fact, many trains had no dining cars whatever. We longed to arrive at Bombay, Madras or Bangalore (those were the names of the cities at that point in time) for an opportunity to splurge. The moment we left the railway station we headed to the nearest restaurant, reputed or otherwise. The long stay on wheels gave us an unexpected lesson in nutrition. Having read a news report that bananas were rich in many nutrients, the friends in our compartment kept an unending stock of bananas hanging from the ceiling fan. 'Please pass me a vitamin' became a standard poor joke among the four occupants of our compartment, when afflicted by pangs of hunger. One sweet use of adversity, then, was the inculcation of healthy eating habits during *Bharat Darshan.*

A second factor that bothered the group was, surprisingly, boredom, which was born of undergoing claustrophobic journeys across peninsular India. There was a limit to the amount of time that could be devoted to playing cards. Further more, the activity had been exciting in the early days at the academy, because it was then a stolen pleasure. Engrossment in card games was now a tame affair, since the indulgence did not involve any infringement of rules. To break the tedium, some members of our high-spirited party managed to create artificial excitement, to the chagrin of Professor Tiwari. I recall one dramatic incident involving (I unabashedly drop names here) Ravindra Sharma and Bhola Nath Tiwari, along with their seconds. The time was midnight. As the train was chugging (remember, it was the age of steam engines for the Indian Railways!) at its customary pace, all the passengers in the carriage were rudely woken up by much loud shouting and screaming. Perturbed by the commotion, and the sound of unmentionable abuse, Professor Tiwari rushed out to investigate, notwithstanding his state of undress. 'Have we been attacked by dacoits?' he enquired anxiously.

'Sir, there is big quarrel between two violent boys,' reported an eye-witness to the episode.

Professor Tiwari effectively separated the sparring leaders, Bhola Nath and Ravindra, whose arms were flailing at each other. 'Desist from this misbehaviour!' he ordered firmly. 'What is the cause of your ugly brawl?'

Bhola Nath's reply astounded the officer in charge. 'Sir, I predict that the next railway platform will be on the left side. Ravindra insists that it will be on the right.' To his eternal credit, Professor Tiwari resolved the impasse with commendable diplomacy. 'Mr Bhola Nath (that is the manner in which the professor addressed all probationers), why fight? If the platform is on the right, we can move out that way, else we can get out from the left side.'

All in all, *Bharat Darshan* helped us to establish many lifelong bonds. In the days to come, we would rise to enjoy much opulence on official tour. As officers of the government, we would have occasion to view the very sights that we enjoyed as commoner probationers. The general sense of well-being and camaraderie developed in those spartan days, however, floats still before 'the inward eye', as Wordsworth puts it. Sightseeing then carried a flavour that money cannot buy. *Bharat Darshan* was an exercise in living together, and tolerating each other as we viewed the country as spectators.

During the training period I was involved, for no fault of mine, in a sensational incident. Had the telecom revolution, which assures instant communication today, embraced our country 50 years earlier, this gloomy incident might never have occurred. As it was, most parts of India of the 1960s depended mainly on the entrenched Morse code to transmit, via telegram, good tidings and bad. And the humble post office, which is now in a state of decay, was the default option for transmitting messages of urgency.

A Second Lease of Life

While yet on *Bharat Darshan*, our batch of probationers was attached with Central Emergency Relief Training Institute, Nagpur, for learning to cope with disasters, especially the role of civil defence. One momentous day the staff at CERTI received a stunning piece of information. The sad news was that three members of our group of trainees had suddenly died. The astounding report of demise of three young IAS officers, and their names, came to notice shortly after the normal training activity in the institute was over. The suspense at Nagpur lasted until dinner time, that is, when a head count revealed that the rumour was based on some misinformation. I myself, along with some friends had gone out to see a film. On our return I encountered, on the faces of my colleagues, strange expressions of shock and disbelief. I learnt only at the dinner table that my name was among those of the three persons declared as gone and born again.

At that time, I noted that my batchmates had discovered in me certain unsuspected qualities of head and heart. This usually happens when one kicks the bucket, as they say in colloquial terms, or passes away, in staid language. Seeing me alive, my friends hastily withdrew their eulogies, and began to accuse me of deliberately misleading them, as though I were myself responsible for feigning my departure from earthly abode. It was uplifting to be praised (albeit undeservedly) in absentia, for good deeds and thoughts, even though the testimonials were rescinded, post-haste.

Within a record period of one week, the mystery of the non-dead IAS officers was solved by the Commissioner of Nagpur Police as an inside job. The sleuths displayed the very same investigative skills that Sherlock Holmes might have astutely used. It transpired that one of our own probationers had sent false telegrams to the homes of the three lucky survivors of doom, as we came to be known. The families, unnerved and panic-stricken, managed to contact CERTI after suspense of many hours, to obtain a reassurance that the alarm was false. The original telegrams were recovered from the post office. The question now was of identifying the culprit. This the police did by ordering every one of the group, including the affected three, to write, in block capitals, the very words used to convey the dreadful news. Imagine my embarrassment at being forced to print, in bold ball point, 'RAJAN DEAD. COLLECT BODY. ACCEPT CONDOLENCES. DIRECTOR CERTI.'

Handwriting experts identified irrefutably the colleague who had misused the technology of the day, the telegram. The suffering, even though short-lived, was that of the concerned families. The three of us were blissfully unaware of the pangs of grief that our parents and grandparents would have endured, if only for a day. Although three of us were the victims of the ghastly prank, it was my family that endured suspense for the longest period of time. This was because the perverse telegram happened to be delivered at my ancestral home address, a remote town in Punjab. My grandmother relayed the doleful false news to my parents in other towns. Many hours elapsed before the falsity of the communication was discovered, to the relief of all. In the interim the numerous members of my large extended family, spread across the country, had been left disconsolate for many hours. For some years they continued to celebrate February 18, the date of the macabre event, as the day of my rebirth.

Retribution was swift. Thanks to the no-nonsense approach of our director, the young man with the perverse streak was discharged from service within two weeks of the incident.

A Civilian in Military Clothing

The experience that I gained during the days at NAA was truly diverse. Along with weeks of educational tourism and orientation in civil defence, I had a firsthand exposure to field conditions in which units of the Indian army operate. Just a few months after the 1965 war concluded the probationers were attached in groups with different infantry battalions stationed in the state of Jammu and Kashmir on the international border. The host for my group of seven IAS probationers was the Infantry Battalion 11 of the Kumaon

Regiment, at a nondescript border post called Jhangar in the Nowshera sector. We stayed for about two weeks in tents, going on patrol with heavy rucksacks and carrying rifles of 7.62 mm bore, accompanied with armed escort. We reported to a burly, outgoing, friendly Commanding Officer named Lieutenant Colonel Chattar Pal Singh Choudhary. The officers' mess, where we took our meals, bore the bullet marks of recent enemy fire from across the border just a mile away. We took part in some activities such as group physical training (PT), firing and played basketball with the *jawan*s (foot soldiers). The CO would engage us in the game of bridge. At dinner, in the officers' mess, we were introduced to military etiquette: proper dress code, no discussion on subjects like women, food or politics, and so on. Those who imbibed could drink to their heart's content. It was true army hospitality. We had a flavour of the tough conditions in which the army operates. *Jawan*s are allowed limited days of home leave, during which they attend to petty problems, such as construction and repair of houses, litigation relating to land, etc. We were enjoined to assist soldiers in need at home. I needed no convincing. I was happy that on my very first posting as a Sub-Divisional Magistrate, I could alleviate some little irritants of soldiers on leave. Using my discretion, I gave priority to soldiers in sanction of building material, such as cement and bricks, and also tried to intervene where possible in land disputes where servicemen were a party.

I learnt much in the short military attachment. I recall fondly the army hospitality during the days spent on the 'hot' border, and the rapport between civil and military authorities; I would like to forget the onerous journey of 200 miles from Jammu to Srinagar, in a massive army truck (a three-tonner they called it) sitting atop bedding rolls and other luggage.

Like all good things the year-long sojourn at the Academy had to end. Truly, we were sad at departing from Mussoorie.

Relating to the physical and mental burden loaded on us I was reminded of what the English poet John Keats, once wrote, 'We hate poetry that has a palpable design on us.' Indisputably the management at Mussoorie was intent in fulfilling some sinister design. The obvious palpable objective seems to have been to keep the probationers severely occupied in a strict routine. Perhaps Mr Pimputkar and his cohorts succeeded in their aim.

I can vouch, though, along with many friends, that our days as probationers in Mussoorie fulfilled an unstated aim. This was to groom us in a subtle manner, in the art of governance. Did the Academy imbue us with special qualities of leadership and problem solving? A moot question! I, for one, would never complain that I am any worse for wear on account of my beautiful days at Mussoorie.

The Ropes in the State

The second year of my training began interestingly with an encounter at the entry of the Punjab Civil Secretariat in Chandigarh. The little incident and its aftermath deserve mention, as an adjunct to my main narrative. As probationers, 16 in number, we were on our first visit to the seat of power of the Government of Punjab. Youthful we were, but not so young in appearance, I am sure, as to be mistaken for sightseeing students. Why, then, did the lift-man query, 'Your pass, Kaka?'[3] Was he roused by our uncomfortable squirming in buttoned-up formal *khadi* suits? One among our group, a leader in his own right, snorted in a lordly air, 'The Chief Secretary is waiting for us at ten', and attempted an out flanking movement into the lift. The bold *sahib* ran into an outstretched arm firmly checking his advance. The unexpected blockade, accomplished with amazing dexterity, obliged us to view with a new respect this remarkable sentry. I observed a tall, trim Sikh, his beard beginning to grey, in spotless white pajama and shirt. Two things about the man's appearance immediately struck me. One was his apparel, which was contrary to the regulation khaki prescribed for his category of staff in the government, and included a satchel, a canvas bag slung loosely across the shoulder. The other striking feature about the liftman was a penetrating gaze, at once quizzical and bemused. It was at this stage of baptism in Secretariat administration that we heard a sharp voice in our ear, 'What is happening, Gurbachan Singh?' Fate had sent the Chief Secretary himself to rescue us from the impasse. 'These boys tried to sneak in, Sir', replied

3 Kaka, in Punjabi, is a form of addressing a young boy. It is a term of endearment, and also of condescension.

Gurbachan Singh, our stout barricader. Adding, with a measure of finality, 'I will not allow it.'

Three years later, my training and Sub-Divisional posting over, I was to meet Gurbachan Singh again as I entered the Secretariat. He welcomed me with deference, but with not a shade of remorse or embarrassment over the last incident. His bearing was upright as ever, the glint in his eye as sharp. In my new assignment in the Secretariat, he ferried me in his lift regularly now, and I grew to know him. I learnt that he was regarded, even revered, as an elder among his colleagues. Punctual to the second, and dedicated to a fault, you never had to wait for his vehicle. It was always waiting for you, it seemed. Other operators often parked their carriages on the ninth or tenth floors, lingering in the nearby canteens, even as hapless passengers waited at landings down below. No such repasts for Gurbachan Singh, nor for him to indulge in idle chatter. It was no wonder then that the Secretariat employees always headed for the lift of the Baba (by which name he was commonly known). My peon swore that the Baba's lift travelled twice as much as any other on any single day.

The Baba was a most popular figure in the Secretariat. The primary reason was his expertise in an unusual discipline. The Baba was a dispenser of eye-tonics. Numerous concoctions of *surma* all personally prepared by the Baba from local herbs—that is what that ubiquitous canvas bag around his shoulder contained. The moment his duty hours ended, the Baba would set himself up in a predetermined corridor of the office building and begin serving his remedies. He had certain rigid restrictions for himself and for his patients. First and foremost, treatment was given totally free of charge, in charity. This was a pledge made by the Baba to his late Guru. Then, the Baba visited the home of no individual, no matter how highly placed. Another quaint characteristic of the Baba's system was that he must personally administer the potion in the patients' eye. This meant long queues for patients who had to wait their turn for the physician's attention. So great was their faith in the remedies that many officials adjusted their duty hours to the Baba's timings. In due course, as the fame of his skill spread and the queues became serpentine, the Baba had perforce to allow the patients to take home his herbal remedies in little phials. The Baba was truly a remarkable man.

Several years later, Baba Gurbachan Singh again met me, in my office room in the Secretariat. I had by now come to look on the Baba not as a low-ranking employee, but as a social benefactor, a man who gave, and did not demand. It was therefore somewhat of a shock when he disclosed that he had come for some help in connection with a personal matter. It seemed that on his retirement the Baba would not be entitled to pension, as he was not confirmed in service. His juniors in the Chandigarh Administration were confirmed, but in his case, some earlier years of service in the state of Punjab before reorganisation of the state had been ignored. It was a knotty personnel problem, which became more and more entangled when I sought to intervene. The man could be confirmed, provided that certain rules were relaxed. The Ministry of Home Affairs of the government of India in Delhi was the competent authority to take this momentous decision, since the employees worked in a Union Territory (of Chandigarh).

The progress of this case showed me how government procedures complicate, obfuscate and oppress. Three walls imprisoned the Baba, and these were the bureaucracies of the State of Punjab, the Union Territory of Chandigarh, and the Government of India. Massive files were constructed, citing precedent, order, regulation, rule and article. The references moved, on reluctant feet, from one authority to another. Many office hands, experienced and wise analysed and expostulated on the issue. Did 20 years of driving a mechanical contraption called an elevator entitle an old man to a pension of Rs 136 per month? The Baba's destiny was somehow linked with me, I began to think. At the Ministry of Home Affairs, where I served in due course, I found that the monumental decision about his pension would have to be taken by the Union Home Minister himself. But the Deputy Secretary needed some clarifications from Chandigarh and Punjab. When I was posted back in the State Government these were duly supplied.

The story has a happy ending. In 1984, two years after the retirement of Baba Gurbachan Singh and after nine years of struggle, a princely pension of Rs 270 (up on account of inflation from the original Rs 136) was finally released to him. Furthermore, the Baba was deemed to be re-employed for two years from 1982 to 1984.

Within the Secretariat, we were received with warmth, at first by Mr P.H. Vaishnav, the Coordinating Officer, and then by the top brass of the state bureaucracy. Mr Vaishnav, who rose to be Chief Secretary in the state and also a Secretary with Government of India at New Delhi, informed us that each of us would be posted in one or other districts of the state. This was to be a short posting of a few months' duration. He invited all of us to state if we wished to work at any preferred station. He also informed us that we must clear certain departmental examinations relating to law and administration and knowledge of the regional language Punjabi. He warned that failure to clear the tests would debar us from increments in our salary. Even as we were in Mr Vaishnav's office, who should march in but Mr Ram Kishan, the Chief Minister of Punjab. It transpired that following some political developments the Government of Mr Ram Kishan had just resigned. Mr Ram Kishan was merely making farewell calls on the officials who had worked with him. The state was that very day placed under the President's rule, that is, for direct administration by the Union of India. The political ramifications did not concern junior officers like us, so we made ready to report for duty in our respective districts. Mr Vaishnav arranged, however, that before leaving Chandigarh we could make a courtesy call on Mr Dharam Vira, an ICS officer, who was the Governor of Punjab.

Compared to the closely monitored activities at the Academy in Mussoorie, the months I spent at Ambala, my place of posting were indolence itself. Me and two other batchmates who had also been posted in Ambala were given office rooms in the District Courts. Unable to shake the habit of discipline inculcated by Mr Pimputkar in Mussoorie, all three of us (Lalit Jain, Rajinder Singh and I) would diligently travel on our two-wheelers , reaching office punctually, and observe office hours. Sadly, there was none to appreciate our dedication to duty. The reason for the atmosphere of lassitude was that the bureaucracy was at that time in some turmoil. The Government of India had decided to break up the state of Punjab in three: the Punjabi speaking area would comprise the new Punjab; the area with a majority of Hindi speakers would be the new Haryana state; the mountainous portions of the original state of Punjab would be merged with the Union Territory of Himachal Pradesh. The government employees of all levels were in a state of suspense. They awaited in expectation the orders determining which state they would be serving. For us, the three new Assistant Commissioners the uncertainty ended soon enough. Rajinder Singh and I were allotted the state of Punjab, while Lalit Jain found himself in the Haryana cadre of officers. Our immediate boss Mr M.S. Gill, who was the Deputy Commissioner, was placed in the Punjab cadre. Since Ambala district fell in the new Haryana state Mr Gill was shifted from Ambala and replaced by another IAS officer V.K. Sibal.

The attachment at Ambala lasted just four months. During the monsoon months of July and August I did worked on flood relief in inundated villages, for which I waded through knee-deep water. On one field visit I travelled on horseback. I learnt how the clerks at the most junior level tackle files. The period was gainfully employed by me to clear the mandatory departmental test, a comparatively easy venture.

In November the entire group, along with a number of officers of the Punjab Civil Service (PCS) reported in what was called the Revenue Training School, to be educated on the fundamentals of management of land records.[4] As I have mentioned in Chapter One, from medieval times, and especially in British India, land revenue had been the mainstay of the state's income. Land records determine right of owners and tenants over all property in rural and urban areas. For this reason, the government always attached highest important to training young officers in preparation and maintenance of basic land records. Also, an IAS officer is vested with power to adjudicate in respect of a number of land laws. As the Collector of land revenue, a Deputy Commissioner controls revenue administration in his district. The best, and indeed only time that a young officer can familiarize himself with the complex laws that he administers is when he or she is still a trainee. When he

---

4 IAS officers in Punjab now receive training in Mahatma Gandhi State Institute of Public Administration. The course content includes revenue administration as well as specialized aspects of administration.

becomes the head of the district, he obviously cannot confess ignorance of his fundamental responsibility. For this reason, we were taught to carry out the duties of the staff engaged in revenue work at many levels in the hierarchy. In ascending order these are the menial labourer, who physically carries metallic measuring chains; the *patwari*, the custodian of the village land records; the *girdawar kanungo*, the inspecting officer; the *tehsildar*, who controls the entire record management and transfer of rights; the Assistant Collector (the first substantive appointment of a PCS or IAS officer) and finally the Collector himself.

The intricacies of revenue law might not excite the lay reader; what would be of interest is the manner in which IAS officers get hands-on experience by carrying out all the tasks of each one of the functionaries mentioned above. Thus, I had to personally map out 200 fields in a village, by geometrical definition, and to propose a consolidation of the areas owned by each small land holder (the *patwari*'s task), physically inspect crops in defined areas (the *kanungo*'s responsibility), sanction or refuse transfer of land by process of mutation (exercising powers of the *tehsildar)* and adjudicate in appeal cases as the Collector. My teachers were two seasoned *kanungo*s in the RTS. By choice I was assigned *tehsildar*'s duties in my ancestral town of Kapurthala. And by chance the peon attached with me at Kapurthala was a man called Atma Singh, the same person who had been attached with my father as a police orderly some 20 years earlier. Atma Singh regaled me with stories of my father's training days in a police academy in the town of Moradabad, in present day Uttar Pradesh. He related an escapade when he gave some liquor to the horse that my father was riding in a competition; the horse turned frisky and became difficult to control, but under the stimulant galloped ahead of the rest of the field. During my two months at Kapurthala I was able to stay in my ancestral house with my grandmother. It was a matter of immense pride for her to have me at home. I travelled to numerous villages, atop my two-wheeler, my trainer *kanungo* riding pillion. I duly completed my quota of sanctioning 200 mutations, exercising the powers of a *tehsildar*. The staff were amazed that I took my lunch sitting under a tree; they were even more impressed that it was my grandmother who fixed my tiffin box for my daily picnic.

The two months that I trained at Kapurthala brought some dolor too, as I reminisced nostalgically about my childhood in the very town. The erstwhile princely state of Kapurthala now stood reduced to a small district. My grandfather, who had served as a confidant of the late Maharaja, had died a commoner four years earlier. In its heyday, Kashi Bhawan, the ancestral house had been occupied by my father and his 10 siblings. Over the years, the mansion was slowly deserted; four brothers and a sister had migrated to the United States, and three brothers had tragically died young. With my father working in the police and another brother, Inderjit, in the army, my grandmother Kalawati (Bibiji, as the family affectionately addressed her) now lived with only her youngest son Hardyal, and the widow and children of another son. Bibiji was the glue that had kept the large clan together, every child pleaded that she come and live with them, but she steadfastly refused to leave Kapurthala. At best she might agree to visit them for a few months at a time.

Having seen glorious days as a matriarch of a huge joint family, Bibiji adjusted remarkably to the loneliness of her new existence. For me, her favourite grandson, to be living with her, even for a short period, filled her with understandable pride. I was only too pleased to accept her request to take her to Beas, a distance of 17 miles, on weekends. In the small town, where everyone knew each other, it would have been startling to observe her nonchalantly sitting behind me on a scooter, with a grandchild standing in front. The irony struck me. 25 years earlier, she had the luxury of taking the very same journey in a motor car driven by none other than my father, a police superintendent. Now, in her old age, her chauffer was her grandson, who perched her precariously on a humble two-wheeler.

As I ruminate about my grandmother, I must go slightly forward in time, to the year 1972 to be exact, to narrate an instance of the amazing perspicacity that Bibiji displayed at a time when my wife delivered our son. Bibiji was attending on my wife Meena, the expectant mother in Chandigarh during the last days of her pregnancy. At an age close to 70 years, Bibiji grasped the assignment lovingly and enthusiastically. In the tradition of extended families Meena and Bibiji stayed with my aunt Dev Kumari Arora in her house in

Chandigarh. As it transpired, when the labour pains began, the two women took a bold, perhaps foolhardy decision to walk together to the hospital post-haste. Apparently the two brave walkers reached the hospital just in time for the baby boy to be delivered. Several babies born that day were tagged with the names of their mothers and taken into an anteroom, which Bibiji was invited to enter. The nurses held out a baby boy to be placed in the arms of his great grandmother. Bibiji glanced just once, and refused to touch the child. 'That's not ours!' she exclaimed. The nurse was astonished. 'How can you be so certain?' she queried. 'Because,' Bibiji added in a tone of finality, 'I recognize the one who is actually ours.' She walked calmly and picked up another baby in a cot. Bibiji was absolutely right. How could she possibly recognize a baby at first sight? The grand matriarch told me later that the new born was the spitting image of his father, myself, whom she had helped to deliver into the world 29 years earlier! In recounting this true old wives' tale we often joke with our son Anurag that but for his great-grandmother, we might have lost him to some other family.

As the second year of my training period came to a close, I was ready to take up my first appointment as a Sub-Divisional Magistrate. As a good manager I used the joining period of seven days efficiently. This was to get married. I was not yet 24 years old.

CUTTING THE TEETH

In the tradition of the colonial Indian Civil Service (ICS), from a young age, IAS officers serve at the cutting edge of governance. In these assignments in the districts, they are charged with considerable responsibility, and also armed with appropriate authority. At the time of its independence the country established the Indian Administrative Service (IAS) as a successor to the ICS. As with the ICS, members of the indigenous IAS are selected via a rigorous national written examination and a personality test.

Every district in India is headed by a Deputy Commissioner (DC), typically a generalist administrator from the IAS with upwards of six years in service. He or she is assigned a variety of functions, of a Collector of revenues of the state, of a District Magistrate for law and order, and of an overall coordinator of the work of other specialized agencies of the government. The tasks include the delivery of public services, and promotional, development and welfare functions, as well as some form of judicial work. The DC is an empowered representative of the state government, and deemed its public face. Furthermore, many other regulatory functions, such as conducting of elections and the management of unforeseen situations, such as natural crises, are entrusted to the DC. Before appointment as the district head, IAS officers serve two years at a junior level as Sub-Divisional Officer (Civil), where they assist the DC and also work as the Sub-Divisional Magistrate.

In the process of their career advancement, the government attaches much importance to the experience gained by young officers in the initial field postings. On my own part, I found these district appointments both exciting and challenging.

Beginning a Career and a Home

Immediately on the conclusion of two years of training, as described earlier, I entered my first substantive office, that of the Sub-Divisional Officer in the town of Pathankot. For me personally it was a piquant situation. As per the posting orders, I joined duty on 5 June, just three days after my marriage. The responsibility of learning the ropes of a new office had to be reconciled with the domestic compulsions of establishing a brand-new home. I was able to manage both tasks because my wife Meena enthusiastically took control of the household, primitive as it was at that stage, and also bore uncomplainingly my long periods of absence from home on account of official commitments. My official house was part of a complex, which included my office and court room, and a jail house for prisoners under trial. Interestingly, touching the buildings was a little used railway track of narrow gauge, that is, one-and-a-half feet in width, which carried a toy-like train from the town to a little hill town by the name of Jogindernagar. Apart from my other duties, I was also Superintendent of the jail, for which additional duty I was given an honorarium of Rs 30 per month. This perquisite was then not an altogether meager addition to my normal monthly emoluments of Rs 540. My duties as Jail Superintendent were defined in the Jail Manual.

My wife Meena and I approached the process of home building with excitement. At the time of our wedding Meena was working for her PhD in Botany in Meerut, her home town in the state of Uttar Pradesh. We agreed that Meena should complete her research work, for which she might travel periodically to her university town, a distance of some 300 miles. Here, just after we arrived in town, we moved from shop to shop to pick up some basic necessities. Since, to begin with, we had no refrigerator, we procured slabs of ice, for which, incidentally, the factory owner refused to accept payment. In those days there was a standard joke among us bachelor friends that a wife brings with her elements of financial support. We called this external assistance PL 480. For the uninitiated, PL 480 stood for Public Law 480 of the United States of America. This was an authorization for the US government to deliver aid in kind to a food-deficient India. In the same manner, as foreign aid supported a country by supplying food aid,[1] parents helped a needy young couple to set up house. Since

1 The disheartening phrase in use then was India's 'ship-to-mouth' existence. I was to learn later that PL 480 was a loan on concessional terms for India, which India duly repaid, and not an outright grant from USA to India. It took a while for the humiliating public perception of India with a begging bowl to disappear.

we had landed in my new place of appointment almost directly from the wedding altar, the components of PL 480, such as furniture, utensils and crockery took some time to arrive. It was an embarrassing moment when my parents paid us an unexpected visit. The rooms being bereft of any furniture, we had to borrow some chairs from the office next door. My father, incidentally, was at that time the Inspector General of Police of the neighbouring state of Himachal Pradesh, and was in his flagged car en route to some destination on tour. Considering the bareness of the rooms and the cupboard, we did not invite the parents to stay overnight. Soon enough the household items arrived, including an old sofa set from my ancestral house in Kapurthala. My parents would have understood our discomfiture. My father loaned to me his small Fiat motor car, which added to the components of PL 480. I think that during subsequent visits of friends and family, we were able to make up for our initial deficiency in hospitality.

At that time, in the year 1967, Pathankot was a low-profile little town of Punjab. True, it served as a gateway to two Himalayan states, Himachal Pradesh and Jammu and Kashmir. Many villages within the administrative unit touched the international border between India and Pakistan. As a military cantonment, Pathankot served as a base for the army as well as the air force. The town did not usually witness sensational happenings. The locals often jested that the only dramatic events that occurred in the town were internal injuries suffered by pregnant women traversing the potholed Dhangu Road (rudely named as 'abortion road'), or the frequent transit of the Chief Minister of the state of Jammu and Kashmir.[2] As per protocol, one of my own uncomfortable duties was to wake up early on winter mornings to receive the dignitary from the neighbouring state at the rail terminus, who perforce travelled by the famed Kashmir Mail train from Delhi. He moved on from Pathankot by road to his state.

My assignment did entail some elements of adventure. For accessing villages in Narot Jaimal Singh, a development block situated across the river Ravi, I needed to tour on horseback. The alternative route for vehicles was a tedious and longer road passing through the state of Jammu and Kashmir. The international border was porous, and there were occasional incidents of infiltration of people from the Pakistan side. As the magistrate I conducted several inquests, which, in common parlance, were magisterial enquiries into the death of infiltrators killed by the security forces in skirmishes.

Early during my tenure, I was surprised to learn that the junior position of the Sub-Divisional Officer figured in the ken of the military authorities. As a 23-year-old, I was in some trepidation at being unexpectedly summoned to his office by no less than the Sub Area Commander, a Brigadier of the

---

2 For many years Pathankot continued to be the rail head for travellers to the state of Jammu and Kashmir. Some 15 years ago, the railway line was extended, first from Pathankot to Jammu, a distance of about 70 miles, and then from Jammu to Srinagar in the Kashmir valley, a distance of 200 miles of mountainous terrain. Pathankot now enjoys the status of a district in Punjab state.

Indian army. I was mystified even more when he began the interview by observing that my posting in Pathankot had come as a setback to the development plans of the services. As I sat across the commander's desk, the mystery unravelled. It transpired that the army was in the process of acquiring land for expansion of the cantonment. The responsibility for legal acquisition of land for the important national project was vested in the Sub-Divisional Officer in civil administration. My predecessor in office had duly begun the initial procedure for acquiring the land. The process was now to be completed by me. The snag was that under Indian revenue law, the government could not invest me with the powers of Land Acquisition Collector until I had gained a mandatory experience of three months in my assignment as Assistant Collector. I assured the military boss that I would complete the job expeditiously as soon as the requisite powers were conferred on me.

For me personally, this visit to the Sub Area ended with unexpected joy. When the Brigadier learnt during our conversation that I was an avid tennis player, he made me a member of the exclusive Officers' Institute. He even allowed me the rarer privilege of parking my humble scooter in the lot marked 'Flag Cars Only.' And so I was to make friends among young army officers.

Half a century on, I am proud to have been a part of the process that brought Mamoon Cantonment, Pathankot, into existence. That is exactly the area that the army needed me to acquire.

While attending to matters concerning revenue and land laws, and also the code of criminal procedure, I was soon to realize the considerable difference between absorbing the fundamentals of law in a classroom, and actually employing legal powers judiciously. While hearing cases relating to land tenures[3] for the first time, I was totally convinced with the arguments put forth by the plaintiff. When the lawyer for the respondent made his submission, I was equally bowled over with his eloquence and arguments to the contrary. Deeper study of case law proved educative, and enabled me to perform my duties with confidence. I had learnt that since my decisions would be contested in appeal, every judgment must be drafted with special care.

A Beginner's Luck

During the period of my posting at Pathankot, an energetic Chief Minister by the name of Lachhman Singh Gill was on the saddle. He had come to power by breaking away, along with some like-minded members of the state legislative assembly, from a coalition of parties that included the Akali Dal, the Jan Sangh and the Communists. As a measure of securing their political loyalty all the 16 members of Gill's group were made ministers. Gill was able to survive with his minority of MLAs with the external support of the

---

3 The Punjab Security of Land Tenures Act, 1953, as amended several times was a major legislation for redistribution of agricultural land. It limited the extent of land that an individual could hold. It ended the domination of large land owners in Punjab. Under this Act the authority for adjudication is the SDO (Civil) exercising the powers of Collector.

Congress party, which was the second largest in terms of members in the assembly. The tenure of Lachhman Singh Gill is remembered for his success in establishing a network of roads linking villages in the state with each other and with the main state roads. I understood in due course the crucial importance of road communication in the economy of the state.

Gill elicited strong emotions, on account of his political position, and for an aggressive approach in administrative matters. On one occasion I was required to intervene to tackle a large group of striking workers of the state-run Punjab Roadways, who had blocked the bus station in the city, and also the adjoining roads. With the support of the Communist Party of India, a party which was strongly opposed to Gill's dispensation, the unions of transport workers had struck work throughout the state. At Pathankot the Roadways had a large depot. It was feared that the agitators might turn violent, thereby endangering life and property. As a magistrate responsible for the maintenance of law and order I took a quick decision, which might today appear to have been foolhardy. Rather than summon a police force I reached the scene of the mob gathering alone and unescorted. With the adjoining roads blocked, it was only my two-wheeler scooter that was able to manoeuvre its way to the heart of the trouble spot. I found myself confronting a mob of over 200 emotionally charged slogan shouters. In that chaotic noise, my voice of reason could not possibly be heard. On an impulse, I decided to climb on top of a bus parked in the square, stepping up the flimsy ladder installed at the back of the vehicle. The ladder is for loading passengers' belongings on to the luggage carrier on the roof top. I think the mob was so nonplussed to see me atop the roof of the bus that the slogan shouting ceased abruptly. Speaking their own language from a pedestal that represented the union's bread and butter I was able to reason with them with assurances that I would convey their demands to the higher authorities. Miraculously, the agitators began to disperse. It was not my words, but perhaps the body language, especially my perch above their own bus, that would have persuaded them. It transpired that Pathankot was one of the points in the state where the explosive situation was defused quietly.

It was several weeks later that my boss Amrik Singh Pooni, who was the Deputy Commissioner of Gurdaspur district, of which Pathankot was a part, commended me for a job well done. It was high praise coming from a person not given to hyperbole. In fact Mr Pooni told me that he had been aware all along about the happenings. He said he was testing my ability to handle a tough situation. He was pleased that I took a decision on the spot, and that I did not turn to him for guidance. He was especially happy that I did not bring in the police, the presence of which authority would have proved a red rag to further inflame passions. Even as the episode ended happily, I am doubtful if I would have displayed that bravado later in life. Here it was, simply put, beginner's luck. Incidentally my wife Meena learned about the dramatic occurrence much later, as she was away from town at the time.

Another Lesson

If the above crisis situation emanated from external political motivation, another noteworthy incident arose from my zeal in enforcement of a certain policy of the government of the day. This was a time when the country was facing shortage of basic food grain stocks, and was heavily dependent on imports. The farmers in Punjab had begun to adopt the new technologies for securing high yields in wheat. This allayed the supply situation somewhat in Punjab, but the neighbouring state of Himachal Pradesh and several other states were still in a position of scarcity. Unbelievable as it appears today, the Government of India banned interstate movement of wheat. The state government had issued orders to all Deputy Commissioners to prevent what was euphemistically termed 'smuggling of wheat' from Punjab. During a visit to Pathankot, Mr I.C. Puri, who was the Secretary of the Department of Food and Supplies, had enjoined the Deputy Commissioner and other district officers to exercise vigilance. It was noted that the market price of wheat in the state of Himachal Pradesh was substantially higher than in Punjab. The price difference certainly proved to be lucrative for traders to move the grain grown in Punjab to the more profitable market.

I had received reports that, with the connivance of the police and the officials of the Department of Food and Supplies, some traders were illegally ferrying quantities of wheat from Punjab to the adjoining Himachal Pradesh. Since there were allegations of collusion of the enforcing agencies,

I decided to personally make a midnight check of a post next to the town that was a link point between the two states. I took along with me some staff from my own office. This was really a shot in the dark. I carried with me the instructions of the state government directing DCs and SDMs to check any suspicious movement of wheat across the interstate points. When I reached the barrier point, which was manned by the staff of the Food and Supplies Department, I met a sight I was totally unprepared for. There were at least a dozen trucks fully laden with wheat parked and ready to cross the interstate borders. It was obvious that, in the dead of night, the precious cargo of food grains was being blatantly moved across the state's border. Evidently, I had stumbled on to an illegal operation, which was conducted with impunity. At the barrier was some junior staff of the food department, along with some uniformed policemen. As I questioned the staff on duty, who should turn up but a Sub-Inspector of Police, the Station House officer of the local police station? My initial sigh of relief at the arrival of the SHO was misplaced. It became clear that the man had come to assist the smugglers, and not to help me in upholding of law. Even as I was directing the police to confiscate the illegally moving goods, another gentleman, whose name I learnt was one Kesho Ram, reached the scene. It transpired that Kesho Ram was the kingpin of the racket, being the owner of the trucks and of the material therein. Accosting me the man began to rave and rant, claiming that he was a respected businessman in town, with several political friends who could vouch for him. All the while the SHO tried to persuade me to pardon the culprits, lamely claiming that there was some misunderstanding.

I found that I was up against a criminal gang, aided and abetted by the enforcement agencies themselves. I noted the registration numbers of the parked trucks, and my staff took the written statements of the drivers. I returned home from the late night jaunt with the feeling that I was in an ineffectual minority in a drama dominated by a crooked mafia. It was about 2 am that I wrote a full report to my superior, the Deputy Commissioner.

The very next morning, the police officer was transferred to the police lines. I do not know what action was taken against the officials of the department who had connived. The incident had an interesting aftermath. A week after that, the food department reported that a truck belonging to the Himachal Pradesh Police had been apprehended as it was carrying three bags of wheat for the policemen of the state. Nothing came of this preposterous action by the local police, as the police truck was merely carrying a petty quantity of rations, for which it had written authority to transport. It was clear that what I had touched was just the tip of an iceberg of entrenched crime. Perhaps the police in my district was hitting back at me obliquely, as my father happened to be the Chief of Police of the state whose rations had been seized. The Superintendent of police of Gurdaspur later told me that he had severely reprimanded his officers for the impasse.

I wondered later whether I might not have been better off tackling corruption with more finesse, instead of personally confronting it head on.

Reaching the Villages

The incidents above were among the interesting happenings during my first assignment as a fresh officer. The area in my jurisdiction at Pathankot was extremely scenic. It was interspersed with a network of canals originating from the river Ravi; one development block called Dhar was entirely mountainous, so much so that one could easily travel from my jurisdiction to the beautiful hill station of Dalhousie, just 20 miles uphill, in Himachal Pradesh, for a weekend holiday. The government expects officers to tour the districts systematically. For this it is prescribed that all SDMs and DCs should spend at least 90 nights and 120 days on tour during the year. Officers now follow these guidelines more in their breach. There being well-appointed government rest houses on canal banks for stay of officers in my sub-division, I was happy to travel and tour. I thus fulfilled the norms. Also I trekked many parts of the hilly block of Dhar, walking on foot to remote villages to understand the local conditions.

While on tour, an officer was required to take along his own provisions for meals. My loyal attendant, who was also a cook, would dutifully pack a steel trunk with essentials including even some kitchen utensils. This was necessary as many rest houses were situated away from habitation. I was to continue the same practice in subsequent postings in the field.

At that time SDMs did not have official vehicles for touring. I would sometimes borrow a jeep from the Block Development and Panchayat Officer, who was allowed the vehicle, as his job needed him to travel extensively in the villages. I recall a scary journey by night in a ramshackle jeep from Narot Jaimal Singh, a block situated next to the international border, driving though territory of Jammu and Kashmir. On reaching home, I realized that the brakes of the vehicle were non-functional. In all innocence I had been castigating the driver for running the jeep in low gear, which he was forced to do as a safety measure.

In the month of May 1968, less than a year into my assignment, my idyllic stay in a beautiful part of the country came to a rude and abrupt end. I was shocked to receive unexpected orders of the government transferring me to Ajnala, a little town in Amritsar district. My successor by the name of Baldev Kapur was a junior officer of the state service. I was astonished when the man walked into the court room where I was hearing some cases, carrying the Government's orders. I met my successor in the retiring room, and assured him that I would hand over charge to him immediately.

I must admit that I was mightily upset with the orders moving me less than a year after I had joined the station. Most IAS officers complete two years in their place of posting before promotion to the next rank. My superiors had expressed satisfaction with all aspects of my work; the orders seemed unfair. My wife Meena reacted with more equanimity, reasoning that it was not for me to question the decision of the Government. It was a mere change of place of work, she pointed out. The move was no reflection on the quality of my performance. Initially I was unconvinced, especially when I learnt that my successor had secured the assignment with the support of some small-time local leaders. The final argument stemmed from what our faith had taught, viz. that a man's role is to perform his duty, not to demand the fruits of his labours. I remembered the acceptance enjoined in Shakespeare's lines in a play I had read:

'Men must endure
Their going hence even as their coming hither.'
(*King Lear*, 5.2.9–10)

The words of the famous Urdu poet Zauq expressed the same sentiment, in relation to life and death as stages of a man's existence:

'Laa i hayaat aaeqaza le chali chale,
Apni khushi na aaye, na apni khushi chale.'

(It is destiny, and not our own will that brought us into the world: likewise, our time of death and departure from the mortal coil will be determined by fate.)

At that anxious moment in life, it was philosophy, then, that rescued me from any feeling of personal impairment, and of bitterness toward the government. I quickly reconciled with the situation. Not only that I vowed that never in future would I resent or protest decisions by the authorities in regard to any assignments. I determined that I would accept every decision affecting me as preordained, a part of my dues or '*karmas*'. The greatest takeaway from my first appointment was inculcation of an attitude of objectivity, and of resignation. Transfers and placements are but minor events in life, I had learnt. It is best to take vicissitudes in your stride: this lesson in positivity would stand me in good stead in later years, when I faced greater challenges.

Incidentally, my successor's stay at Pathankot proved to be short. Within months the man was involved in an ugly incident where police fired at a mob at the railway station, killing several persons. The SDM was indicted for rashness and mishandling of the situation. He was unceremoniously removed from his chosen position. I wondered whether, in shifting me from Pathankot, providence had not saved me from possible ignominy.

At 24 hours' notice my bags and belongings were packed and dispatched to Ajnala, a distance of some 70 miles. I received an emotional send off from my office staff, but did not stay on to accept any other farewell parties which the local citizens and friends had arranged in my honour. Ironically, on reaching Ajnala, I found that the house there had not been vacated by Baldev Kapur, the officer who had been so keen to replace me in Pathankot. Consequently my wife and I decided to spend a week in Simla with my parents. In the event, the government revised my posting orders, and directed that instead of Ajnala I should report for duty at another sub-divisional town, Ropar. I duly complied. So it was only our furniture and baggage that stayed in Ajnala, and that too for just a week.

Moving Laterally

I was to spend three-and-a-half years in the districts, two years in the post of SDO, and one year and a half as Deputy Commissioner. In between, I worked for two years at Chandigarh, handling work relating to rural development and agriculture. This was a critical time for the economy of the state. During this early part of my career, I observed at first hand a remarkable transformation of the agricultural economy and of the lives of the residents in the rural sector. It was professionally satisfying to be a part of the surge that was to lift Punjab to become India's most prosperous state, and India's bread basket.

After a stint at Pathankot, it was not difficult for me to adjust in my new assignment as SDO Ropar. The duties were similar, as also the systems of work. One small difference was that my immediate superior, the Deputy Commissioner worked at the same station as I did. While at Pathankot my boss was from the IAS, three years senior to me. Here, the DC, named Captain (retired) Gurdarshan Singh, was a venerable elder from the state service (called the Punjab Civil Service, PCS). I was in fact to return to Ropar as the Captain's in-office Deputy Commissioner after a two-year posting at Chandigarh. My residence was a palatial bungalow surrounded by a tract of cultivable agricultural land. For me the only drawback in the new post was that my attendant could not cook, which was inconvenient when I had to make an overnight halt during a tour. My wife managed the kitchen, but a problem arose when she had to leave Ropar for a longer period (she was in the family way then). During her absence, I tackled the irritant by making weekly visits to Chandigarh city, located just 28 miles away, to replenish my refrigerator with cooked food from my aunt's house. This was the aunt with whom I had spent four years as a house guest during my university days.

In most places in Punjab, especially those remote from the state capital, it is possible to find domestic help, which is indeed essential for officers working in the field. Such support is difficult at stations near Chandigarh. For the Deputy Commissioner, of course, support staff is available, but junior officers need to have the good fortune of the company of a wife with the talents of a skilled and competent cook. But apart from minor inconveniences, my experience as the SDO was pleasant enough. I now had at my disposal an official jeep for touring duty. I gained first-hand experience of conducting an election of a member of the legislative assembly. General elections for the state legislative assembly were held in the year 1969. As SDO, I was the Returning Officer (RO) for election to the local constituency of Ropar. The RO is personally responsible for critical action at every stage of the electoral process. These include the registration and revision of the electoral rolls of voters, the scrutiny of eligibility of candidates, the establishment of polling stations where votes are cast, the detailing of staff for election duty, observing the actual polling, and the counting of votes. The RO is to act as an unbiased observer, to prevent any fraud or malpractice by candidates and finally to declare the results.

In India the procedures are clearly laid down and understood by all aspirants, as well as the staff which comprises the machinery for elections. It is taken for granted that every official, especially the RO, will display utmost impartiality and competence. My own role as RO was fairly straightforward; there were no complaints of malpractice of any kind. The result was duly declared and accepted without demur.

While I was yet a junior officer, certain circumstances at home led to an unexpected enlargement of my family. It happened that my father, who was working as the Inspector General of Police at Simla in the northern state of Himachal Pradesh was suddenly transferred in the same capacity of IGP to Imphal in the north eastern state of Manipur, bordering Burma, which was situated some 1400 miles away. This exigency presented a complex problem for our well-knit extended family. It transpired that my father's younger brother Partap had died recently, leaving behind his widow Nirmal and young school going children. After Partap's demise, Nirmal and her two daughters were staying with my father at Simla. My parents did not find it feasible for Nirmal and the girls to move with them to the distant station where he was transferred. As a practical measure it was decided that Nirmal and her daughters, my cousins, should move in with me and Meena. Both of us were happy with the arrangement. We welcomed that our own daughter, then one year old, would enjoy the benefits of a joint family. Later my son too, born three years later, enjoyed the affection of caring young aunts at home. History seemed to be repeating itself. For many years, both my children received the doting attention of a senior generation of relatives, just as I myself had done during my early childhood at Kapurthala. Meanwhile my career, and that of my father, proceeded concurrently in two different states, Punjab and Manipur.

For a period of time, some seven years, I was blessed to boast of a largish family with us. True, there were some piquant moments. On one occasion, at a public function, the organisers mistook the two young girls to be my daughters. They were incredulous that while I was just 26 years in age, my children should be teenagers. Meena had to clarify that we had been married two years, and that the girls were not the progeny from any child marriage! (At that time the legal age of consent for marriage for males was 21 years, and for females 18).

A False Start

I began my tenure as Deputy Commissioner Ropar on a somewhat unpropitious note. With the benefit of hindsight, I admit that in my first interface with an important political leader, I managed merely to needle him, rather than gain his confidence. The fault was mine. It was in the middle of a heavy monsoon that I had driven from Chandigarh with my wife and two-year-old daughter to assume charge of the new post. The SDO Ropar, an officer named V.V. Kohli, had kindly hosted lunch for us. Just as we finished lunch, a political leader whom I did not recognize, stepped in. Mr Kohli introduced us. The gentleman was Giani Zail Singh, the top leader of the Congress party, of whom I had heard but vaguely. Welcoming me to the district, Giani *ji* observed that the heavy monsoon rain had caused much damage in the area of Anandpur Sahib. A seasonal river had inundated many villages and destroyed standing crops. Giani *ji* urged me to visit the distressed villages immediately and to provide some relief to the affected farmers. This was a perfectly reasonable request. Instead of reassuring the leader, I remarked that I had yet to assume charge as DC, and that I would soon attend to the matter. My response might have struck Giani *ji* as churlish. Probably he read my body language to state, 'Why should I take orders from a politician? I know my business.' Of course I did not say as much, but the impression that Giani Zail Singh could have gathered of me was that of a young, brash officer. Instead of winning over an important leader, I had, by a single reaction, alienated him. It is another matter that the first action that I took that afternoon was to visit the site of the ravage caused by the flood water. The local leaders were effusive in their appreciation of what little relief I arranged on the spot. Here I was doing even more than what Giani *ji* had requested, but in the process, not earning his goodwill. Giani Zail Singh was to become the Chief Minister of the state. After some years he would be elevated as the President of the Republic of India. I doubt if he would have forgotten the slight. I started my tenure then, with success in making an enemy of a potential friend, and as it transpired, a possible benefactor. I recalled the sage advice of the Maharaja of Kapurthala, mentor of my family, described in the first chapter of this book '*Mulaqat karamat*!' A meeting can work miracles. That had been his recipe for success.

I was to learn later that Giani Zail Singh was a highly regarded freedom fighter against the British colonial rule. He was a fervent supporter of a nationalist movement called the Praja Mandal, which defied princely rule, especially in the erstwhile state of Faridkot. This party had in due course merged with the nationalist Congress Party of India. On account of his direct confrontation with the rulers, Giani Zail Singh had been punished in a bizarre fashion. According to a legend, Giani *ji* was dragged by his hair tied to the back of a moving jeep. Giani Zail Singh's home was in Faridkot district, but it was from Anandpur Sahib that he was seeking election to the State legislature.

When I joined my appointment as the DC, the state of Punjab was under the President's rule. Elections to the assembly were scheduled about six months later. In this period of run up to the state elections Giani *ji* assiduously cultivated his chosen constituency, which consisted almost entirely of villages. It was undoubted that Giani *ji* had an ear close to the ground. He would often intercede with me on behalf of his constituents, for speeding up development work in some segments. In the event of the Congress Party winning the state elections, Giani Zail Singh was tipped to be the Chief Minister of the state. It was not surprising then that many departmental officials in the district treated him with great respect. In fact, a number of middle-level staff had been posted in the district at his behest. I recall a visit to

Ropar of Mr Ashwini Kumar, Inspector General of Police. Mr Kumar knew my family well, as he and my father were service colleagues. Mr Kumar hinted that Giani *ji* was likely to become the Chief Minister shortly.

Mr Kumar was correct in his prophesy. When the state elections were held sometime in February of 1972, the Congress Party secured a clear majority. Giani Zail Singh was duly elected from Anandpur Sahib and became the CM of Punjab. The defeated candidate, a leader named Shiv Singh Bela, challenged the outcome in an election petition in the High Court of Punjab and Haryana. He alleged that Giani *ji* had adopted an unfair practice, viz. using government machinery, consisting of key officials in some departments to help him. Such litigation in the courts continues over many months. The CM was unfazed with the proceedings before the court. Even as he was busy with his vast responsibilities as the head of the state government, Giani *ji* found time to visit Ropar quite often. As the DC I would travel with the Chief Minister in his car when he toured the district. I observed the care that Giani Zail Singh took to make a special call on local leaders, especially the *harijans*,[4] and those belonging to the poorer sections of the community. He enjoyed an immediate rapport with the grassroots leaders and the common village folk. Despite the initial impasse that I described earlier, we

4 'Harijan,' in Hindi-Punjabi, means literally the child of God. The nomenclature was coined by Mahatma Gandhi for those depressed castes (untouchables) that were engaged in occupations traditionally regarded as unclean and demeaning. Gandhi had severely opposed the evil practice. Untouchability is legally banned in India.

had a good working relationship. He accepted my suggestions for allocation of funds for a number of development projects in the district. He appreciated and supported my efforts, and in public meetings he praised me openly. In a very short period of time, we were able to complete some crucial projects, such as construction of an all-weather road to the economically backward Nurpur Bedi block, which was situated across the river Sutlej. This tract had remained cut off from the main district during the rainy season. A sports stadium was constructed in a record period of six months, which Giani Zail Singh himself inaugurated and christened Nehru Stadium after India's first Prime Minister.

While the Chief Minister's periodical visits were for initiation or completion of specific development works, other activities on my plate continued alongside. I found myself learning the process of rural development at the grassroots, the village.

At that time only two passenger cars, named Fiat and Ambassador, were manufactured in India. The demand for cars far exceeding the number available in the market, there were long queues of customers awaiting delivery of cars. In that controlled economy, the manufacturers placed a few vehicles at the disposal of the government that could be allotted for purchase by individuals at the discretion of the government. When I received orders of appointment as DC, I pleaded with the Chief Secretary that I may be allotted a car from what was called the 'government quota'. A Deputy Commissioner is authorized to fly a designated flag. I pointed out that since

I owned only a motor scooter, it would be embarrassing if I were to place a flag atop its mudguard. Mr S.S. Grewal, the Chief Secretary, had a good laugh, and allotted me a small car out of turn. This was a minor perk of my office. I was also loaned an amount to cover part of the cost. The official car, an Ambassador, was for official tours, the Fiat for any personal chores.

Green is my State

During a two-year interregnum between my positions of SDO and DC, I worked in the Punjab Secretariat as a Deputy Secretary for Development and Agriculture. At state headquarters, I could understand the strategy of the Government of India and also the Government of Punjab for ushering in the so-called 'Green Revolution' in agricultural production. In the district I was directly involved with the implementation of the policy through a multitude of agencies.

Miracle seeds of wheat and rice developed by the Nobel laureate Norman Borlaug in Mexico and Manila had demonstrated potential for enhancing crop yields manifold. The state of Punjab was at the forefront in adoption of the new technologies. The technology required heavy infusion of inputs of irrigation, chemical fertilizers and insecticides. Conventional practices limited operations to a level of subsistence farming, which generated no surplus that could be invested in procuring these additional items. It was thus imperative to arrange agricultural credit to fund the cost of the inputs vital for the new technologies. The existing sources of credit were private money lenders, and direct government lending via a century-old system of called *taccavi.* Credit from private lenders was available at exorbitant rates of interest. After a great amount of research by professionals, the government had decided to dismiss *taccavi* as 'little else than the ill-performed disbursement of inadequate moneys by an ill-suited agency.'[5] In the year 1968, the state government abolished the system of *taccavi* loaning, and strengthened institutional loaning through a system of cooperative societies. Thereafter, the top priority for the state was to ensure adequate agricultural credit to all farmers to meet the heavy investment in all inputs that the new technology demanded.

Enterprising as the farmers of Punjab were, they responded avidly to plant the new varieties. More and more cultivable area was brought under irrigation. Ground water for irrigation was delivered via additional tube wells, for which power supply was assured; networks of cooperatives were built up to supply chemical fertilizers and plant protection items. The Agriculture Refinance Corporation (ARC),[6] a national institution supported by the Reserve Bank of India, provided all sums required by the cooperative banks for long term credit (for tube wells and machinery) and short-term loans (for inputs like fertilizers and pesticides). Along with the arrangements for farmers'

5 Reserve Bank of India (1954), 'All India Rural Credit Survey'.

6 ARC was reorganized in 1982 and is now called National Bank of Agriculture and Rural Development (NABARD).

education, the demands of credit and marketing were met with alacrity. The Development Commissioner (Agriculture Production), my immediate boss, reviewed the progress of all institutions involved in a weekly meeting. I remember that I drafted the minutes of these crucial discussions, held punctually every Tuesday. The farmers of Punjab were quick to avail the linked facilities for credit and other inputs on convenient offers.

In a single year (1968–69) the quantum of crop loans jumped eight times, and the area under wheat crop doubled. By the year 1971 additional tube wells numbering two lakh had been put up by individual farmers in the state. Between 1968 and 1969 the market arrivals of wheat rose from 8 lakh tonnes to 16 lakh tonnes. In those heady days, the state of Punjab generated so much marketable surplus of wheat that going from managing shortages, it now faced the problems of managing surpluses. Overnight the country became self-sufficient in so far as wheat was concerned.

If the macro policy formulation was by the Government of India and general direction for implementation proceeded from state headquarters, the cutting edge for execution was the district. Unfailingly, the fifth day of every month, there was a comprehensive discussion with district officers on all aspects of agriculture and development by the Deputy Commissioner of the district. I reviewed at length progress on items such as installation of tube wells, the supply of seed and institutional credit as well as the recovery of dues, farmers' training, marketing arrangements, etc. There was much enthusiasm among the representatives of departments and institutions to highlight their performance against the set targets.

During these meetings, and in my interaction with the public, I discovered two factors which proved critical for success of the strategy. These interlinked factors contained inbuilt incentives for the farmers to make investments, which was a hallmark of the input-driven movement towards modern agriculture. Firstly, consolidated holdings, in other words the pieces of land owned by farmers being contiguous to one another, and not dispersed physically. Secondly, easy access for farmers to markets to sell the agricultural produce.

In the year 1948, it had been decided[7] to remap the entire area of the state, to align all holdings in a proper north–south direction, and to consolidate all holdings of individuals into contiguously owned land. By the year 1961, the entire cultivable area of the state had been systematically mapped and aligned, and segments of land holdings owned by farmers across the state brought together. With the success of this bold exercise, the landowners could manage their land in a single block efficiently, and had an incentive to make investments for irrigation and machinery. A happy, not-unexpected consequence of the ambitious process of consolidation was that, on the map, a small share of land belonging to every

---

7 The enabling legislation was The Punjab Consolidation of Holdings Act, 1948. History tells us that the agrarian revolution in England of the 18th century had as its foundation a structure of consolidated holdings of farmers. The process of consolidation has still not been completed in several states in India.

owner was set apart for a common purpose, viz. village roads. In due course, roads were constructed exactly as per the map markings. The provisions in the Act were stringent, and binding on all land owners. Consequently, the placement of every link road was set in stone.

The advent of the 'Green Revolution' in Punjab proved to be coterminous with the establishment of the network of village-link roads, which provided connectivity with district and state roads. This was also the period when markets came up in the bigger villages and small towns. The village-link roads were therefore essential to the enhancement of agriculture. According to one piece of legislation, named the Punjab Agricultural Produce Marketing Act, 1961[8] *mandi*s, or markets for sale of agricultural commodities were notified, where the surplus food grain was sold. The market fee levied on grain arrivals in the *mandi*s yielded large surplus of revenues; these amounts could be spent for stipulated purposes, the most important of such purposes being the construction and maintenance of market linked village roads. Thus a virtuous circle of rural economic regeneration was created. Market revenues funded road communications, which in turn boosted the volumes of market arrivals. The village community played a crucial role in the success of the village road project. So great was the demand for establishing village roads that the sanction of every such road was contingent

8 In the wake of greater sophistication in marketing arrangements the efficacy of the Act is now being questioned on the ground of the *mandi*s acquiring a monopolistic role. In the 1960s and 1970s, when facilities for marketing were primitive, the Act benefitted the rural economy.

upon the local community using their own volunteers to physically prepare the foundation of the planned village road. This meant that the engineers of the State Marketing Board (the institution responsible for the project) began proper construction as per engineering norms only over paths where the local community had completed what was called 'earth work,' a preliminary non-technical activity.

While most activities, adjunct to the modernizing of agriculture, were undertaken by the authorized institutions, public participation in the process had to be catalysed by the Deputy Commissioner. Motivated with the promise of connectivity of the respective villages, the panchayats vied for initiation of roads to benefit their respective settlements. A substantial part of the labour component being contributed by the villages free of charge, the Board's liability in the total cost reduced. At the same time the local leaders pressurized the Government and the Marketing Board to complete road construction expeditiously. Good road communication in the state was an important factor for the comparative prosperity that the farming community in the state came to enjoy.

A stickler for rules, I was determined to adhere to the norms stipulated for disposal of court work as well as touring. Every month a certain minimum number of appeals in revenue matters had to be decided. Guidelines mandated the DC to remain on tour for a minimum number of days and nights. Every week I set apart two days, Monday and Tuesday, for court work and other work at the district headquarters; Wednesdays and Thursdays were assigned for field touring. Members of the public were free to approach me in office or in the field, except when court work or official meetings were in progress. Moving out to small towns and villages, meeting farmers, local leaders and officials was truly an education in itself.

Ropar district falls at the foothills of the lower Himalayas. It is crisscrossed by a network of canals emanating from the Bhakra-Nangal hydroelectricity project (India's largest) and from Ropar itself. There were many well-maintained rest houses on canal banks and within the Bhakra-Nangal project for stay of officers on tour. Touring for me was not a chore, but a pleasant experience. I would normally move out of Ropar in the late evening of Tuesday, and return on Friday morning. At Ropar I could indulge myself in a game of badminton, which we played outdoors under lights, as there was no covered badminton hall.

An Abrasive Civil Servant

One special project in which I was involved was that of a new institution called the Marginal Farmers and Agricultural Labourers' Agency (MFALA)[9] in Ropar district. In 1971 the Government of India established agencies in selected districts in the country to support small farmers in economically viable activities, and to generate employment

9 The agencies for small and marginal farmers and agricultural labour were initially in four selected districts of Punjab. Building on the success of the experiment, all districts in the state now have District Development Agencies, which carry out the same work.

for the landless. The Project Director and Chief Executive of MFALA was a colleague, a fellow IAS officer named Karl Reddy. As the Deputy Commissioner I was also the Chairman of MFALA. Karl, trained as an engineer, was endowed with a brilliant and incisive mind, and also an ability to think out of the box. Even as his senior by two years in the official hierarchy, I think I learnt more from him than the other way round. In his student days at the Osmania University in Hyderabad, Karl had been a firebrand student leader who fell out with authority. Joining the IAS had mellowed him slightly, but here also he would not conceal his contempt for mediocrity. So much so that he rubbed some of his superiors the wrong way and early in his career was dubbed a potato too hot for many officers to handle. I myself had observed his unusual combination of erudition, analytical skills and practical orientation, and went out of my way to support his endeavours. On his part, Karl continued to thumb his nose at authority. Despite my own conviviality, he did not hesitate to point any shortcomings that he perceived in my approach. I respected him for his bluntness. This incidentally earned me the reputation of an officer who could tolerate and motivate.

On one occasion, when the Development Commissioner, Mrs Sarla Grewal, one of the senior-most officers of the state government, was to visit my district, I planned to showcase Karl Reddy's successful projects for establishing small farmers in viable businesses. Karl told me bluntly that he had no time for the meeting, which he regarded as merely a PR (public relations) exercise. He was also cut up as Mrs Grewal had not approved some scheme for development that he had posed to the state government. It was with much cajoling that Karl reluctantly called off his proposed boycott. During the review meeting I was at pains to laud Karl's bold drive, but his demeanour in the interaction was sullen. Mrs Grewal remarked to me later about Karl's unusual behaviour. Instead of Karl receiving credit for some remarkable success, I was hard put to justify what Mrs Grewal would have viewed as strange petulance.

That was Karl Reddy then, a man with a razor-sharp mind, and a down to earth practical approach to boot, who displayed a rare quality of needling official personnel.

Karl Reddy initiated some unique projects for economic uplift, for the funding of which he persuaded locally active commercial banks. He also designed some community projects for environmental protection and soil conservation, which generated employment for the locals. There was one novel scheme for installation of deep tube wells owned and managed by the village community. These innovations entailed public participation and a break from ponderous official management. The projects were a departure from conventional government-run programmes. Borrowing from commercial, rather than cooperative banks raised the hackles of officials of the government department of cooperation, who felt that the monopoly of cooperative banks was threatened. The scheme for soil conservation entailed the installation of small check dams to trap the run-off of water that was inundating precious cultivable land. During the course of the project, I realized that it was in conflict with the conventional practice of the Irrigation Department (the Drainage wing). On the one hand the engineers were spending huge amounts in channeling the flow of excess water in the fields, to deliver the same into the nearby rivulets: on the other MFALA was building small dams to check erosion of soil, and using the stored water to recharge the underlying aquifer. The Forest and Soil Conservation departments aimed at a long term environmentally judicious goal for productive use of surplus water, and the Irrigation Department pursued a short-term goal of fire-fighting seasonal floods. The success of MFALA projects brought Karl Reddy into conflict with entrenched interests of several government departments. I think in many matters Karl was ahead of his time.

Even as Karl's reputation for excellent planning and execution was somewhat tarnished by his deliberate slighting of official authority, in personal life he displayed a streak of romance. During my stay at Ropar, a lady IAS officer Satwant Sidhu was doing her district training with me. I requested Karl to allocate some substantive work of MFALA to the young officer. This would be part of the training schedule for the new recruit. In the process I inadvertently played the role of Cupid. Shortly after I had left Ropar the two young officers decided to tie the knot. I am sure Karl would not give any credit to me for helping in furthering the romance.

A lesson I learnt was that small focused projects initiated by competent persons can succeed, but require the pilots to accept great accountability. In a bureaucratic hierarchy responsibility is usually dispersed; individuals can manage to pass the buck. I used the experiment in development by MFALA at Ropar as the subject of a dissertation for a degree of Master of Philosophy that I pursued at the University of Cambridge in the United Kingdom a few years later. In a later Chapter I have tried to place the work of MFALA at Ropar in the perspective of academic research.

Fascinating Personalities

As the Deputy Commissioner, there are multiple occasions for meeting a variety of distinguished people. By the virtue of his position, the DC associates with public spirited individuals in diverse fields of activity, many of which are beyond his routine official functions. Compared to larger districts where there is much industrial activity, Ropar's was a small, mainly rural-based economy. At Ropar, I met some eminent personalities with unusual qualities, like Uma Daulat Singh, wife of one of India's great army generals. Lieutenant General Daulat Singh, regarded as a hero of India's war with China of 1962, had been killed on duty in November 1963 in an air crash in the state of Jammu and Kashmir. Uma Daulat Singh's life ambition was to develop the village of Bhabat, the ancestral village of the late general, which fell under the district of Ropar. Uma had decided to invest the life savings of her late husband to help the residents. On my recommendation her request for renaming of the village as Daulat Singh Wala (village of Daulat Singh) was easily accepted by the state government. More difficult was motivating the residents of the village to adopt some schemes for their economic uplift. The hidebound, traditionally conservative villagers refused to try out a number of small schemes for their benefit, even when the cost was being borne by Mrs Daulat Singh.

Uma Daulat Singh was a frequent visitor to our home. From the whiff of delicate perfume that Uma used, I could sense when she was in the vicinity. With her aristocratic lineage, Uma was happy to spend days with unrefined village folk in unhygienic surroundings. She was frustrated that she could not persuade the villagers to accept her financial support for the uplift of the village. The only condition Uma stipulated for the beneficiaries to avail her munificence was that the money should be gainfully spent in viable activities. Meena and I enjoyed meeting the charming Uma. I shared Uma's disappointment that she could not change the mindset of the intended beneficiaries. From the Government side I could offer some projects of rural business activity for the residents of the village. No amount of cajoling by Uma, or by government officials could break the resistance of the locals to the adoption of sensible activities that were on offer. Sadly, some years later, when Uma departed from the scene, the state government reverted to the old name of the village. It is called Bhabat again. Most of the land owned by the village residents has been acquired by the government, and is now part of the expanded international airport. Perhaps General Daulat Singh, who perished in a helicopter mishap, would have been happy with this ultimate denouement.

A second distinguished person who came to me with a specific project of social benefit was a retired Colonel named D.S. Vohra. His unusual project required the establishment of a centre for development and production of what came to be known in medical circles as artificial limbs, including the 'Jaipur foot' (a prosthetic leg). Vohra was a retired officer of the Electrical and Mechanical Engineering Corps of the Indian army. He had acquired expertise, rare at that time, of creating artificial limbs for soldiers who were incapacitated during war. During his army career, Vohra had established the Indian Army's institution for artificial limbs in Poona. After his retirement from the army, Vohra wanted to set up a prosthetic unit to carry forward his mission. He wanted the state government to assist him in acquiring land for the project. The colonel had identified some land belonging to a panchayat in a village close to Chandigarh city. I was able to persuade the panchayat of Bhabat (the very same village patronized by Uma Daulat Singh), to place with Colonel Vohra five acres of land on long lease. Colonel Vohra was surprised when I told him that his demand had been processed and accepted. 'But I only need two acres!' he exclaimed. I urged Vohra to take the larger piece of land on offer, which he might need in future for possible expansion. Vohra's reaction was typical of a straightforward military man. He regarded the project as a place where he could help wounded soldiers, not a base for commercial activity. Vohra Nevedac Prosthetic Clinic is now internationally regarded as a leading institution for research and development and production of artificial limbs. Whenever I met Colonel Vohra, years after he set up the institution, he regretted that he did not avail of the opportunity that had come his way in the year 1972. In recognition of his contribution the Government of India awarded Colonel D.S. Vohra the prestigious Padma Shri.

The most celebrated citizen in the district of Ropar was Dr Mohinder Singh Randhawa, a former ICS officer, who lived in Kharar, a small town on the outskirts of the city of Chandigarh. I considered it a signal honour to be invited to Dr Randhawa's farmhouse. An amazingly versatile personality, Dr Randhawa was an eminent botanist and academic, and also a brilliant administrator. He had authored numerous books on plants and the environment. At the time of India's partition in 1947, when he worked as Deputy Commissioner of Delhi, Dr Randhawa personally organized the rehabilitation of thousands of Hindu and Sikh families uprooted from their homes in the new Pakistan territory, in Delhi. During his tenure as the Chief Commissioner of the emerging city of Chandigarh, he did pioneering work in horticultural development. The city owes its name of 'city beautiful' to Dr Randhawa's imaginative selection of tree species and their methodical plantation, and the creation of numerous parks and green belts. Likewise, during his appointment as the Vice Chancellor, Dr Randhawa raised the stature of Punjab Agriculture University to that of a world class institution. His achievements were legion, but what struck me most during my visits to his home was his sense of discipline and management of time. In accepting an invitation, you arrive punctually to the minute. In the case of Dr Randhawa, even the time of your departure was determined meticulously by the host. On my first visit to his home, I arrived punctually at 7:30 pm, enjoyed snacks and dinner, and lively conversation on such topics as the contouring of the landscape of Chandigarh. He offered to help me in preparing plans for greener urban areas in the district of Ropar. As I was warming up to blow my trumpet on what I was doing in the district, Dr Randhawa stood up abruptly, observing, brusquely, 'It is ten minutes past nine now. I have to be in bed at nine thirty.' The evening ended with him presenting me his book on the forests of Kumaon, if I remember correctly. Even as he gave me the volume, he tasked me with absorbing the contents. Behaving as a mentor, he promised that he would discuss a strategy for urban renewal on our next encounter. It dawned on me that our discussion had not been merely small talk. Dr Randhawa expected some of his academic rigour and administrative acumen to rub off on his young guest. Here was a man both stern and humane. It was a lasting regret that I could not give practical shape to Dr Randhawa's vision. Under orders of the government, I was suddenly moved out of Ropar before I could get going.

During a senior district posting an officer gets to many such distinguished figures in public life, and he has opportunity to associate with worthy causes, as in the aforementioned cases.

Some Excitement

My time at Ropar was marked by two different episodes that generated some excitement. One was the outbreak of war between India and Pakistan in December 1971, and the second an unusual incident of police firing in the month of January 1972, when some nine members of a violent eccentric group were killed.

Details of the events in the war between December 3 and December 17 in the year 1971, that led to the birth of Bangladesh as a new nation are a significant part of military history. Conspicuous bravery displayed by members of the armed forces is chronicled in military folklore. I confine myself here to the impact of the war in a district like mine. In Punjab, the scene of hostilities was the areas abutting the international border. The imminence of war was announced by the then Inspector General of Police Mr Ashwini Kumar in a midnight meeting in the district town of Sangrur, where all the Deputy Commissioners had been summoned. Certain standard operating procedures were laid for district officers in situations arising out of armed border hostilities. The guidelines, based on experience gained in the Second World War, and from the recent battles between India and Pakistan in the year 1965, included air raid precautions, management of blackouts, dispensing relief in crisis situations and the like. In the run up to the war it transpired that the civil administration did not even possess basic equipment like sirens that could warn citizens of likely air attack over civilian areas. The theoretical guidance that

I had received in the Central Emergency Relief Training Institute (CERTI), Nagpur was now put to use. In the event, the theatre of war operations was limited to military targets, besides tactical advance and retreat across the border by the antagonists.

While civilian areas in Punjab, especially in hinterland districts like Ropar were mainly unscathed, the war casualties included as many as 42 soldiers hailing from parts of Ropar district, who died in the war. The armed forces, of course, delivered relief to the bereaved families in due course. As an immediate measure, Meena undertook a heart-rending task, namely, of personally visiting the widows and next of kin of every brave soldier killed in action, and delivering some relief in cash from the district Red Cross funds to the bereaved families. By this gesture, the DC's wife, viewed as an emissary of the government, could condole individually with every young widow and grieving parent. In their tragic condition the young widows could relate better with a woman in their midst. She could observe the condition of the distraught families at first hand. The wife of the DC is ex officio President of the Hospital Welfare section of the District Red Cross Society. In that capacity Meena motivated several institutions and many individuals to donate for gifts for soldiers on active duty on the borders. I remember that she and other female members of the group personally prepared large quantities of pickles at my official residence.

After the hostilities were over, we were able to visit the troops of an Indian army unit who temporarily controlled an area near Gurdaspur district by the name of Shakargarh.[10] This small portion included a few villages of Pakistan, which remained in control of the Indian army for some months. It was an interesting experience to be in 'enemy territory', so to speak. We delivered some gifts to the battalion commander of the unit. One small contribution to the national effort at Ropar was to arrange a large blood donation camp, where we collected some 250 units of blood to help injured soldiers convalescing in hospitals. It was the first time that I myself donated blood. After Ropar I became a regular blood donor, and even marked my retirement many years later by donating on the day I demitted the office of Chief Secretary of the state.

The incident of police firing on 21 January 1972 was a scene from the theatre of the absurd, grotesque in the extreme. It resulted entirely from a display of wanton and aimless aggression by an inebriated mob. I happened to be in Chandigarh that evening for the marriage of a colleague. In fact, the family was enjoying a spicy plate of potato *tikki*s from a roadside vendor, where a uniformed police officer located me to report that a number of people had been killed in a police firing at Ropar. Needless to say, I rushed back to Ropar, apologizing profusely to the bridegroom that I could not stay for his party.

---

10 During the war of 1971, the Pakistan troops retreated from some sections of the theatre, leaving possession of some blocks of land with the Indian army. Most of such areas were returned to the opposing country after an agreement between the Prime Ministers of India and Pakistan was signed in Shimla in the year 1972. Of course Bangladesh had become an independent nation.

It was almost midnight when I reached the hospital where the injured persons were admitted. As many as nine members of a group of *nihangs*—warriors of the *panth*, as they called themselves—had been killed. Many policemen had suffered injuries from weapons like swords and spears. Here I saw both groups of antagonists lying next to each on adjacent hospital beds, like exhausted football players of opposing teams after a hard-fought friendly match. Both parties expressed joy to receive my commiseration at one o' clock in the morning. All that I had done was to assure them that they would be fairly treated and looked after, but even this little gesture was appreciated. It also defused the charged atmosphere somewhat. At the same time, at that late hour I issued a formal order that the local Sub-Divisional Magistrate should conduct an enquiry into the happenings.

To grasp the events that had such tragic consequences it is necessary to understand the peculiar culture of the *nihangs*, their psyche and the historical development of the *nihang* tradition. The *nihangs* have no fixed abode, but are seen to be wandering on horseback in the area surrounding Anandpur Sahib. Even in the 21st century one can sometimes see groups of ferocious Sikh riders on horseback, wearing their traditional, antiquated robes of deep blue. A turban of the same colour is fortified with heavy steel ringlets. They carry weapons in the form of antique swords and spears. Having no ostensible sources of income, they travel from village to village, seeking alms in the name of the last Sikh Guru, Guru Gobind Singh. They have quaint habits, and their own vocabulary describing items of food, clothing, weapons and the like. A *nihang* does not beg for alms, or food items: he seizes any offerings as a birth right. Thus, a donor is obliged to place on the ground any amount of cash offering: the *nihang* will pick up the offering with the tip of his spear. He lives with such dramatic illusions. The villagers indulge these fantasies as harmless eccentricities of a passionate, if uneducated sect. In their retinue, their weapons and their bearing, the *nihang*s live two centuries in the past. People in the area are so used to seeing the *nihang*s in their quaint attire and on horseback, that a *nihang* looks quite comical, and out of place if seen, say on a two-wheeler motor cycle, rather than astride a usually emaciated pony.

To truly grasp the status of the *nihang*s in society, it is important to know how the Sikh religion took birth and developed over several centuries. The area comprising the district of Ropar, where the *nihang*s are most numerous, is the venue of important events in Sikh history. Guru Nanak Dev (1469–1539), founder of the Sikh religious faith, was followed in the line of succession by nine Gurus. The Sikh religion preaches ideals of peace, universal brotherhood, equality and a spirit of service. Beginning as pacifists with a strong spiritual mooring, the adherents began to suffer persecution at the hands of the Mughal emperors. The persecution began around the middle of the 17th century. The fifth Guru, Arjan Dev (1563–1606) was tortured for his belief and burnt alive. The ninth Guru, Tegh Bahadur (1621–1675), was tortured and beheaded. It was in the year 1699 that the community of followers of the faith was transformed into a body of militant fighters for their faith. Anandpur Sahib in Ropar district was the town where Guru Gobind Singh (1666–1708), performed the symbolic act of baptism of the first Sikhs, and created in the year 1699, the *Khalsa panth* (literally 'the path of the pure') to fight the oppression perpetrated by Emperor Aurangzeb (1618–1707), often reviled as the most bigoted of the Mughal emperors. During protracted warfare, which was mainly hand-to-hand physical combat, Guru Gobind Singh and his family suffered grievously; two sons of the Guru died in battle, and the two younger sons, aged seven and nine years, were walled up alive. The entire district is dotted with Sikh shrines (*gurdwaras*) that commemorate important events in the resistance by the Sikhs to the cruel and intolerant regime.

The bravery of Guru Gobind Singh and his followers inspired Sikhs to continue their armed resistance to the regime. Many bands of followers adopted guerrilla tactics of attacking the Mughal troops sporadically, inflicting lethal blows. In the 18th century the Sikhs consolidated numerous armed units, called *misls*, into a formidable fighting force. In the early 19th century Maharaja Ranjit Singh established a strong Sikh empire, which encompassed most of the areas of north and northwest India, and even present-day Afghanistan. Even as the Sikh empire had become a reality, many small bands of armed horsemen, calling themselves the soldiers of the Guru continued the bohemian existence of their precursors, right through the 20th century. The successors of the knights errant of the guru, as they have been colourfully described, are the *nihang*s of today.

There is no centralized leadership among the *nihang*s. Several separate groups, each with an individual leader, are visible at an annual festival held at Anandpur Sahib in the month of March, called the *Hola Mohalla,* or grand gathering to commemorate the founding of the *khalsa*. On *Hola Mohalla,* various competitive events of horsemanship, fencing and hand-to-hand combat are arranged at Anandpur Sahib, where the *nihang* groups display a spectacle of feats, witnessed by large gatherings of spectators, for which they receive rewards.

It was one such group of *nihang*s headed by their leader named Sucha Singh that entered at midnight a prominent Sikh temple of Ropar called Gurdwara Sadavart, and forcibly took possession of the premises. Apparently, Sucha Singh and his followers, numbering perhaps 50, had moved from one gurdwara to another all night, looking for shelter. The local managers of the shrines, all situated within a radius of about 20 miles, refused to entertain the large party. They finally descended on Gurdwara Sadabrat, and made themselves at home. The unarmed Sikh priest in charge of the gurdwara was terrified at the presence of an armed lot of warriors, who seemed to be under the influence of drugs. He called for police protection. He was obviously convinced that this violent mob was determined to seize ownership of the shrine.

By the time a police party reached the venue, Sucha Singh and his cohorts were fully entrenched in the premises, which they considered that they owned by convention, as the Guru's foot soldiers. During a later enquiry the police deposed that the *nihangs* were drunk and under the influence of a potent drug called *sukha*, a drink from concentrated, home-processed opium. Taken in excess, *sukha* causes hallucinations. Initially the police officers felt that they were dealing with a group of eccentric, but harmless, hooligans who could be persuaded to remove themselves from illegal occupation of the gurdwara. Imagine the chagrin of the protection force of policemen when choice abuse and invectives were hurled at them. Sucha Singh's warriors had psyched themselves into a state of frenzy. The crazed mob had been hypnotized to a state where they were convinced that the police force was an opposing regiment of infidels, which was intent on devastating the Guru's army. Bellowing slogans like 'Death to the Turks!' (at the start of the 18th century, the Guru and his successor warriors had battled the army of the Mughal emperors, who were descendent in the line of Timur, the Turk conquerer), the passionate horde armed with swords, spears and machetes, charged the police party as in a pitched battle. Sustaining grievous injuries caused by the primitive weapons, the police party opened rifle fire. As many as nine *nihangs* were killed on the spot; some were injured. Many policemen were seriously wounded. These details emerged in the testimonies presented before a judicial commission that investigated the happenings.

This could well have been a scene from the famous Cervantes' novel, where the protagonist, Don Quixote, beset by hallucination, charges at the windmills with the notion that he is confronting an attacking army. Whereas the incident in the novel is a comic interlude, here in Ropar the absurd behaviour of the inebriated mob had tragic consequences.

My decision of a magisterial enquiry was announced to the public at large and to the media. It also conveyed a message that the government was determined to have an objective assessment of the causes of the fracas and to fix responsibility for any lapse that might have occurred. The state government viewed this incident with utmost seriousness. Before the SDM could begin his enquiry, the government decided to set up a Commission of Enquiry, headed by Justice R.S. Narula, a sitting judge of the High Court of Punjab and Haryana to hold a comprehensive probe into the incidents.

Justice Narula completed the enquiry within a few months. His Report castigated some police officers and also some doctors for errors of omission and commission. I was to learn more than a year after Justice Narula, later Chief Justice Narula, had submitted his Report, that the Honorable Judge had commended my role as District Magistrate in taking quick action to bring the volatile situation under control. It is necessary to mention the aftermath of the unfortunate events. I could not benefit in any way from the positive remarks by the Judge. My role was never formally recognized. For this I do not blame the bureaucratic procedures so much as my own propensity to have sought credit for myself as a matter of right. When I learnt about the contents of the Report I was working as Joint Secretary, directly reporting to the Chief Secretary, Mr R.S. Talwar, my immediate boss. I addressed a written submission to the government, quoting the following extracts from Justice Narula's Report:

'I appreciate the promptness of Mr Rajan Kashyap, IAS, Deputy Commissioner, Ropar, in the SDM immediately on the 20th of January 1972 to hold an enquiry into the incident—', and further adding, '—I appreciate the frankness, truthfulness and sense of devotion to duty of Mr Rajan Kashyap—'.

I was technically correct in requesting that the commendatory remarks should be brought on official record. This might have benefited me in my future career. I was disappointed that Mr Talwar, the Chief Secretary, refused my request. He was probably displeased that I had placed before him an official demand for recognition, rather than requesting the grant of a favour. Possibly Mr Talwar expected me to approach him personally. I had again been remiss in man management: this was my lesson as a bureaucrat. Ironically, I had behaved like the very *nihangs* whose actions were examined in the judicial enquiry. Just as the eccentric group demanded, rather than requested alms, I too had sought support of official rules, instead of making a personal submission.

As with my first posting as SDM, I received abrupt orders transferring me from the high-profile post of DC to a routine assignment of a Deputy Secretary in the Civil Secretariat. When the Chief Secretary informed me on the phone that he was bringing me to Chandigarh, my immediate response was 'Sir, when do you want me there?' The Chief Secretary clarified that he was not summoning me for a meeting, but was transferring me mid-season. To this I rejoined that I had understood, and I was merely seeking directions on when I should report at the new job. The Chief Secretary advised that I could leave charge at Ropar in consultation with my successor.

The truth is that the sudden transfer orders did not upset me, as I was prepared for a change. I knew that the Chief Minister had some regard for my work, which he had seen for himself. I had realized, though, that a number of local leaders, who owed allegiance to the Chief Minister, were unhappy that I did not oblige them in certain small matters, which they brought before me. I knew that the Chief Minister's inner circle of supporters in the district would be pleased at my departure from the local scene. In the month of December 1972, the petition challenging the Chief Minister's election to the legislative assembly had been withdrawn by Giani *ji*'s opponent, so the Chief Minister was on firm ground politically.

I had had a satisfying spell as DC. I had also learnt some lessons in boss management. I resolved that, in future I would be more discreet and tactful, especially where matters of personal interest were concerned. It is a moot point, though, whether tact is an inborn human trait, or a quality that can be developed.

On 1 January 1973, I was back in the pavilion, so to speak, of the Secretariat, to begin a new innings. The advent of a new year is the time for making resolutions. And there is time enough during the rest of the year to break them. My own resolution was to develop a modicum of tact, and try not to upset superiors needlessly.

Moving home from one station to another, especially to the capital city, is usually trying. In government one is provided on nominal rent an 'official residence', the size of which is determined by one's status, but such a habitat is not available at short notice; sometimes months elapse before a displaced officer is fully rehabilitated. As they rise in seniority, officers working in Chandigarh move from an apartment to a bungalow, with which is attached substantial garden space. On transfer from Ropar to Chandigarh I could conveniently move immediately into a small house built by my father over 500 square yards of land in Sector 10, Chandigarh. The house was mine to use, the pater assured me; the only rider was that I must maintain it, and not rent it out. This was an entirely win-win situation. Throughout the years at Chandigarh, I did not occupy a government house, even though my colleagues preferred the luxury of bungalows. 'Why not maintain good relations within the family?' was my rejoinder when a fellow officer queried why I refused larger accommodation offered by the government.

A SMALL FISH IN A BIG POND

Some 10 years into my career I found myself working in New Delhi, a part of the Government of India, Ministry of Home Affairs. The move from Chandigarh was not my own choice; it was a decision of the state government. As a matter of fact, I was with the Chief Secretary, Mr H.S. Chhina when I overheard him speaking on the phone to the Cabinet Secretary in New Delhi regarding the posting of an officer from Punjab in the Government of India. It seemed from the conversation that the central government had selected another IAS officer from Punjab (the person concerned was a friend and colleague) for the particular assignment. Mr Chhina informed the caller on the line that the Chief Minister did not wish to spare the chosen officer, but that the state government was happy to suggest another person (the name was mine) who was equally good. In speaking about the matter in my presence, the Chief Secretary had, in not too subtle a manner, conveyed to me that the decision to transfer me to Delhi was that of the Chief Minister himself.

At that point in time the transfer was actually quite inconvenient to me personally. My wife Meena had just begun to work as a lecturer in a government college in Chandigarh. Were she to accompany me to Delhi, she would need long leave of absence from her teaching assignment. In the event of her plea for leave not being allowed, she could be compelled to give up her job altogether. The move from Chandigarh thus entailed financial loss to us, besides disruption in Meena's teaching career. I faced a dilemma. The choice was to comply with the orders unreservedly, or to plead with the Chief Secretary, and even the Chief Minister, to review the orders placing my services with the centre, on the ground that my wife's career was at stake. Governments usually try to accommodate couples by posting them together, at the same station. After discussion Meena and I agreed that I would accept the decision by the state and central governments, and not appeal for cancellation of the orders on 'compassionate grounds.' I had decided early in my service career that I would not question decisions of the government in regard to my placement, nor seek any personal favours from my superiors. The Chief Minister had seen my work as Deputy Commissioner in Ropar, which he visited often. He would clearly have reasons for shifting me, which were not mine to question. I decided that I would consider the change as a routine step in my career.

The very day I sought an appointment with Giani Zail Singh, the Chief Minister, which was quickly given. During the brief meeting I thanked the Chief Minister for his trust, and assured him that during my stay in New Delhi my loyalty to my home state of Punjab would be unflinching.

For good measure I added that I would see my role as that of an envoy of the state of Punjab. From Giani *ji*'s expression I detected an element of surprise. He might have expected me to request a review of the orders. He was disarmed with my response, viz. that I accepted his decision ungrudgingly. After all, transfer is no punishment. And who can predict what the future holds? I began to view working at the national level as a new opportunity.

And so began another chapter in my life. The distance from Chandigarh to Delhi is just 160 miles, but there is a world of difference in the working environment of government in the state and at the centre. Even more startling is the contrast between the living conditions of the head of a district and those of a Deputy Secretary in New Delhi. As the key functionary of the state, a DC is invested with ingrained executive powers of administration. Along with authority over men and affairs, the DC enjoys several perquisites of office, in the form of a large earmarked residence, a dedicated official car and household help and attendants. For the state government the Deputy Commissioner is the go-to man for execution of projects and schemes at the district level. The institution endows the holder of the office with a high position in the society. In so far as education of children is concerned, the best schools in town consider it a privilege to admit the children of their DC in their institution. Call it a feudal legacy, or the consequence of a decentralized structure of public administration, but the position of a Deputy Commissioner in a district continues to be *numero uno*.

A Deputy Secretary at the centre, on the other hand is one among some 200 officials of similar rank working in the various ministries and departments of a huge establishment. True, all IAS officers with equivalent years of service behind them carry home the same emoluments, irrespective of where they happen to work in India. The assignments at the national level deal with issues of national and international import, but do not offer any special facilities or conveniences to the incumbents. In my case, the creature comforts attached with the office of DC had already vanished when I was shifted from Ropar to the Secretariat in Chandigarh. Proceeding from the state capital to Delhi was not too drastic a move. I was quite happy to adjust to the changed milieu. We now had two children, a girl aged seven years and a boy aged four. They would surely get to study in the best schools in the country, to participate in many activities available only in a metropolis and to prepare for the life to come. Such was my expectation as our family of four moved to Delhi.

Bringing up the Young

In their personal life young officers joining an office in Delhi face two immediate challenges. One is in regard to living accommodation, and the other in respect of education for their school-going children. In the year 1976, decent living quarters in the form of independent houses or flats with two or three bedrooms were available only to senior officers of the level of Joint Secretary and above. The best that the Department of Urban Estates could offer me was a two-room hostel tenement in a multi-storied condominium called Asia House. Asia was located quite close to the Secretariat buildings and to Connaught Place, New Delhi's premier shopping area. We moved in at once. The apartment being so tiny, the children's room had to serve as a bedroom at night and as the living room during the day. Obviously the living premises were quite cramped. While we were in Delhi there were frequent occasions when house guests, including parents and relatives, visited us. Both Meena and I had been brought up in a culture where guests were to be welcomed at all times. Once in a while the living room perforce became the guest room, and the children moved into our bedroom. The household could overflow with inmates to the extent that one or two younger guests slept on the floor of the makeshift dining room. On the obverse side of the coin, our receiving relatives as house guests strengthened bonds with members of our extended family. The style of community living also accorded us an opportunity to mix with families of colleagues from the IAS as well as many other services from all parts of the country. In those days it was rare for middle class families to own a television set of their own. Common entertainment consisted in whole families, with children in tow, watching the weekly film on the black and white TV set in the common room. The children in particular enjoyed the new form of interaction with their peers, playing excitedly in the common grounds. Surprisingly, neither our daughter Bini nor our son Anurag demurred at the discomfort they faced in the limited living space at home. I think both the children imbibed subtle lessons in caring and sharing space and material goods, both of which were at that time in short supply for them.

Delhi boasts of the highest quality of school education in the country, but obtaining admission into any prestigious school is extremely difficult. Every top school exists in a seller's market, the demand for admission outstripping in multiples of ten the number of seats available. It is well-nigh impossible for parents to even gain entry into the office of the redoubtable schools' principals. Numerous personal visits and pleas fall on deaf ears. The travails of desperate parents seeking admission for their children in quality institutions have become the stuff of stories and have even been dramatized in popular Hindi films. Bini had studied at a Christian missionary school in Chandigarh. Thanks to a testimonial from the Principal of the school in Chandigarh, the Convent of Jesus and Mary deigned at least to meet me, but she held out no assurance of admission. Eventually a colleague whose daughter was a student in the same school, managed to prevail on the Head, so at least one child gained entry into a good school.

For my four-year-old boy we aimed at securing admission in St. Columba's school, which is situated next to the girls' school that my daughter joined. In the coming session there were as many as 250 vacancies in the lowest class called kindergarten (KG) for boys in the age group of four to five years. I took it for granted that the boy would be among the selected children. Some friends advised us to enroll the boy in certain coaching classes in advance of the admission. It is a mystery to me as to what form of specialized coaching can equip a young child of four to face a selection panel. Apparently some teachers did prepare children to bear up to the forthcoming ordeal. Imagine my disappointment when the boy did not figure in the first list of children admitted. We were fed vague assurances that some children might be accommodated in a second round of admissions. At this stage I decided that I would muster what little influence I could gather to achieve my formidable target of primary education for my son. I simply requested my immediate boss, Mr S.S. Sidhu, who was the Additional Secretary in the Ministry to intervene on my behalf. I was immensely grateful that Mr Sidhu intervened successfully. What a lesson was learnt! The system of education in the country required the assistance of a top bureaucrat to gain admission for a child in a nursery.

The teething problems of establishment at Delhi over, we now determined that the children must gain maximum benefit from their stay in the metropolis. In real life many people pass through their youth without excelling in their fields of interest, such as sports or the performing arts. In time they encourage their children to train in the very disciplines which had enthralled them, but in which they could not indulge, for whatever reasons. My special interests were sports and music. Since my days in college I was a reasonable, club level tennis player, even earning university colours, but I had not had professional coaching lessons, so I never played the competitive tennis circuit. Likewise I had a goodly collection of music in the form of vinyl records and spools of recorded tapes, but had not received training in classical Hindustani music, which was for me a passion. Like other parents I wished that my daughter and son should receive specialized training from a young age in the areas of my interest. Perhaps this was an attempt to vicariously enjoy the success of the children in the chosen fields. My daughter joined classes for learning classical music and dance in a highly regarded academy by the name of Sangeet Bharati, which was located at a walking distance of just one kilometer from Asia House, and my son was enrolled for lessons in tennis and swimming in the National Stadium, also situated close by. In Delhi, Meena was a full-time housewife, attending to all household chores and the children's needs. The extra-curricular activities of the children did not incur heavy costs, as the charges in the institutions were nominal. A chaperone had to, however, accompany the children to the academies. As our limited budget did not allow travel by hired taxi, Meena walked daily with the children to their destination. A situation in which walking to a destination in Delhi is mandatory is probably unthinkable for most IAS officers today. In any case, since the children were so young, they were cajoled to join their lessons. On some occasions I was able to accompany the children in these pursuits.

As I began to write this chapter I chanced upon my pay slip issued by the Home Ministry in the year 1977. I was astounded to find that the sum total of my monthly emoluments during that year was exactly 1700 rupees. Even accounting for the low prices prevalent at that time, this was a small amount for meeting the needs of a middle class family. In order to live within one's means one had perforce to develop the habit of thrift. In my years in the service I had of course gone up in life. In Delhi I was the proud owner of a small motor car, and also of a two-wheeler scooter. Driving the car was treated as a luxury to be indulged in on rare occasions. My sturdy two-wheeler (of the make Bajaj) was the default option for transportation to office and also for most family outings. I carried forward my habit from Punjab of being home for lunch every day. It took me exactly four minutes and fifty seconds to drive between Asia House and the North Block, where my office was housed, so commuting was easily done.

Being in Delhi offered me some unexpected benefits, and it transpired that these were free of cost. I became a member of the tennis club for government officials which had dozens of grass courts as well as clay courts. The tennis courts are on Brassy Avenue, just a few hundred yards from the North Block of the Secretariat which houses the Ministry of Home Affairs. The 'game' being a love of my life, I tried not to miss an hour on the courts, irrespective of any pressing official tasks. I simply carried my playing kit and racquet to office. Even when pressed for time it was child's play to wheel my scooter, play a couple of sets and be back in office in the space of an hour and a half. At the same time, I enrolled myself for a two-month training programme in Yoga at an institution called Vishwayatan Yogashram on Ashok Road, again located just a five-minute driving distance from home. The Ashram, spread over several acres in the heart of Delhi, was run by a well-known personality, by the name of Dhirendra Brahmchari. My hour long yoga sessions began at five in the morning, so I could indulge myself in the fitness regime well before office began. What I learnt in the Ashram has stayed with me for life. After my lessons in the Ashram, I adopted Yoga as an essential component of living. No matter where I might be, I never miss my exercises on any single day in the year. The Asia House hostel is also close to a number of cultural centres, where again, at a nominal cost, one could witness plays and musical recitals by world famous artistes. I recall that in the year 1977, my wife and I watched a play in the Kamani Auditorium, whom should we see seated close by but Mrs Indira Gandhi, then a defeated ex-prime minister of India? It speaks volumes of the polity of the time that such an important international personality could enjoy entertainment unescorted and in so unobtrusive a manner.

National Officialdom

I served in the Home Ministry between the years 1976 and 1979. This period witnessed great political turmoil and upheaval. In June 1975 the government of Prime Minister Indira Gandhi had declared an internal emergency in the country. Many civil liberties had been suspended, the media muzzled, and many opposition leaders imprisoned under laws of preventive detention. During the abnormal conditions the Home Ministry was the nodal point for stringent legislation, and for monitoring the implementation of the policy directives by the state governments. In this background the work of Centre State Relations, which was assigned to me had suddenly acquired importance. I found that the role of a Deputy Secretary is quite crucial, as policy proposals begin at his desk to be sent up for approval at the appropriate level, which could be the Home Secretary, the Home Minister, the Prime Minister or the Union Cabinet. I was thus privy to the work of the government during the days of the emergency, to the installation of the new coalition government of the Janata Party in March 1977 after the defeat of Mrs Gandhi's government and to the steps taken for lifting the emergency.

Even as the dramatic changes at the national level were in progress, within the Ministry it was business as usual. The very procedures of disposal of official business adopted by the Congress government continued with the new regime of the Janata government. The original decisions on authoritarian use of power had been approved at top levels, after due confabulation between the Ministries of Home and Law. Exactly the same levels superseded the contentious empowerment made by the outgoing dispensation. After the emergency was lifted, many vocal critics averred that the outgoing government did not permit any dissent whatsoever by the civil services. Being close to what was termed the 'hot seat' in the Government of India, I found that my superiors did not silence discordant notes; indeed they allowed us to speak our mind objectively.

I relate a sample of the working of inter-ministry consultation on a crucial issue. At a time when the government was pursuing a policy of forcible sterilization to control the population explosion, the Ministry of Health and Family Planning, as it was called, proposed that the two-child norm be strictly enforced on all citizens, and that legal penalties be stipulated for couples who failed to abide. The proposal of the Health Ministry came to the Home Ministry for concurrence. The subject was directly in my charge. I recall that I raised legal and conscientious objections to the proposal. In a nutshell the position I took was that it was not within the legal competence of the state to enact a legislation limiting the number of children that a citizen of India could have. The government could not compel a couple to adopt measures of birth control. At best the government could lay down that an infringement of the norms on the number of children per couple could deprive the offender of any special facilities, such as eligibility for grants of welfare, etc. I recommended, accordingly, that the proposal of the Health Ministry be dropped, or substantially modified. To my surprise, my note was endorsed by the Home Secretary. The Union Home Minister too agreed with my view. He recorded that he had apprised the Prime Minister of the view of the Home Ministry. Our Ministry's view prevailed over that of the Ministry of Health.

At a time when the impact of the Emergency was at its height the Union Government decided to activate the dormant National Integration Council, which was headed by the Prime Minister, and included key ministers of the Union Government and the Chief Ministers of the states. I had myself drafted the agenda and notes of this meeting, which was held on 27 November 1976. The five topics discussed, which were approved by the Prime Minster herself, gives an idea of the priorities of the government even during the period of autocratic rule. The topics were:

- Elimination of violence—communal and general
- Minorities, including the problem of their employment
- Discrimination and atrocities against Harijans
- Adivasis
- Regional Harmony

From the level of seriousness with which discussion on the agenda was held it was clear that even during the troubled times, basic democratic ideals of inclusiveness and national integration were enjoined and pursued.

On a personal note, as I handled matters of national integration and centre–state relations, it was an opportune time to gain proficiency in a new language, Urdu, which had fascinated me from childhood. For those in my father's generation, Urdu had been their first language. The connoisseurs, including the professors at the university who taught me English Literature, considered Urdu poetry as rich in all respects as poetry composed in English. While in the Ministry, I discovered an additional motivation to take up the language. As a step for promoting national integration, the government paid an incentive amount of 2000 rupees (a substantial amount at that time) to IAS officers who cleared a test of proficiency in any language other than their mother tongue or the language of the state in which they served. I signed up to take the examination in Urdu, and worked seriously on the script. I was soon able to read passages passably, but developed cold feet as the date of the written test approached. I failed to lay claim to the promised prize money, but managed to develop more than a nodding acquaintance with the choice language. I thus enjoyed the journey, although I missed the monetary reward. Thanks to my limited determination, I am able to enjoy Urdu lyrics and *mushairas* and *quawaalis*.[1] I can decipher the land record, which in the state of Punjab, had been maintained for centuries in the mandatory Urdu. Indeed the terminology for revenue documents continues to be from Persian based Urdu, now written in the Punjabi (Gurmukhi) script. Among friends I sometimes affect superiority, claiming to know four languages: English, Hindi, Punjabi and Urdu.

Immediately after the installation of the new Janata Party government in March 1977, my charge in the Home Ministry, the Centre State Division, unexpectedly came into the limelight. The new government considered the results of the national elections, in which the ruling Congress party was decimated in numbers, as a referendum on the performance of the established governments in the states.

---

1 *Mushaira*: a symposium, where poets recite their own verse, usually without any accompanying musical instruments. *Quawaali*: a style of rendering noted poetry in a chorus, sung in *ragas* of Indian classical music. Both forms emerged as performances in the courts of Mughal emperors in India, and before provincial chieftains of the day.

The Union Cabinet decided to recommend to the President of India that under Article 356 of the Constitution, the legislative assemblies of nine states be dissolved, and fresh elections be conducted to those nine assemblies. The reasoning was that the governments of these states, led by the ruling Congress party, had lost the confidence of the voters, as evidenced by a near total rout of the Congress party in the elections to parliament. At that time Mr B.D. Jatti was the acting President of India, since the elected President Mr Fakhruddin Ali Ahmed had died in April 1977. There was high drama for two days as initially the (acting) President did not approve the recommendations of the Cabinet on dissolving the state assemblies. Eventually the will of the Cabinet prevailed, and the President conveyed his approval to the government. The episode is mentioned here as it shows how euphoria engendered by the dramatic results in the national elections impacted governance in the states. Subsequently, less than three years later the tables were turned, when the Janata government lost the electoral mandate in the elections to the Lok Sabha. The winning political party used the precedent set by its rival to similarly disband the state assemblies and order fresh elections in the same states.

This narrative aims primarily to present an insider's picture of the functioning of bureaucratic systems. The objective is to unravel the tape that fastens the frame of governance. The canvas here does not attempt to evaluate the complex legal issues regarding the imposition of the emergency, or the political developments that led to the formation of the Janata government, or even the dismantling of the set up established by Mrs Gandhi's government. On all these aspects there is considerable authentic literature by distinguished writers from India and abroad. I confine myself therefore to how civil servants handling such matters responded to the changing environment of governance.

During the period of the emergency, June 1975 to January 1977, the Union Home Secretary was Mr S.L. Khurana, a distinguished IAS officer of the Rajasthan cadre. When Meena and I called on them, as was then customary, Mr and Mrs Khurana received us graciously at their home on Ashok Road. During our training period at Mussoorie we had been instructed on the various aspects of social behaviour, such as interaction with families of the seniors. The convention was that normally junior officers should make a social call after due appointment. Calling without prior appointment was also permitted, but in the event of the host not being at home, the callers should leave two visiting cards in token of the young officer and his spouse having paid their regards to the senior and his spouse. The seniors would reciprocate by inviting the juniors and their spouses to an evening meal. Such social customs were the legacy of the British colonial rule. In today's time, the little graces have all but disappeared. Most top officials have little time for such social niceties. On their part the younger generation of officers would much rather cultivate such political bosses as can help them in the advancement of their career than complete the formality of socializing with their seniors.

The Ministry of Home Affairs had a peculiar tradition of the highest ranked staff remaining in office until late evening, that is, much beyond the closing hour of 5 pm. It could be that during the emergency the Ministry was in a kind of 'crisis mode', where any dramatic occurrences in any part of the country required immediate attention. It was almost a routine for all Additional Secretaries and Joint Secretaries (I think the number was eight or ten) to meet over a cup of tea after normal office hours, and stay on in office until eight or nine o' clock. I personally considered the practice a sign of inefficiency. If the hours for office work were eight, I reasoned an efficient work system should ensure that the work, no matter how critical, gets completed within the stipulated period of time. There might be odd occasions when key personnel need to burn the midnight oil, but the habit of senior officials routinely sitting late hours reflected poor time management. At risk of being judgmental, I wholeheartedly agreed with the Scottish novelist Robert Louis Stevenson, who labelled 'extreme busyness—a symptom of deficient vitality.'

As part of the machinery of the government, one has to adjust to the environment in which one is cast. The Ministry of Home Affairs seemed to revel in its importance, as it lurched from crisis to imagined crisis. As a Deputy Secretary it was difficult to obtain leave for proceeding on holiday. On some weekends I did manage to drive the family to the city of

Meerut, a city situated about 45 miles from New Delhi, where Meena's parents lived. The children, of course, were delighted to be spoiled by their doting grandparents, Vishwamber and Vimla Puri. Meena's parents were distinguished academics, and at that time headed as principals the best-known boys' and girls' colleges in India.

Even as we could make occasional short trips to Meerut, a long planned visit to the hills of Mussoorie was scuttled at the last minute, on account of some exigency in the office. The car was packed and ready to move, when I announced the cancellation of the trip. The children were in tears. This holiday had been promised to them months in advance. I myself was upset at the disruption of the well-laid plans, especially as the reason for cancellation of my leave was a trifling matter of protocol. It transpired that a foreign delegation visiting New Delhi had to be received by representatives of several Ministries. As luck would have, I was named to represent the Home Ministry in the official event. Meena and I tried to console the distraught youngsters. I assured them that instead of the hills, they would get to view the Dussehra celebrations in the famous Ram Lila grounds. Although we could not go to the salubrious hills, we would visit a friend's flat on Minto Road, which overlooked the Ram Lila grounds where the effigy of the demon Ravana was to be ceremoniously put to flame. Imagine my consternation when I could not join the party even to enjoy this little pleasure, as the very moment of the finale of the Dussehra event was chosen for the reception for the visiting VIPs. Ironically, my own presence at the official event was not even noticed (nor would my absence from the scene have been observed), as I had no role to play in the proceedings. The children witnessed the fiery event from my friend's balcony with their mother. All that I could do to compensate their disappointment was to take them on the subsequent day to a musical dance drama that condensed the story of the epic *Ramayana*. The little episode brought home to the children that their father placed duty above all other commitments.

Questioned years later both my daughter and son averred that apart from their short term chagrin at the above small episode, they fully enjoyed their stay in Delhi. In order to balance the domestic budget, Meena and I had to resort to considerable stinging in our daily expenditure. At that impressionable age the children were just not bothered with any curtailment of their needs. Indeed they profited considerably from the lessons in school and in the academies, besides the attention that they received at home. In retrospect, we did not really face adversity. The trying Delhi days were packed with several sweet uses.

In the Ministry my work required me to report to several officers as my immediate superiors. There was a wide difference between the working styles of various officers. On the one hand was S.S. Sidhu, my Additional Secretary (Mr Sidhu went on to be Governor of several states). Mr Sidhu was most encouraging as a mentor. He would take me along to important meetings with the Home Secretary and with ministers, introduce me to them and on occasions laud some policy notes that I had presented. For such a broad minded and positive person I would happily plod and research beyond the call of duty. Mr Sidhu was satisfied with the timely output of work and did not concern himself with the office timings that I maintained. I was punctual in arriving in office, and usually left the office at five, the normal closing time, for a game of tennis on the Secretariat courts. In contrast another Joint Secretary, who I will not name here, had a habit of summoning me late in the evening. Finding me absent he would nag me the next day, making it appear that I was shirking duty. He was particularly riled that I was enjoying a game while he was slogging, as he put it. One other irritating habit this officer had was of not only denying credit to his juniors when it was due, but of claiming personal credit for the performance of his staff. I realized that when I presented some papers on policy, as for the Cabinet of Ministers, he would quietly remove my signature from the document, add one or two sentences, and pose the document to the superiors as his personal effort. A form of bureaucratic plagiarism, I considered the act!

When the relations with my immediate boss threatened to descend to the level of bickering, I sought a direct appointment with the Home Secretary, and apprised him about the needless tension that was afoot. Instead of making a complaint, I merely submitted that my Joint Secretary and I were temperamentally incompatible. As such, could I be shifted to any other assignment within the Ministry? I must admit that my request for a change was immediately granted, and I found myself working with a more understanding superior.

Mr S.L. Khurana had been handpicked for the assignment by the then Prime Minister. In early 1977, as the election results began to pour in, it became clear that Mrs Indira Gandhi had not only lost her election as a Member of Parliament; her party, the Indian National Congress, had been decimated at the polls. Even before the final results came in Mr Khurana called a meeting of all the officers of the Ministry. In a short address Mr Khurana thanked us all for our hard work and cooperation and announced that he would be leaving charge immediately. He ended by stating boldly, 'We are proud of the manner in which we performed. I have no regrets.' Here indeed was a leader that I could admire, a person who stood firm in his conviction and belief.

Working in the Government of India enabled me to appreciate the delicate relationship between officials and the political leaders. While quality of performance of an officer is always appreciated, the primary motivation for a politician is enhancement of his public image and acceptability of the electorate. Most officers, on the other hand aim at securing positions of authority and patronage. True to human nature in general, key appointments at the centre and in the states are determined by the ability of incumbent officials to please the political masters. The test for conscientious officials and politicians is to strike a balance between the personal and public interest.

The Indian Administrative Service plays a pivotal role in governance at the centre and in the states. At the time of India's independence in the year 1947 it was Sardar Vallabhbhai Patel, the first Home Minister of independent India, who took a firm decision, duly endorsed by the Prime Minister Jawaharlal Nehru, that the IAS should be a successor service to the Indian Civil Service, which had constituted the steel frame of colonial bureaucracy. The IAS was seen as an institution for national integration, as its members from all the states could be required to serve in any part of the country. The Government of India is the appointing and controlling authority for IAS officers, but every officer is placed in a different state cadre, and each state government is designated the cadre-controlling authority for IAS as well as IPS officers. The Central Government has no cadre of IAS officers of its own; it borrows from the pool available nation-wide. These officers serve for fixed tenures at the national, central level and thence return to their own states.

A typical career civil servant serves an initial 10 years or so in his state, and then is appointed to work in one of the Ministries of the Government of India, usually for a period of five years. During their period of service, officers move between the state of allotment and the centre. The key level of appointment in the Government of India is considered that of a Joint Secretary, for which there is a rigorous screening process. Ambitious officers aim at appointment as Joint Secretary, preferably in a ministry of their choice, and thence go higher. Some officers work in their states at equivalent posts by choice, or because they have not cleared the screening for higher appointments. In the hierarchy of the Government of India, the status of civil servants is determined by the designation of the position they hold, Deputy Secretary or Joint Secretary or Secretary, etc. Even so many ambitious incumbents prefer to work in certain high-profile ministries, such as Economic Affairs or Commerce or Industrial Development. Such postings are perceived to enjoy greater authority, or patronage, than similarly designated jobs dealing with matters such as languages or social security, which are not regarded by officials as attractive assignments. The classical situation in economics, greater demand than supply of desirable goods, prevails equally with the elite bureaucracy serving across the ministries of the Government of India. The number of officials vying for the posts being more than the number of prized jobs on offer ensues a rat race for the coveted posts. The winners are sometimes determined by their skills in the management of their own superiors, be they civil servants like themselves or powerful political leaders. In some cases luck plays a part, as when the performance of an officer happens to be recognized by an important benefactor.

In the famous words of English essayist Francis Bacon, success in public life demands three skills. 'Reading maketh a full man, conference a ready man, and writing an exact man' (from 'Of Studies'). Ambitious civil servants have to inculcate qualities of reading and writing on their own. For acquiring expertise in conference they would do well to watch the performance on stage of their successful seniors.

RENAISSANCE

While I was in Delhi, the government recommended my name for joining the University of Cambridge in the United Kingdom for a nine-month-long course in Development Economics. I was absolutely thrilled when the university accepted my nomination. To be at one of the world's oldest and highly regarded institutions was for me a dream come true. Having been a student and also a teacher of English literature, plus as a bibliophile to boot, I was excited to join the famed 800-year-old university. In my mind's eye was the picture of a campus that had bred some of the greatest writers, philosophers, scientists and economists that the world has witnessed. What a privilege it would be! Economics was for me a new subject academically, but relevant to my work as a civil servant. Meena was keen to accompany me. For her, this was a unique chance of returning to research in Botany, in which field she had earned a PhD degree. As soon as my admission was confirmed, Meena applied to the Cambridge University Botanic Gardens to be enrolled for post-doctoral research for the period that I was to be at Cambridge. With her academic credentials, the university readily accepted her too. For good measure we decided to take the children along, who at ages ten and six years respectively, would assuredly benefit from studying abroad. Meena's sister lived in London; being able to meet her was an added bonus.

I travelled from Delhi to London by British Airways on a ticket that had been arranged by British Council, the sponsoring agency. Meena and the children travelled separately a day earlier than I, by another airline, which offered lower-priced tickets. This led to a minor embarrassment for Meena when she arrived at London airport. In regard to the purpose of visit on the form of entry into the UK, Meena had naturally stated that she was accompanying her husband, who was on an official government visit. The immigration officer was understandably mystified to find no trace of the husband as mentioned. It took a few minutes to explain the situation. The officer smiled and waved the three of them in.

My sabbatical was sponsored by the Government of UK under a project called the Colombo Plan. During the course, I was entitled to a small stipend of exactly £194 a month. This amount was deemed enough for subsistence of one student, for that is what I effectively was. Whether it was a sample of male chauvinism on my part, or in an act of mutual cooperation, Meena agreed to work to earn some extra money. At the age of 35, we were both adventurous, and we went prepared to rough it out if needed. Initially, for a few days, Meena stitched clothes at home, for which she was paid a pittance. Years later, my daughter told me that, surprisingly, she never felt that any stigma was attached to a person toiling manually for a living. She viewed her mother as one of the hardworking heroic characters she had read about in fiction. Meena then courageously accepted a job in a small factory to augment our income. Here she made life-long friends among her colleagues, all working women. In the social system prevalent in the country, there was absolute dignity of labour. She found the atmosphere at the factory cheerful and convivial. Her fellow workers could never imagine that Meena, who was in fact the only foreigner in the group, was professionally a highly qualified academic. She would work half the day in the factory, visit the Botanic Gardens for her research project, and thereafter teach Hindi to a student at home. With the added task of running the household, Meena had a life busier and more varied than mine as a full-time student. Having herself done research, she could guide me in the intricacies of documentation in my academic tasks.

A New Milieu

In Delhi I had faced immense problems in securing admission for the children in school. I was prepared to face similar obstacles here too. To my astonishment, when I made a telephone call, the education office on its own selected the school most convenient for my children. The office advised that young children should join a school situated closest to their home. Furthermore, since most children in the city walked to school, the route to school should not require them have to cross a busy highway. The very next day we met the headmaster of the chosen school, and the children began to attend classes immediately. As this was a state school, no fees needed to be paid. Here then, was my first encounter with an efficient system of primary education. From day one, the children walked unescorted to school and back. This would build in them much self-confidence. As for studies, neither child found any difficulty at all to adjust to the curriculum, which was found less rigorous than what they were used to back home in India. Many years later, they visited with nostalgia their old school Brunswick, as it was called.

Equally smooth was my search for living accommodation. According to a century-old tradition, all students, no matter what their academic discipline of study, are admitted to one or other of the numerous colleges in the university campus. My college, Wolfson, offered hostel accommodation to students and their spouses, but had no arrangements for children. Fortunately, I had written in advance to a family friend, Bob Fields, who lived in the city to help in finding suitable living quarters for my family. This he had promptly done, so the very day we arrived, I signed a contract of tenancy and moved in. It was a neat little independent cottage on Montague Road, fully furnished. The rent was £108 per month, which constituted a major portion of my monthly stipend. We could afford the expenditure on lodging as Meena was earning independently. At Cambridge, students move from building to building for lectures in different departments linked to their course of study.

These buildings were situated just two miles or so from our cottage. Like everyone in the university, both teachers and students, I decided to acquire a bicycle for commuting within the city. From the college notice board I identified a machine that an outgoing student had advertised for sale. I paid £20 for a second-hand bike. Cambridge is hailed as England's city of bicycles. Many parts of the city, especially the city centre, are closed to motor cars, but cyclists can move freely everywhere. It was a time-honoured convention, my professor told me in jest, that unless a student could produce evidence that his bicycle had been stolen at least once during his stay, he would not be granted his degree.

Academia of Tradition

The arrangements for students in the campus are a marvel of prompt management and service. Within a day of joining, Meena and I were issued identity cards, which entitled us to numerous facilities, including entry into departments, membership of libraries, travel by train at concessional rates, and medical attention. We were armed with complete information and maps of the city, especially the location of the colleges and buildings that housed the various departments. I retain as a souvenir *The Cambridge Pocket Diary 1978–79*, three inches by two inches in size, the maroon colour, form and style of which has remained unchanged over many decades. The diary contains in 300 compact pages complete information about all activities in the campus during the year, from examination schedules of all departments, library facilities, sports and social occasions, even the schedule of trains and bus services to London. The dates for every single activity are published a year in advance. The schedule is meticulously observed in practice during the academic year. The diary cost £1.

Within the student fraternity at Cambridge, members mainly unknown to each other display unusual cooperation and innovation for mutual benefit. Outgoing academics advertise for sale items such as television sets, cars and the like, all of which are quickly picked up at bargain prices by others who need them. Meena purchased an electrically powered sewing machine for stitching at home. I was able to procure a second-hand motor car, a Ford station wagon, at a laughable price of just £80, and a used black and white TV set for £20. Rajinder Singh, a colleague from India in the same course as I, shared with me the cost of purchase of the vehicle. Rajinder's wife stayed with him in the college hostel. The serviceable jalopy sufficed for both of us and our families to travel together or separately to many parts of England during the vacations between terms. Indeed, at the end of the course Rajinder even drove the car to Europe. On departure we sold the faithful car at the same price as we had paid to buy it. Truly, like the majority of students, we had to squeeze the best out of a shoestring budget.

Within the IAS, Rajinder was regarded as the epitome of honesty and fair play, which he could carry to an absurd extent. The two of us were like-minded on most matters, and shared a lifelong warm personal relationship. The only difference that we had at Cambridge was on a matter that I derided as a non-issue. This was the issue of sharing of expenditure on the running of our jointly owned car. He insisted that a log book be maintained of all journeys performed by us. When our two families travelled together the cost was equally shared. If either party travelled alone, the respective user bore the expenditure of travel. This much was easily accepted. Rajinder raised a subtle point of accountancy. The hostel where Rajinder and his wife Agya stayed was situated about two km away from our cottage. The intricate question that my dear friend raised was this. Which partner should pay for the journey between cottage and hostel? I averred that I would be happy to bear the burden but Rajinder Singh determined that even this petty liability be equally shared by both parties. I was forced to acquiesce silently. I wish I had have kept a photo copy of the meticulous log book, as a poignant instance of fair accountancy. No wonder that the staff of Rajinder Singh were terrified of his eagle eye, which detected the minutest irregularity in official work. It was a sad day in my life when Rajinder Singh, whom I considered one of my dearest friends died suddenly of a heart attack at the age of 53, at the peak of his career.

The city of Cambridge is a tourist's delight—many grand cathedrals and stately buildings designed by famous architects seven centuries earlier retain their lofty dignity. The lush green lawns are maintained immaculately. It is forbidden for ordinary mortals to tread on the grass. Just a handful of 'fellows', as some distinguished senior professors are labelled, have the privilege of walking on the lawns, but even this exclusive tribe of intellectuals never exercises their titular entitlement, so the expanses of green remain forever untrodden, to provide perennial delight for spectators. During its history from the medieval times, Cambridge has had numerous distinguished members, such as pioneers in science Isaac Newton and Charles Darwin, philosophers of the eminence of Bertrand Russell, economists J.M. Keynes and Thomas Robert Malthus and poets like Milton, Wordsworth and Coleridge. Cambridge is regarded the world over as a fountainhead of fundamental research in Mathematics. It warmed my heart to discover the awe in which the Indian mathematical genius Ramanujam, who worked in the University, is regarded. In an entirely different field, Cambridge provided the inspiration for another alumnus, Florence Nightingale, who is considered the mother of the nursing profession. I myself saw Stephen Hawking, the most famous physicist of the modern era, wheeling his chair in the streets of Cambridge. I had an occasion to attend a lecture of the famous economist Joan Robinson.The list of luminaries that have been through those hallowed portals is spectacular. Is it the ambience of the university, built over centuries, that inspires creativity or is it that the best minds find Cambridge a habitat for nurturing genius? I wonder.

With no fewer than 88 winners of the Nobel Prize in various disciplines among its former students and teachers, the university confesses that it is unable to dedicate a museum to do justice to the achievements of all its eminent alumni. If you visit the rooms where some of these personalities lived in the distant past you would find the quarters cold and dingy; the 'digs', as the living quarters are called, have been consciously preserved in their original state over centuries. In those times, the guide will tell you, there was no provision for running water or heating of the rooms, so many students went through entire terms without taking a bath. I myself saw a rickety writing desk in Trinity College on which the debonair Lord Byron had carved his name with a sharp instrument. One of the libraries that I frequented overlooks a feature called Newton's Bridge. The father of modern physics, as Isaac Newton is regarded, had constructed the bridge without using nuts and bolts to hold the structure together. Legend has it that, many years after Newton was buried, some brilliant young engineers attempted to unravel that marvel of structural design. To the misfortune of the university and an affront to the legacy of Newton, the engineers managed to dismantle the bridge, but could not restore the structure to its original pristine form. The bridge retains the shape that Newton imparted three centuries ago, but now it is held in place with screws and nails!

Cambridge offers an amazing variety of sights. The river Cam, which runs through the campus, is like a small canal less than 10 metres wide. Many of the old colleges are constructed on the banks of the river, with the rear of the ancient buildings almost touching the river bank. Those segments are appropriately called the 'backs'. The students of all colleges are permitted to do some rowing over the surface: actually the raft is called a 'punt', and the sport is named 'punting'. The little boat is maneuvered with the help of a single long pole. I found that punting is not as simple a skill as it appears. In the hands of an amateur the punt can go into a spin, and members of some enthusiastic rowing parties find themselves splashing in shallow waters. Many a picnic ends with unexpected drenching, to the merriment of onlookers.

The period of my stay at Cambridge was in one way unique—every member of the family was separately engaged in some form of study. We had all convinced ourselves that we would treat my sabbatical as a prolonged foreign holiday. As we settled down in the little house, it was as if the household had shifted base seamlessly from India. We had a variety of friends, including some fellow students who loved to visit our family home, and my friend Dr Bob Fields, an alumnus of the university, who had arranged the tenancy of our cottage. Meena's guide, Professor Walters, the Director of the Botanic Gardens, and two of my supervisors whom we invited to a Christmas meal at home, were wonderstruck that we had established a running home so quickly. They were delighted when Meena treated them to Indian cuisine from our own kitchen. We thus had the best of several worlds; a home, a social circle of friends, and the flavour of life in a university town in which we had absorbed ourselves.

Our financial resources were paltry; these had, perforce, to be used economically. Throughout our stay all meals were cooked at home, including picnic baskets that we carried during our outings. The children enjoyed accompanying us to the nearby Cooperative Store for shopping for groceries; for them there was fun even in collecting little coupons and stamps that were offered on the purchases. These bits could be exchanged for little trinkets and sweets. Both had realized that the toys they eyed were beyond our reach to purchase for them. Away from home, we did not even miss the Diwali festival; my friend Bob Fields took us to witness a grand display of fireworks on the river bank to commemorate Guy Fawkes' Day, 5 November, which fell close to the day on which the Indian festival of lights is celebrated. In British history, Guy Fawkes had conspired to blow up the Houses of Parliament in the early 17th century. The attempt, called the Gunpowder Plot, was foiled.

On weekends there were short outings to nearby tourist spots like the Ely Cathedral. In the peak of winter, trudging to school over frozen ponds held its own delight for the young ones. The only apprehension that my six-year-old son had was what would happen if the surface of ice collapsed. We were constantly penny-pinching, but we could still enjoy some of the best things in life at minimum cost. Such was an unexpected lesson in austerity and adventure for the younger generation, as it was for us, their parents.

The participants in the course hailed from many different countries, including the UK. Age wise, we were all in our early 30s. Most of my colleagues had travelled alone for the programme; a few were accompanied by their spouses. I was the only one who had brought along both wife and children. The university has innumerable activities for students, including sports, the performing arts and pure festivals and feasts. Cutting across academic disciplines, all are encouraged to take up pastimes of their choice. There is never a dull moment; a vast variety of intellectual and social pursuits is scheduled over the year. One can attend music and dance recitals by celebrated artistes that the university hosts. Sports buffs can witness matches featuring stars, or personally engage in competition or as a pastime; others are free to socialize, or indulge in hedonistic pleasures if they so fancy. All categories of students, researchers and teachers are equal members of their respective colleges. During my stay at Cambridge, I did attend several obligatory official events. At the annual college dinner, my little daughter and I even presented an item highlighting Indian music and dance. I also visited the tennis courts occasionally to impart basic lessons in the game to an English friend. Involved in some activities beyond academics, my stay of nine months at Cambridge was all the more fulfilling.

Researching

During our stay we did socialize a little, even beyond the precincts of the campus. I admit, however, that I was unable to find time to enjoy many a high-quality spectacle that Cambridge had in store. The reason for my diffidence was that I let myself in for a course of study that demanded a kind of sustained application far beyond what I had bargained for.

The course for which the government had sponsored me led to a Diploma in Development Studies. Almost all my colleagues were similarly working for the same Diploma. On the day of my induction, the coordinating tutor called me aside and enquired if I would like to work for a degree of Master of Philosophy. He informed me that a few of my fellow students, who had already done preliminary work in advance of the start of our course, had enrolled for the MPhil degree. Aspirants for the degree required to attain a level of performance much higher than those for the Diploma. Thus, MPhil candidates need to score at least 66 percent in the written papers, whereas 50 percent suffices for diploma students. Additionally, the degree of MPhil entails the writing of a thesis. Most of the researchers for the MPhil degree had a head start over me, as they had begun work on their theses several months earlier. It would be a challenge to complete the research work within the scheduled time of less than nine months, I was warned. Professor H.W. West in the Department of Land Economy confided that on the strength of my academic record he was prepared to go out of the way to offer me opportunity to join the MPhil programme. Such an option was rarely open to the majority of students. Professor West cautioned that he could merely recommend my name. The final decision lay with an authority called the Board of Graduate Studies. I admit I was flattered to receive such unexpected recognition even before I had begun studies. Cambridge is exceedingly selective in admission to its courses. On an impulse I responded that I would accept the challenge. The expectation that the University has of all researchers is encapsulated in a few phrases in the official guidelines of the University of Cambridge. The stiff stipulations are that the thesis of a candidate accepted for the degree of Master of Philosophy (MPhil) should make 'a contribution to learning' in the chosen field. A thesis by a successful candidate for Doctor of Philosophy (PhD), on the other hand, is expected to make 'a significant contribution to learning'. The subtle nuances regarding the standard of research work demanded highlighted the magnitude of the task that I had before me.

I think my professor was pleased that I had responded positively to his unusual initiative, of inviting me alone from the entire batch to vie for a prestigious programme. 'It will be no picnic!' were his exact words as he enjoined me to prepare within two days a synopsis of the topic that I wished for my research project. The first lesson Dr West gave me was this: if you get the title right, you will probably define the scope of the synopsis adequately. Further, if you are clear, concise and incisive in the drafting of the synopsis, you would have charted the direction and content of the thesis proper. I hung on to every word that the he spoke. Dr West seemed to suggest that acceptance by the Board of my synopsis would vindicate the faith that he had knowingly posed in me. The synopsis was to be evaluated by the powerful board. In our very first meeting Dr West had bowled me over and presented me a heady challenge. I determined that I must live up to the expectations of my new found motivator. In the short period given to me I went to work with passion to prepare a paper as succinct as I could. Admission for the degree course on the basis of the critical document, my synopsis, became for me a matter of prestige, as it was for my mentor.

During my assignment as Deputy Commissioner, I had worked for providing institutional credit to small farmers for viable projects. Why not base my research project on my practical experience, rather than select an abstruse topic relating to fundamental economic concepts, I reasoned. I had written some papers concerning the experiment that me and my colleague Karl Reddy and I had undertaken in the Marginal Farmers and Agricultural Labourers Agency (MFALA) Ropar.[1] In the two days allowed to me to prepare my synopsis, I managed to piece together a three-page document titled, 'The Role of Agricultural Credit in Rural Development: Analysis of Facilities for Small Farmers in a District in India'. I mentioned in my paper that I would procure the empirical data for the research project from my sources in India.

Within a week of submission of the synopsis, to the satisfaction of Dr West, no less than mine, the Board approved my candidature for the MPhil degree. I was amazed that the meeting of the Board was held on the very day, 16 October that had been announced in the Cambridge official diary. Being allowed to research is just the beginning of an academic battle, I realized soon enough. Now began the

---

1 The scope and working of MFALA project Ropar are mentioned briefly in Chapter Five.

real task, of grasping the issues of economic development, of submitting at least two analytical papers every week, of moving from library to library to locate relevant books and reading material, of absorbing ideas enunciated by brilliant minds in path breaking lectures and of adducing data from multiple sources.

The written examination was just as crucial as the thesis. My papers included General Economics and Theories of Development, along with specialized study of issues of Land Economy and the Environment. The university was prophetic in including in its syllabus concerns that were to occupy centre stage in economic development worldwide years later. The course of study highlighted the political and social systems that conditioned economic development. It was fascinating to study how systems of management of land could impact progress in developing countries and how the oil boom was affecting the economies in the Arab nations of the Middle East. One could appreciate the manner in which internal and external factors within national economies held the roots of future conflict. Likewise, issues concerning environmental degradation and climate change, which are dominating international discourse today, were considered so critical that the university assigned a full paper to Environment. At that time, in the year 1978, India and China had more or less the same level of Gross Domestic Product per capita. It was also the time when the Cold War was dividing the Western democracies and the communist giants China and the Soviet Union. Brilliant economists like

John Toye, V. Fitzgerald and Ajit Singh gave us a perspective on the imminent rise of China as an economic power and the likely collapse of the Soviet Union.

Civil servants in India are engaged mainly with issues of administration and policy. I will attempt to describe the travails of a career administrator in an academic setting, especially adjustment to the demands of academic rigour. It might be of interest how the milieu of study in an institution of excellence could have conditioned my approach to real-life situations.

For imparting academic skill, the University adopts several modes, including traditional lectures for groups, a system of one-on-one interaction between teachers and students in tutorials and capsules of concentrated inputs on specific topics. In the conventional format, eminent speakers deliver talks on relevant topics to a group audience. Depending upon the veneration with which the lecturer is regarded, the number of persons in the hall could vary between 20 and 80. The presentation is followed by a lively interactive discussion between the lecturer and members of the gathering. There is absolute freedom for every person to challenge the speaker on content as well as quality of submission.

Systems and Motivation

The university has a system, refined no doubt over centuries of its existence, of tutorials. Here at least two or three times every week several different supervisors guide and appraise a group comprising a maximum of two or three students. Along with freewheeling discussions on the topics prescribed in the syllabus, it is the obligation of every candidate to submit a paper of around 500 words on a specific aspect of the topic under discussion. Each paper requires consulting numerous books. The tutorial is designed to inculcate in students a spirit of inquiry, an in-depth understanding of the topic at hand and skills in concise writing. For preparing the essays, my tutors suggested considerable reading material, including many books and would often provide thought provoking notes and articles from their personal collection. At Cambridge so much reading material is conveniently available in the libraries that one is spoilt for choice. Indeed, there is danger of a student being overwhelmed with the magnitude of books and publications on the topics of relevance. The university library boasts that it possesses every single serious and worthwhile publication in the world. Other libraries of the Departments of Economics, Applied Biology and South Asian Studies which I frequented, were well-stocked and met my needs. The writing of every essay necessitated study and more importantly absorption of a wealth of literature. As I delved deeper in the volumes at hand, I found that the limits of my knowledge were expanding. In the process of reading I observed, in the words of the poet Alexander Pope that 'Hills peep o'er hills, and Alps on Alps arise.'

Writing papers was merely a first step. The second stage, which initially made me less than comfortable, was the critical evaluation of my work by the tutor himself. Some tutors were guarded and subtle in their written and oral comments. Others, like one Mr Cathy in the Department of Land Economy, were scathing in their appraisal. We all dreaded sessions with Mr Cathy, who was capable of tearing your laboriously crafted paper to shreds. In one of my essays on agriculture in India, a subject that I thought I had some knowledge about, I had extolled the partnership between the farmer and the government in achieving the goal of a Green Revolution. 'Where did this revolution come from?' Cathy questioned. 'And what is green?' I realized that I had casually brought in terms used by the Indian media, without defining them. A politer instructor like Dr West would remark that my essay was a good paper for presentation by an official spokesman of the government. The implication was that it lacked academic rigour, and that he did not deem it sufficiently incisive and analytical. Another tutor enjoined, 'It's not verbiage you want, but cogent argument, all the time backed by facts and convincing references.'

These sessions could be quite onerous, at times even humiliating. To do justice to each essay I would usually have consulted a dozen books and several publications, all of which I dutifully quoted as sources. This entailed hours, indeed days of labour. To find that the end result was deemed less than satisfactory was personally demoralizing. I have retained dozens of papers that I had submitted to the tutors, God bless them. I found I needed to unlearn some of the methods that are commonly employed in paper work by government officials. If, for example, when the Minister has to answer an awkward question in Parliament, the skill of his staff lies in evading the supply of information that the government does not wish to divulge. The draft that the Secretary submits for the Minister's brief is usually such that it forecloses any further discussion on the subject, while managing to adhere to the guidelines for parliamentary proceedings. In a nutshell, government systems, at least in respect of replies in the parliament, intentionally avoid responding directly to queries of opposition leaders. The presentation of the dilemmas tackled by ministers and their officials in the BBC TV series called *Yes Minister* is a dramatic exaggeration of real-life situations within the government. The technique of answering a question, without giving information, enables the ministers to avoid pitfalls, like exposing the government to possible future criticism in the media. If an officer prepares drafts that help his boss to avoid commitment on facts and information, he is regarded as a skilful bureaucrat. In the atmosphere of learning at the university the same style is labelled as 'obfuscation.' Likewise, official papers are expected to justify the government's policies, whereas in the academic world you are expected to critically measure the same policies against objective parameters.

As the weeks went by, I began to play by the accepted academic rules. I also developed a thick skin when facing abrasive evaluation by the supervisors. Indeed, my resilience gradually developed in me the ability to defend my position stoutly. I was surprised that, far from taking umbrage at the confidence of my assertions, the interlocutors appreciated any principled stand, when they found it logical. I have retained all my papers from Cambridge, along with the remarks recorded by the guides in red ink. The observations of the tutors are seen to become less and less critical, culminating in a rare appreciation from one of them, 'Your work has shown considerable improvement. If you can get this down in 40 minutes in the exam, you're okay.' At Cambridge most teachers are given to understatement. Any form of outright commendation of work of a researcher is a rare occurrence. I found that within the very first term of eight weeks I had successfully acclimatised from the dusty bureaus of the state to the rarefied academic world of rationality and precision.

Compared to the systems that prevailed in universities in India, the pattern of terms and vacations at Cambridge appeared to me quite novel. An academic year at Cambridge from October to mid-June comprises three terms, each ten weeks in duration, interspersed with two breaks of six weeks each. At first blush I was delighted at the schedule, anticipating that I had free time of close to three months to holiday in various parts of the United Kingdom. My teachers quickly disabused me from any idea that I could expect a long spell of leisure. Dr West, who was by nature cautious and unassertive declared, 'The weeks of vacation are meant for students to complete their unfinished tasks. These are set apart for in-depth study. Furthermore, you have to get down to writing the thesis.' The time was my own, he observed, and as a mature researcher it was for me to utilize it wisely. He advised, in short, that I could assign at most one or two weeks for holidaying. The university expected students, especially postgraduates to devote the major portion of both vacations to study.

I admit that the observations of my teachers were a dampener. Here I was with a family all dressed up to leave for sightseeing in a country with unlimited attractions for a tourist. Would my academic commitments deprive us of a lifetime opportunity of visiting exotic destinations waiting to be explored? I had acquired a modest motor car. I also had a driving license valid for the country. I had promised Meena and the children that we would enjoy the stay in England to the hilt. We planned to see the sights in London, visit Scotland and the beautiful Lake District of Wordsworth and Coleridge, and tour Shakespeare's Stratford-upon-Avon. We also planned to visit some holiday resorts on the sea coast. I did not mention to Meena that my supervisors had suggested that I should curtail the planned holiday. I adroitly latched on to the words of Dr West in regard to effective management of my scarce resource of time (I was now attuned to the jargon of economics). I determined that extended holidays we must all have. I would efficiently apportion the time available between study and sightseeing. If not the entire period of the two vacations, a substantial part would be for leisure activities. To make up for any lost hours, I would find time even during our stay in London to do some reading and writing.

Eventually, the dream holidays did materialize. For some part of the winter vacation, we were in London with Meena's sister Anita and her husband Gurbax. Apart from their great hospitality at home, our hosts drove us around to the famous tourist spots in the city.

With careful management of time, I visited many parts of England, without really impairing my studies. Despite the exhortations of my supervisors, I was able to treat the family to some memorable holidays.

Writing a Thesis

If the first term at the university was spent in establishing my academic credentials with my teachers, the second and third terms had to be devoted partly to the work on my thesis. I use the word 'partly', because the pressure of writing essays continued unabated even as the tasks of structuring the thesis, the assembling of empirical data for the research project, and the actual writing, were proceeding concurrently. My guide was Dr R.B. Riddell, by birth a New Zealander, a senior member of the faculty of the Department of Land Economy. His easy going and informal manner was disarming, as he was a subtle task master. He encouraged me to call him by his first name Bob, but I never took the liberty of doing so. 'What is agricultural credit?' he would begin and then proceed to give me a reading list of more than 20 books to help me get my ideas straight. Initially I had intended to describe the economic conditions of farmers in India, and then add data on the government-sponsored schemes that enabled the small farmers to access institutional finance for their operations. As I began to write, I realized that at the outset it was imperative to enunciate the very concept of credit as an instrument of empowerment of the farm community. It took me several weeks to define the function and role of credit in various socio-economic settings.

Thereafter, it was necessary to survey the stages through which India's policy on agricultural credit developed during the course of a century. Strangely, I learnt more about the cooperative movement in India and the development of credit facilities in a foreign university than I had while practically supervising the delivery systems for credit in the field in India. The initiatives of the Reserve Bank of India and its organs in shaping and refining the structure for cooperative credit came home to me in an alien settling. It was necessary to explain how agricultural credit plays an increasingly vital role in a rural economy poised for absorbing expensive but potentially profitable technical changes in farm practice. I never once used the term 'Green Revolution' in the research paper. I did, however, make an analysis of the strengths and shortcomings of the informal credit arrangements offered by private money lenders. The money lenders charged usurious rates of interest, but their loans were timely and involved minimal paper work. From successive rural credit surveys of the Reserve Bank of India emerged an all-encompassing structure of cooperative banks. The transformation of the agricultural economy in India, especially in the state of Punjab was fuelled by efficient credit arrangements.

At Ropar, we had offered the beneficiary farmers a choice between alternative sources of credit, that is, from commercial banks as well as cooperative banks. I needed to look critically at the experiment and not merely laud the projects for their efficacy. I must admit that the analytical habit inculcated during the course of my study helped me in making a critical appraisal of the work that I had undertaken as part of the project. In this way the conclusions in the dissertation could stand on a firm objective foundation.

To my dismay, I found the actual process of writing my dissertation somewhat onerous. It seemed that my guide was perennially dissatisfied with the draft of the chapters that I wrote as part of the main document. On seeing the first draft of my thesis, Dr Riddell remarked that it was certainly a fine paper on the credit policy of the government in India, but, he added meaningfully, it might not find acceptance in academic circles. Without being outright dismissive at my effort, he would comment obliquely. Thus he would commend my command of the written word in English, and in the same breath he would suggest that the presentation needed to be refined on lines expected of economists. The technique is similar to that employed by some English satirists of the 18th century in respect of their opponents, who would 'damn with faint praise, assent with civil leer', as Alexander Pope put it.

Even as I was struggling with the task, Dr Riddell advised me to show the draft of my thesis to Professor B.N. Farmer, who headed the Department of South Asian Studies. Having worked in India, Prof. Farmer would be able offer me valuable guidance, as Dr Riddell reasoned. He also suggested that I should consult Mr Cathy, who had worked on credit systems in several countries. Cathy was the supervisor whose demeanour I had initially found repellant, but a person who had gradually begun to value the papers I submitted. All the referees spoke the same language. I had undoubtedly worked hard, was the consensus, but I wasn't ready to be considered MPhil material. It was Dr West, the instructor with whom I had closest rapport, who accosted me with a form of plain talk. My writing was good, he assured me, but by trying for an MPhil degree in a short period of nine months, I was taking a huge risk. If I did not clear the test, I would return home empty handed. I would have neither a degree nor a diploma to show for my time spent in the University. Dr West assured me that a diploma was well in my grasp. So, in conclusion, enquired Dr West, would I like to lower my ambitious target? If I wished to persist, I was assured, the university would recommend an extension of time for submitting my thesis. On his part, Dr West offered me a deal. In order to refine my skills, he and the other supervisors would spend more time to help me. My task would be to write at least four papers every week, which would be monitored and evaluated.

On these observations I was touched to the quick. In my own assessment, I was certain that I could tackle the written papers adequately. In their own written remarks, as well as in oral observations, the tutors had begun to express open satisfaction with the numerous papers that I was routinely writing. Even a man like Cathy, the most acerbic of all the interlocutors, could discern no tangible deficiency in the essays. In the month of March 1979, near the end of the second (Lent) term, the university had conducted mock examinations to assess the level of preparedness of the examinees. In these tests, too, the supervisors had evaluated my performance positively. How then, I reasoned, could they fault me of not being ready to face the ultimate exam in the coming month of June? Could it be possible that the supervisors were playing at intimidating me to work harder still? I learnt that at that belated stage some of my fellow researchers decided to withdraw from pursuit of the MPhil. It is possible that they too had been subjected to a battle of nerves like me. At Cambridge there were gory stories that April is considered a cruel month for researchers and students alike; sometimes students resort to an extreme step, suicide, in that month because at that time the pressure on their performance reaches its zenith.

Face to face with the dilemma, I weighed several factors. First, it was possible that the supervisors were merely testing my resolve. Second, I considered that in facing the challenge, the prestige of my country was at stake. Here in a foreign land, among peers from other nations, any surrender might be perceived as a blow for my country. Having come thus far, might it not appear cowardly to abandon my quest mid-stream? An added impetus for my resilience was the presence of my wife and children. They had seen me slogging for months, and had cooperated unstintingly to remain out of my way when I was busy. I could well imagine the impact my chickening out at a crucial stage would have on them.

Whether it was my ego or self-belief, I made a fateful decision, viz. that I would not lower my target to settle for a diploma. I would not even seek an extension for submission of my dissertation. I was prepared to accept any challenge that my supervisors held out. 'Arrange to reach a peak of efficiency by May,' was Dr West's injunction.

As it transpired, I kept my part of the bargain, and my professors and supervisors did likewise with theirs. As the pressure grew, the months of April and May were excruciating. I approached the examination as a man possessed. At that time, in the year 1979, computers were not commonplace, although there were photocopy machines and electric typewriters. Successive drafts of the thesis had to be penned in longhand. I then searched for a skilled typist who could prepare the manuscript on an electric typewriter. The one that I settled on was a lady who lived a few miles away from the town, on a farm. As I delivered the papers to her, we spoke about the farm that her husband was running. I was astonished to learn that the landholder employed just three workers for all farm operations over an area of land measuring 200 acres. This was a sample of the level of mechanisation in agriculture in an advanced economy like that of England's!

After the typing was done, three copies of the thesis were neatly bound and delivered to my guide. If accepted, one copy would be given pride of place in the departmental library, another would go on record in the University library and I could carry my personal copy home.

I wrote my papers during 5–7 June, the dates announced in the Cambridge diary a year in advance. In the oral examination, viva voce, on 9 June I held my own against examiners who were at once belligerent and courteous. During the oral examination, one member pointed out a grammatical error on the last page of the thesis. I firmly stated that I had phrased my sentence on the lines of a similar usage[2] in a play by William Shakespeare. I think the interlocutors were quite startled at this highly unusual enunciation. They could well have commented that only a genius poet was entitled to such grammatical liberty, not a researcher. As it is, my own stars might have decreed that they should accept my assertion.

On my return to India, I received a personal, handwritten letter from Dr H.W. West, in which he conveyed that the University was conferring on me the degree of MPhil (Cantab). Uncharacteristically for the normally taciturn Professor, Dr West even wrote, 'You fully justified your self-confidence.' The story had a happy ending after all.

During my stint at the university, I had come to enjoy the work of research. Perchance, my first assignment on return to India was as Chief Executive of a large cooperative institution engaged in the marketing of agricultural commodities. The fundamentals of cooperative credit,

---

2 The exact lines under reference read,
'It is the stars
The stars above us, govern our conditions.' (*King Lear*, 4.3.33–34)
The Bard had omitted the conjunction 'that' or 'which' before the word 'govern'. I had taken similar poetic license.

the topic of my thesis and my assignment of cooperative marketing are closely tied to one another. As I worked in my new role, I made bold to approach Dr West, my mentor at Cambridge, if I could enroll for a degree of Doctor of Philosophy in the related field at Cambridge. I even sent to Dr West a synopsis of the study that I wished to pursue. My idea was to take up the research work alongside my official work in India. Dr West responded positively. My proposition could be considered, he assured me. As per University regulations, a candidate for PhD must work for at least three years for a research project. Dr West was prepared to recommend that the academic year spent for my MPhil may be counted toward my work in research for the PhD. I could be allowed to spend one year for the new research work in India, provided that I revisited Cambridge for a year to conclude my project. This was an attractive offer. I could not however pursue it. The tasks attached with the new assignment were overwhelming, as the next chapter describes. Dr West was disappointed that I severed my academic calling, and continued as a career administrator.

Postscript: A Forgettable Adventure

The return from London to Delhi in July 1979 turned out to be unexpectedly traumatic for our family. As on the outbound journey from Delhi to London, Meena and the children, then aged ten years and seven years, travelled back on cheaper, more affordable, tickets by Ariana Afghan Airlines, which flew from London to Delhi via Kabul.

Reaching home uneventfully ahead of the rest of the family, I was at the Delhi Airport to receive them at the time scheduled for their landing, watching expectantly as many disembarking passengers passed by in the arrival lounge. Imagine my consternation when I realized that the three I awaited were not among them! The duty staff could provide no clue to their whereabouts.

When I flashed my official card the airlines manager was forced to admit that some passengers had been offloaded at Kabul. He assured me, somewhat sheepishly, that the airlines had arranged hotel rooms in Kabul for stay of the passengers left behind. They would reach Delhi by the next flight from Kabul, which was to arrive two days later.

For me this was a stunning shock. At that time, in the year 1979, Afghanistan was embroiled in political turmoil. The country had been rocked by violence among several warring groups. The Soviet Union had decided to intervene militarily and politically. The press reported that the country was effectively under Soviet control. Amid such chaotic happenings the Soviets had taken control over the capital city of Kabul and were intent on consolidating hold over the rest of the country.

For me in Delhi, the stress was unimaginable. It was distressing to imagine the plight of a hapless mother, accompanied by two young children, stranded in that violent city. It was frustrating in the extreme to find the family incommunicado, as Kabul was suddenly cut off from the rest of the world. Distraught, I requested the airlines to deliver to Meena a small note, in which I sought to reassure her, lamely, that all would be well. The note was sent by the Ariana plane returning to Kabul, as I waited at Delhi in overpowering suspense.

The unplanned adventure (aren't all adventures unplanned?) in the troubled country lasted more than two days, a period of unimaginable stress.

During the interregnum, I vainly knocked at the counters of the airline office. Being in the Home Ministry of the Government of India, I pleaded with colleagues linked to the Intelligence wing to establish some form of contact. They too were unable to help, as all communication links from Kabul had been cut.

Eventually, after two days of excruciating suspense, the missing family arrived safe, but shaken. There were tears of joy and gratitude to the 'Unseen Power' of the Almighty that would have looked after the loved ones at the time of tribulation. After we reunited, I could gather the details of what would have been a harrowing experience in a troubled land. They were put up in a seedy hotel room. Soldiers were everywhere. It was providential that Meena met two fellow Indians who were staying in the same hotel, facing a similar predicament. She was quite relieved that they were young Sikhs, obviously from our own state of Punjab. Having the company of the new friends, Meena felt somewhat more confident. Along with the new companions hailing from their own country and speaking the same language, Meena and the children strolled nonchalantly through the streets of the nearby bazaar. The children were oblivious to any possible dangers in a disturbed land. On return from the brave walk in the bazars of Kabul, Meena found that her hotel room had been ransacked. It transpired that the paranoid security agencies had confiscated two seemingly suspicious items from the belongings, a toy plastic gun and the note that I had sent from Delhi. The security men must have been obviously ham-handed and ill-trained for surveillance. They might have feared that the toy gun was a hazard in flight. Perhaps they tried to decipher any malicious content in my personal note delivered by the airlines. On their part, the children were disappointed, Anurag at losing a favourite toy, and Bini at not meeting in the city a single Kabuliwala, like the one immortalized by Rabindranath Tagore in his famous short-story.[3] But, heaven be thanked, Meena had found reassurance among strangers from her own state of Punjab. While the tension endured was by all four of us, the indomitable courage in trying circumstances was that of Meena. As for the airlines, an official complained to Meena, 'Madam, your husband has been giving us hell from Delhi!'

---

3 Kabuliwala—literally 'the man from Kabul'—is the title of a well-known short story in the Bengali language by Rabindranath Tagore, a Nobel laureate in Literature. The story romanticizes the character of a Pathan dry-fruits seller from Kabul, who befriends a little girl in the city of Calcutta. The poignant story, and its translations are included in several anthologies for children.

ADVENTURES IN MANAGEMENT

The shift from the pursuit of academic excellence in a foreign university to the practical management of a commercial entity was for me a major transformation of functions. The three years I was to spend in the corporate institution formed a turbulent part of my career. This was also a time for relinking with family and friends.

Back Home

On return to Delhi from abroad, I encountered an unforeseen problem on the home front. During my assignment with the Union Government, Meena had been on unpaid leave from her teaching job in a government college in Chandigarh. We had reconciled that if Meena and I were to be together, she would be deprived of salary for any period of time she remained absent from the college. It now transpired that Chandigarh Administration, her employer, refused to extend her period of leave. This implied that she had to immediately rejoin her position, or to resign. I requested my Ministry to curtail the period of my deputation at Delhi, which was to last another two years and to transfer me back to my home state of Punjab. The Home Secretary, my boss, was sympathetic and recommended my case to the Government of Punjab. To my pleasant surprise, within two weeks of my request, the state government appointed me in a position at Chandigarh. After an absence of three-and-a-half years, Meena resumed her teaching career. This was a happy event. It was doubly satisfying, as it happened that, among the teaching staff of her college, she was the first to have a PhD degree.

In contrast to the struggle that we had faced in Delhi regarding living arrangements and schooling for the children, the return proved a soft and smooth landing. On my father's superannuation as the Inspector General of Police in the state of Manipur, my parents had set up home in Chandigarh. They were delighted to receive us in the family house. Just after I took up the new assignment, my parents moved from the city to their spiritual centre at Beas. In true official terminology, my father stated that he had all along been waiting 'to hand over charge' of the home to me, as he and my mother shifted to their retreat. There he was immersed in honorary social work for a long period of 36 years until his demise at the ripe age of 98. Indeed he never retired from active life, enjoying a longer active tenure outside government than the period he had worked within it. For me, homecoming meant that I was established in residence in the city, even as I could often visit the parents, as they lived in the state that I served, just 200 km away. Few are blessed to have such a fortunate existence.

Fringe Advantages

A small town holds several benefits. Distances to be traversed are manageable; it is easier to chaperone children to school and other places. Old friendships are revived. Outside office, more time is available for pursuing one's interests. In Delhi, my work had been confined to the office. The new job carried variety: it entailed travel in various parts of the state, and interaction with people within and outside government. The children were quickly admitted in schools of choice, both managed by Christian missionary groups. Academics apart, I was keen that the children should continue to cultivate their potential in such areas as music and sport. My daughter Bini was gifted with a good singing voice, and the boy Anurag was keen on sports.

At Chandigarh, I learnt of a celebrated professional musician by the name of Professor Yash Paul, who had set up the Department of Music in a girls' college. Later he was to found the department in the Panjab University too. Yash Paul was a doyen of the Agra *Gharana*,[1] a school with a renowned tradition in Hindustani (north Indian) classical music. Beyond his routine teaching work at college, Yash Paul's stated ambition was to build classical singers to their

---

1 *Gharana* literally means 'house' or a 'household'. In the field of music it implies a tradition, a school, of training and exposition that has been carried forward over centuries, as in the case of the Agra *gharana*. Each of the well-known *gharanas* in India has its individual distinctive style. An essential component of the gharana tradition is the close association between teacher and disciple, called the *guru-shishya* tradition, whereby the *guru* (master) imparts specialized training to a few deserving *shishyas* (pupils), expecting them to advance and enrich the musical legacy.

potential of excellence, artistes who could carry ahead the lofty tradition of his *gharana* (school) of music. Along with the national radio and television networks ranking him among the top-grade artists in the country, Yash Paul was also recognized abroad as an eminent vocalist. He was, however, known to be extremely selective in accepting trainees for individual lessons, which he imparted at his home; he would take in only those in whom he spied some spark of inborn talent. When I approached Yash Paul in his spartan home in an outlying sector of the city, I was apprehensive if such a renowned teacher would agree to tutor a child of barely ten years. At our first meeting, he asked Bini to sing just three notes: *sa* in the lower octave, *pa* in the lower octave and *sa* in the higher octave (equivalent to the notes do, fa and do in Western music). That little evaluation was sufficient for him to gauge potential. He agreed to accept the young trainee, on condition that he would accept no remuneration for his labours. He stated that if the child fulfilled the promise he had observed, he would consider her success as adequate compensation. Such was the professor's altruistic habit.

Needless to say, this outcome delighted me, but the circumstances presented a dilemma and posed for young Bini a great challenge. She knew that she would need to work with double her normal diligence as her tutor had declined to charge any fee. Since Meena did not wish to drive, it was my task to take Bini three times a week for her lessons.

A fringe benefit was that, over the ten years that I accompanied Bini for her training, I clandestinely picked up the rudiments of Hindustani classical music. It was an education in itself to watch at first hand the master's training systems. Yash Paul focused for months on the fundamentals of voice modulation. He taught that a singer must intone as she normally speaks, at the same pitch, and determine for herself her range for capturing the highest and the lowest notes. He professed that voice culture helped even public speakers, who might not be oriented to vocal music, to declaim more comfortably. He insisted that the sound of music emerge from the throat and not superficially be produced by the tongue. He aimed at an ideal of effortlessness in audition. Two attributes he highlighted were economy of facial expression and management of emotion. He refused to lay down any set pattern or combinations of notes for Bini to learn, or to practice by rote. He expected in his disciples spontaneity and creativity in exposition of every *raga*.[2] Yash Paul moved in the company of the most celebrated exponents of Indian music. With him I met such renowned figures as Ustad Vilayat Husain Khan and Yunus Husian Khan, and even a star of yesteryear Pandit Amar Nath at the age of 90, who came to perform in the city.

---

2 A *raga* is a musical composition where a combination of the basic notes follows a prescribed pattern. Within the perimeters of the discipline, the singer or instrumentalist is free to evolve with spontaneity. There are hundreds of ragas, each characterized by its mood, which usually conforms to the time of the day or night when it is rendered. The *raga*s have evolved over many centuries.

Bini was able to repay only partly her debt to her teacher when she was awarded a national scholarship for music by the Ministry of Culture, Government of India. A small return on the master's invaluable investment over several years! On my own part, I tried to find time daily for a few minutes of *riyaz* (musical practice).

While studying at Sacred Heart Convent School, Bini was profoundly influenced by the teachings of Christianity. On one occasion, Meena received an unexpected visit by a group of teachers from the school, including the school principal. Meena was apprehensive that they had come to complain about some misdemeanour by the child. She was startled, first at a disclosure by Sister Superior, as she was addressed, that our daughter had expressed a desire to join the Christian order and to become a nun. Even more astonishing was the Sister's urging that Bini's mother should dispel the child's notions, which might have been born in an impressionable mind at a tender age. The Sisters advised that if the child wished, she could live by Christian values without any thought of formally joining the order. For us at home, the little incident provided an insight into the systems within missionary institutions.

Meena taught Botany, which included home gardening, in an institution called the Government Home Science College, which admitted only girls, to prepare them to run households scientifically. Lest it appear that I was a male chauvinist, or that the family revolved solely around me, I must proudly aver that, at that point in time, I was happy to participate in my capacity as a husband in some activities at the college. This meant consorting the wife to frequent college functions even in the late evenings. A task that I thoroughly enjoyed was to adjudge the quality of home management displayed by the students. Miss Sherry Dongaji, a dynamic Parsee lady who was the then Principal, would invite selected guests to dinner prepared by the inmates of 'cottages', as they were called and require them to solemnly evaluate the quality of décor of the cottage, besides the taste and presentation of the food dishes on offer. On one occasion, while thanking Miss Dongaji, I casually remarked that I would have enjoyed the proceedings even more had I been invited some years earlier, when I was yet a bachelor. Live wire as she was, Miss Dongaji laughed heartily, an equal partner in such banter. Sadly, the tradition of cottage demonstration has now vanished from the girls' curriculum. Disappeared also are the links of spouses in college activities.

During my official touring, I was able to visit my parents at Beas. Here one could savour the serenity of a tranquil atmosphere. The spiritual colony, called Dera, is like a picturesque park, verdant with trees, flowers and shrubs. Even until the year 1950, Dera was like any primitive village of Punjab. Over the years, as the number of followers grew, the institution created modern infrastructure, including housing, water supply and sanitation for permanent residents, numbering just 15,000, as well as for large congregations. As many as 300,000 seekers now visit Dera to attend periodical *satsangs*, when the spiritual master discourses. The township is a model of community participation. All facilities for the visitors are offered free of charge. Thousands of volunteers work in harmony in the self-reliant colony on the banks of the river Beas. On being accepted as *sewadars* (honorary workers) my parents were provided basic living quarters consisting of a small two-bedroom cottage. *Sewadars* do not own the lodgings; living space is allotted to them for life, rent free. For me every visit to Dera was invigorating. I could imbibe the essence of the philosophy and teachings. I also spent quality time with my parents and with my uncle Dev Prakash to enjoy his choice collection of Urdu poetry.

No visit to the city of Amritsar was complete without my meeting a unique personality by the name of Brij Bedi, a friend who lived there. Brij was the husband of a celebrity, Kiran Bedi, who had broken gender barriers to become the first woman to join the Indian Police Service in the year 1972. I had played tennis with Kiran, who had been Asian champion, and it was she who had introduced me to Brij. Many people viewed Brij in the shadow of his wife, who was making waves as a bold, no-nonsense police officer in whichever assignment she was entrusted with. Being allocated to the Union Territories cadre, Kiran's postings were in various union territories, which included Delhi and other remotely located regions administered directly by the government of India. Brij and Kiran had reconciled to long absences from each other and lived for years as a divided family that was united periodically. Kiran's career was a priority and Brij was tied to Amritsar city to manage his interests there.

As Kiran excelled professionally in the police, Brij was independently ploughing his own furrow. Starting as a one-man army, he took up worthy social causes in Amritsar. These included a drive against mismanagement and corruption in the local municipal corporation, protests against obscene posters wantonly displayed at city crossings and an open challenge to police authority, which often failed to take cognizance of criminal complaints. Brij institutionalized his energies in setting up a NGO which targeted the rampant problem of drug abuse. Brij was an extremely versatile person, boasting of myriad talents. He ran a successful industrial unit manufacturing carpet making machines, producing films (he himself was an ace photographer) and managed his agricultural land situated in an adjacent district. Brij Bedi gathered around himself like-minded social activists and led movements that were decidedly anti-establishment. To my dismay, he withdrew from all these ventures when they were commercially prospering and finally devoted his life exclusively to projects relating to drug abuse and its tragic consequences. Such was his missionary zeal that he sold all his valuable agricultural land and donated the proceeds to his NGO. He highlighted in the media how hundreds of drug users in a section of the town succumbed to their addiction. Brij Bedi's NGO adopted, for rehabilitation of the residents, their entire locality, Maqboolpura, dubbed by Bedi himself as 'the colony of widows', as many young men had died from drug abuse. His work did not stop at efforts to rid the users of their fatal attraction. Brij dedicated himself to rehabilitating the widows and the children, especially the orphans. Schools were set up, as were vocational training centres for the unfortunate children. The NGO even charted the career of hundreds of girls, enabling them to work gainfully in society. On one occasion he proudly introduced to me two girls who had attained distinction as national sportswomen. Brij received accolades and recognition from national as well as international institutions; many came forward to join his noteworthy cause that earned him unsought fame.

Every visit to Brij Bedi's home was for me an inspiration. It was ironic that even as Kiran had caught the headlines as a great police officer, Brij was quietly toiling, without fanfare, to serve a section of hapless humanity in his beloved city. I was constantly in touch with Brij at Amritsar. I was saddened that I could not be at his side in the year 2017, when he passed away in a hospital in Delhi, as it transpired.

A proverb in Portuguese goes, 'Of oil, wine and friends, the oldest is best.' It was around the year 1980 that I could visit one of my oldest friends, Sukhdev, in his farmhouse in his ancestral village Kila Raipur, near Ludhiana. Sukhdev and I had been class fellows from schooldays, having spent six years together in Patiala. We were together even at college and university. At school, I had hero-worshipped Sukhdev for his achievements as the ideal all-rounder, brilliant at studies and a champion in several sports. After a romance at the university, Sukhdev had married Sohinder, our mutual classmate. Meena and I are both close to the couple. On that memorable visit to Kila Raipur I was invited to witness what was charmingly touted as the 'Rural Olympics', a unique sports festival held at Kila Raipur every February. The event features major traditional sports of Punjab, including *kabaddi*, tug of war and bullock-cart races. It was eye-opening to learn that the bullocks are genetically bred, and prepared for years to compete in a showcase event akin to the chariot races of ancient Rome. I witnessed amazing feats of endurance such as a man pulling a tractor with a rope held between his teeth and unusual games like kite flying, rare martial arts and forms of wrestling, which might be seen only in films. The athletes compete not for monetary reward, but for small-time recognition in the state. There is additional entertainment in the form of music and folk dances of Punjab, in which both men and women participate with gusto.

Kila Raipur, which lies at the heart of the most productive agricultural belt in the country, is populated mainly by families of Grewals. The Grewals (Sukhdev was one), excel in agriculture and in the industrial sector too as entrepreneurs. Sukhdev has a thriving transport company in Calcutta and visits the village in Punjab several times every year to supervise farm operations. The games provide the audience, which runs into tens of thousands, a flavour of the style of living and entertainment of Punjab. The vista is far from what one envisions from reports of the department of agriculture. I await eagerly the visit of Sukhdev and Sohinder to their winter place. They are not your stereotypical couple invested in farming. Urbane and sophisticated, Sohinder is wedded to social causes. She supports women artisans in

Calcutta in production of handicrafts and also works with the Missionaries of Charity of Mother Teresa.

I enjoyed scouring the state, even as I was busy with my responsibility as the chief executive of a public undertaking. My work in the corporate sector was dramatic and eventful in itself.

MARKFED

My appointment at Chandigarh was that of Managing Director of the Punjab State Cooperative Supply and Marketing Federation (MARKFED). With matters of home and hearth resolved satisfactorily, I was to spend three extremely eventful years in an institution that was at the heart of transformation of the agrarian economy of the state of Punjab. In this narration a modicum of factual detail was inescapable.

MARKFED is a giant among cooperative institutions in India. It is at the pinnacle of a network of some 1300 cooperative marketing societies[3] in the state of Punjab. Through its constituents MARKFED supplies essential farm inputs, such as fertilizers and pesticides, to the entire institutionally linked farm community in the state, and also markets their agricultural produce. MARKFED also runs a number of industrial plants for processing agriculture-based products for commercial sale. In the year 1979,

3 The figures, turnover and activities are mentioned as they existed around the year 1980, when I worked at MARKFED. There has since been expansion of the institutional network. The number of member societies have increased manifold. The activities have also enlarged, as also their financial turnover.

when I joined the enterprise, its annual business turnover was around Rs 1300 crores[4] (thirteen billion rupees). The management of MARKFED is vested in a board, which comprises elected members from districts and a nominee of the state cooperative bank. The state government nominates three members and also the Managing Director.[5]

The complex structure of shareholding and relationship between the constituents conforms to the basic cooperative principles of autonomy, self-help and mutual support. The state government, which is one among several hundred shareholders, dominates the decision-making process. Within its cooperative network, the institution functions as a corporate public sector enterprise of the state government.

In India the cooperative movement was sponsored and nurtured by the government. Successive studies conducted by the Government of India and the Reserve Bank of India, starting with the Report of the Committee on Cooperation in India, 1915, accepted unapologetically that the cooperative 'movement in India owes its origin entirely to government and is clearly dependent on state support.'[6]

---

4 One crore equals 10 million. In 1979 1 US dollar $ was worth 16 Indian rupees. In the year 2020 one US dollar equals around 75 rupees.

5 Over the years the basic structure of the body has remained unchanged. As districts and societies are periodically reorganized the number of elected members on the board has been changing.

6 Numerous successive official documents of the Government of India, brought out in the years 1931, 1945, 1959, 1971, 1973 and 1976 highlight the same compulsion for the government to play a proactive role in the work of cooperation. Likewise the Reserve Bank of India, in *All India Credit Survey, 1954* and *Report of the All India Rural Credit Review Committee, 1969* has justified a preponderant role for government in assuring the success of the cooperative movement in India.

Many years after my tenure with MARKFED, when I worked as the Financial Commissioner for Cooperation in Punjab I was involved in a study[7] to identify controls of the government over the cooperatives in the state, and to suggest how the controls considered as undue could be removed. Without wading into the intricacies of government controls over the cooperatives, I confine myself here to my experience in the undertaking entrusted to me. The prevalent role of Government in the management of cooperative marketing at that point in time is taken as a given.

By the year 1979, the state had come to be recognized as the country's bread basket. The gross domestic income per capita income in Punjab had become the highest among all states in India. In the year 1978–79 the average yield of wheat per hectare at 2715 kilogrammes was as high as anywhere in the world, as was that of rice (averaging 2938 kilogrammes per hectare). In the year 1980 the state of Punjab occupied about 1.5 per cent of the cultivated area in India, but contributed over 60 per cent of the wheat and 70 per cent of the rice to the marketable surplus of grain in the country. This surplus food grain went into a central pool that supplied the needs of the nation.

---

7 The Report, titled, *Structural Reform in the Cooperative Sector in Punjab (1998)*, followed by other studies are the basis for ongoing reform measures in the state.

Marketing Pains

The mainstay of marketing operations was purchase of food grains, which was a price-stabilization measure. This was a time when widespread adoption of new technologies by farmers, especially in Punjab, had brought the country to food self-sufficiency. For various reasons, producers in all states did not show equal alacrity in adopting the new technologies. The national policy aimed to balance the imperative of a remunerative price for the producers with the goal of delivering food grains at a reasonable price to the consumers, especially the poor. This was accomplished through the system of state trading in food grains. In Punjab the state agencies procured grain from notified markets at a minimum notified price, and delivered the same to the authorized central agency, the Food Corporation of India (FCI). FCI moved the food grain mainly by rail to the deficit states, which delivered to consumers via a country-wide network of fair price shops. Taking into account relevant factors, an empowered Agriculture Prices Commission[8] determined annually a fair support price that the state government agencies[9] paid to the producers. Private traders could purchase grain only at a price higher than the minimum procurement price.

---

8 The Agriculture Prices Commission (APC), established in 1965, renamed Commission for Agricultural Costs and Prices in the year 1985, fixes the minimum support price for commodities, annually.

9 Apart from MARKFED several other agencies of the government were authorized to make purchases. These were FCI itself, the Food and Supplies department and some smaller corporations. MARKFED was the dominant player in the marketing of wheat and paddy, and later in other commodities such as cotton and pulses.

At first sight it might appear that, with the cost price and selling price being predetermined, there was little scope for commercial enterprise within the marketing organization. In actual practice the operations had to be conducted on sound commercial principles of financial viability. To exercise corporate discipline and work within a budget was no easy task. The assembled data showed that over the years FCI had been imposing heavy quality cuts and penalties on wheat delivered to it by MARKFED. The magnitude of the losses to MARKFED on this account was so large that handling of wheat was proving to be a losing proposition. Within the organization it was accepted that that the storage arrangements were deficient, supervision was lax, systems of scientific monitoring were weak, accountability for storage and management was poor, and leakages in the system were being exploited with impunity by some individual members of the staff.

There was immense pressure from the government for prompt purchase and payment to the sellers. The producers demanded, naturally, the maximum price for all grain, even where it was poor in quality. The norms stipulated a graded lower price for grain that did not fulfil the specifications. Amidst huge arrivals of grain in the market and beset with local pressures, the staff often failed to adhere to stipulated guidelines for purchase. At times the lower-ranking staff colluded with the producers of grain and accepted bribes for purchase of substandard produce. These lapses impaired the quality of stocks delivered. FCI eventually penalized MARKFED accordingly.

Further, poor supervision of storage led to damage to stocks, which eventually resulted in financial penalties on MARKFED. As space in the warehouses was found inadequate,[10] many stocks had perforce to be stored in the open, over temporary wooden plinths. Subject to drenching by rain, substantial quantity of stock suffered damage, despite huge tarpaulin protection coverings. Early in my tenure I learnt that one single aspect of storage could impact the entire viability of operations of MARKFED. Over a period of time all stored wheat stocks gain in weight on account of moisture content in the atmosphere. Scientifically stored and aerated stocks could gain in weight by as much as 2 to 3 percent. A quantity of, say 100 tonnes of wheat in a single warehouse could enhance by as much as 3 tonnes during a single season of storage. Through its network of branches MARKFED purchased about one-fourth of the wheat arriving in the markets in the state. This comprised about 1.1 million tonnes out of the total marketable surplus of 4.5 million tonnes. The financial implications of the impact of storage conditions on the quantity of stocks were mind boggling on paper. No scientific study had been made of the phenomenon. MARKFED had thus to rely on the general level of skill and honesty of its staff. On my own I requested the Punjab Agriculture University to conduct an empirical

10 Unbelievably the demand for storage had grown so rapidly that many enterprising farmers decided to divert part of their fertile land for construction of warehouses. The storage space was rented to agencies, including MARKFED for accommodating stored grain. An unexpected consequence of the spurt in production!

study into the impact of storage conditions, especially ambient moisture, on wheat stocks.

Visiting the markets at the peak of the hot summer months of May and June was an education, and also an adventure. My institution being the mainstay of marketing of wheat, I visited hundreds of *mandis* to observe the operations. During my first inspection, I was intrigued at a peculiar action of my staff engaged in conducting the purchase. The man would take a few grains from a heap of the purchased lot, and chew the raw stuff. My immediate reaction was that the man was performing some form of a ritual, akin to a bus driver who begins his journey by touching the steering wheel with his forehead, a gesture seeking God's blessing before beginning his daily work. Could the man, whose profession is grains, be supplicating the goddess of prosperity, I wondered. The mystery was quickly unveiled, when the supervisor suddenly began to admonish his junior. In his verbal lashing he berated his junior for purchasing a stock that had moisture content beyond the permissible limit. At some *mandi*s my people were armed with mechanical moisture meters, which accurately measured the percentage of moisture in every lot of grain offered for sale. Cross checking with the scientific gauge confirmed the efficacy of the rough and ready method of the expert, who had merely chewed some grains. In a bid to demonstrate my own familiarity with the intuitive method of verification, I too began to taste samples of fresh grain. I might have impressed my staff with a supposed proficiency at this low form of technology. I did not dare to confess to them that all I could discern during the 'inspection' was that wheat tastes differently in the raw than what it does when cooked into a pizza!

In summer the markets are hot and dusty. In contrast, the climate is comparatively benign in autumn and winter, when the crops of paddy and cotton arrive in the market. Visiting the *mandi*s in the south western districts of Punjab in the season of purchase of the cotton crop is a unique experience. Even my children enjoyed frolicking over huge mounds of raw cotton spread out in the open in such small unknown *mandi* towns like Goniana, Gidderbaha and Sardulgarh. The fluffy cotton looked like a mountain of soft snow, only there was no danger of a meltdown of icicles.

The Pains of Reform

This chapter is not intended to detail the complex processes of management and reform in an enterprise. Of some interest might be the dramatic fallout of the exercise, which led to industrial unrest, including a general strike in the organization, accompanied with violence and a physical attack to which I was personally subjected.

In its report, called 'Management Information and Stores Accounting Systems', a reputed company engaged for the purpose suggested certain fundamental changes in the methods of monitoring of activities and financial management. The recommendations increased accountability of staff at all levels to such an extent that the union of employees labelled it MISA, after a controversial law (the Maintenance of Internal Security Act, 1971) that the Government of India had at that time adopted for strengthening security arrangements within the country. This derisive comparison with MISA was in fact a left-handed compliment, which indicated that the new systems were beginning to bite. Following the study, systems of internal audit and stricter financial control were adopted. These entailed the recruitment of more than a hundred qualified accounts staff at middle level, along with a number of chartered accountants.

Of greater visibility than the induction of accounts staff was the engagement of young holders of the degree of Masters of Business Administration (MBA) to work as heads of districts. All the posts of District Manager were upgraded to Senior District Manager, which carried a monthly scale of Rs 1200–Rs 2000, up from the earlier scale of Rs 350–Rs 900. Half of these crucial posts were reserved for the existing cadre of District Managers and the remaining went to young MBAs directly inducted from the open market. In order to motivate the existing cadre, the District Managers could also be considered for the senior position, provided that they qualified a written test. Agricultural degree holders were brought in to enhance the technical cadres. Dozens of young scientists with degrees of Master of Science (Agriculture) were inducted as Manager Quality Control.

On behalf of MARKFED, the universities, which were independent bodies, conducted the initial entrance tests for selection. The personnel were mainly qualified graduates and postgraduates in agriculture and commerce. Overnight, the institution was served by several hundred new faces, young and energetic. Expectedly, some candidates approached the political leaders in power for their support. It transpired that the universities had completed their task of evaluation so promptly that in most cases orders appointing the new personnel had already been issued by the time the ministers spoke to me. Many of the individuals named by the political leaders were found to have been already selected on merit. I recall that both my minister and the Chief Minister were satisfied with the process of selection. It was fascinating to observe the socio-economic profile of the batches of new recruits. Many of them came from humble backgrounds. One particular agriculture graduate, the son of a waste picker, was in tears and incredulous when he was handed his order of appointment within a month of applying for the advertised job. The selection drive showed that sufficient qualified manpower for marketing, commerce and management was available in the state.

Dramatic Conflict

The drastic measures for recruitment and for enforcing discipline elicited sharp adverse reaction among the employees. Some apprehensive groups complained to the Chief Minister and to the minister for cooperation about what they termed wasteful expenditure on high paid staff. They also took umbrage at several disciplinary proceedings against employees. In the month of January 1980, groups of disaffected employees began to demonstrate in front of MARKFED office, which at that time functioned in a rented building located in the heart of the city's main shopping complex in Sector 17, Chandigarh. I became quite used to a reception committee consisting of slogan shouters greeting me when I entered or exited the office premises. The major grouses were against the new controls over operations, and to the induction of technical staff. They raised a populist issue, namely, that some senior professionals belonged to states other than Punjab. One amusing complaint against the management was that comparatively junior staff was allowed to sit in air-conditioned comfort, in preference to their seniors. It happened that MARKFED had installed computers to handle the work of monitoring of reports. The hardware of the day needed an environment of controlled temperature. Hence the computer room, where the computer operator sat, was air-conditioned. As the protests continued the happenings had to be reported to the government. The demonstrations were initially peaceful, although the slogan shouting became loud when they sighted me.

For the demonstrators, the last straw was a decision to terminate the services of a number of field employees on account of proven charges of corruption. It happened that among these dismissed employees were two individuals who were the President and Secretary of the powerful union of employees. The protestors viewed it as a deliberate attempt by the management to bully the trade unionists. In those days I chose to travel to office on my two-wheeler, despite my driver urging me to use my designated official car for duty. One afternoon, on returning to office after lunch, I was surrounded by an infuriated mob, which tried to physically attack me as I was parking. It was the presence of mind of Bali Singh, my loyal driver, a burly ex-serviceman that protected me from serious injury. Displaying rare courage, Bali Singh single handedly pushed aside the irate crowd and escorted me safely into my office.

The marketplace being the venue of my office premises, the public was witness to the daily demonstrations there. Physical assault on an officer was a sensational matter. The incident was widely reported in the local press. While covering industrial disputes, the media is seen to sympathise with employees and often castigates senior management. Here was an exception: as head of management, I received uncommon support in the local media. The reason was peculiar. The fact that at the time of the assault, I had been riding my personal two-wheeler to office and did not have any form of security or protection, convinced the reporters that the aggressors could not possibly be the aggrieved party. My personal image in the public received an unexpected boost. As a single person attacked by a large group of hoodlums, I was considered more sinned against than sinning. On its part the government viewed the incident with great seriousness, an attack on the established order of the state. When I reported the matter, both my Secretary Mr K.D. Vasudeva and the Chief Secretary, Mr K.S. Narang insisted that the criminal act must be formally reported to the police for suitable action.

The moment a criminal case was registered, some mobsters were arrested by the police. This led to escalation of unrest, so much so that there was a sudden general strike across all offices of MARKFED over the entire state. For a week I worked from home. As happens in such cases the union of employees enlarged their litany of complaints and demands. Their major demand was that the office bearers of the union who had been discharged from service should be reinstated. To this they added many other issues relating to working conditions, a perceived conflict of experienced older employees pitted against 'young academics drawing fat salaries'. For this they approached the highest levels in government, including the Chief Minister, but received little sympathy. On my part I insisted that the orders of termination of guilty employees could not be revoked. While I was hoping against hope, I was surprised when the unrest lost steam within just a week. Political emissaries from the government intervened to give some form of face saving for the striking staff to withdraw their agitation. It is possible that the union realized that their cause was weak, and so the strike petered out. The law took its course in the matter of the violent incident; the terminated staff was not redeemed and the policy of professionalism within the institution continued. In due course the people who had been dismissed from service on corruption charges challenged in court the orders of punishment imposed. The trial courts disallowed the challenge and appeals too were eventually dismissed even in the High Court.

Incidentally, as I was facing problems with the trade unions, especially violent demonstrations, I tried my best to insulate my family at home from the happenings. At the time of a general strike, I had to give some lame explanation to the children as to why I was not going to work in office. They might have been upset to learn that their father was the butt of slogans and that impassioned protesters were burning his effigy.

I learnt several lessons from the episodes. First, that the head of an organization should avoid becoming a personal target of suspicion and distrust. If possible, the backing of superior authorities for unpopular decisions should be ensured. In actual practice such diversion of responsibility is difficult, as it is at the door of the Managing Director that the buck stops. Second, good managers must carry along sections of employees when seeking to enforce drastic change. This could be done by involving threatened groups in the very processes of restructuring, and also by engaging the staff in positive group activity beyond the office doors. In this regard, when it was decided to organize sports events and cultural activities, there was enthusiastic response. We successfully organized competitions in a number of sports disciplines between three teams, representing the field staff, the staff of the manufacturing plants and the employees at the headquarters. Being keen on sports I was able to assemble several teams that played local sports leagues. I myself joined the employees in athletics and several other team games. Likewise, the annual variety entertainment programme revealed unsuspected local talent. Our Establishment Officer Balbir Singh was a skilled Bhangra[11] dancer, who had even performed in Hindi films. In an impromptu move, Balbir Singh managed to bring on stage the Minister of the department, to join the dancers, to the delight of the audience.

The most important lesson that I imbibed was to be gracious after the conflict had abated. I went out of the way to build bridges with as many groups as possible. For this the team of senior managers was exceedingly effective. Comparative industrial peace prevailed after the cathartic impact of the strike. Alas, this tranquility turned out to be a false dawn. There were now fresh challenges of a different nature altogether, which led to a continuance of turbulent days. The reasons were political.

The Political Dimension

Given the structure of cooperative enterprises, it was inevitable that politics should play a significant role in control and management at the top. It happened that around January 1980 elections for the members of the Board of Directors were held. Theoretically cooperative institutions are neutral to changes in political leadership in the state, and at the centre, that is the Government of India. In practice the members of boards of the cooperative institutions have strong political affiliations. The voters usually return through

---

11 Bhangra is a vigorous dance, performed mainly by males, in the state of Punjab.

the election process cooperators affiliated with the ruling party in the state. It transpired that almost all the twelve members who were elected to the board from the districts belonged to the ruling Shiromani Akali Dal party in Punjab.

In February of the same year, 1980, a piquant situation arose, as the ruling political party was replaced by a Congress government. It transpired that at the national level the Janata coalition government had collapsed, and a Congress government headed by Mrs Indira Gandhi was back in power. The new government decided to dissolve the legislative assemblies in nine states, including the state of Punjab, on the grounds that the ruling party in all these states had lost the mandate of the people. The victorious party of the Congress relied on the very precedent established by the opposing Janata government in the year 1977, when state assemblies were similarly dissolved. In the fresh elections to the Punjab legislative assembly in February 1980 the Congress party returned to power. The new Chief Minister was Sardar Darbara Singh.

The political upheaval in the state was to impact MARKFED in an unexpected way. The elected members of the Board had strong links with the Akali party, whereas the Congress party now headed the state government. As per the bylaws of MARKFED, the state government was authorized to nominate three members to the Board, along with the Managing Director. Loathe at the prospect of members from the opposition Akali party controlling the Board, the state government nominated as chairman of the Board the serving the Administrative Secretary for Cooperation.The elected members of the Board were politically hostile to the government.

The powers of the Managing Director and of the Board of Directors are defined in the bylaws. The Board is supreme on policy matters, but individual members do not enjoy executive authority, which is entrusted to the Managing Director. The elected members often opposed proposals presented in board meetings, but the Chairman blocked any attempts to politicize issues of management. In one board meeting it was agreed to confer the designation of Vice Chairman on one of the more articulate members by the name of Harcharan Singh Hero, but even the Vice Chairman enjoyed no powers whatever. Mr Hero had set his sights on the position of Chairman, but since he was an active member of the opposition party the government could never allow him to occupy the coveted chair. The consequence of the hostility of the members was that meetings of the Board could turn ugly. At times, wild allegations and irresponsible statements were made, but the Chairman firmly put down these attempts. It was not a placid environment for serious discussion on strategy in the business enterprise.

The main interest of most of the elected members was in such matters as appointment and placement of employees within the organization. For this they might approach me occasionally. The members were upset when some of their requests could not be accepted. Many disgruntled employees, who had been subdued in the aftermath of the unsuccessful strike, now made common cause with some of the elected members. Following the aborted strike by the employees, demonstrations at the gate had ceased. The elected members felt aggrieved that the government did not allow them to dominate the Board. They lent the unhappy groups a sympathetic ear and the latter found their voice. Around the dates on which the Board was to meet, the demonstrations intensified. At this stage there was more grist for their mill. With better systems of management and control in position, skeletons had begun to roll out of MARKFED's protected cupboard. The newly adopted systems generated unexpected data. MARKFED's internal auditors carried out an annual stock checking of all the warehouses in the state within a record period of three days. The exercise revealed large volumes of missing stocks of fertilizers and food grain in the warehouses. Following the revelation of heavy shortages, the balance sheet for the year showed financial losses, rather than improvement. The employees used the figures of profit and loss to allege that the newly inducted professionals were responsible for a downturn in profitability. There was thus a strange sight of protestors outside the building and hostile members inside the board room. The real cause of dissonance was that the elected members were affiliated with a political party opposed to the government in power in the state. They carried their political dissatisfaction into the board room. Should this be how India's premier cooperative conducts itself, one wondered?

When I met Mr Darbara Singh, the Chief Minister to apprise him of the situation I was astonished how cool and unperturbed he was. As a seasoned public leader, he was already aware of the political motivation behind the attitude of the members. Possibly, the Chief Minister was secretly pleased that a group of cooperators from the opposing political party were uncomfortable in the prevailing situation. His assurance of support in the reform measures underway inspired confidence and comfort.

From the year 1978, MARKFED was assigned the task of marketing rice. Despite it not being a traditional crop, the agriculturists in Punjab began to adopt eagerly the high-yielding varieties of paddy. Overnight huge quantities of raw paddy flooded the market. The procuring agencies were required to process its stocks of paddy into rice for delivery to the Food Corporation of India. All the rice mills in the state (they were then 900 in number) were in the hands of private traders. The marketing agency was at the mercy of the individual owners of rice mills, both in regard to the quality of the end product (rice) and the period of time taken for processing. The state government stipulated a minimum yield of the end product rice from original weight of the raw paddy. This ratio was around 65 per cent for millers all over the state. During the season the miller was merely required to deliver a certain amount of rice in proportion to the paddy processed. The entire arrangement was fraught, as the handler of grain did not control the manufacturing process. There were complaints of an unholy nexus between the lower staff of MARKFED and the rice millers. The processed rice grain was found to be compromised in quality and quantity. Over the years state agencies like MARKFED have continued to be locked in disputes with rice millers. The government would dearly love to withdraw from the business of procuring paddy, but to the day it seems unlikely that it would happen. In the meanwhile, the agencies perforce have to make the best of a bad bargain.

The focus now was on ventures that could be commercially profitable. While the revelation of missing stocks clouded the figures of profit and loss for the year 1979–80, the position improved considerably in the year 1980–81, showing that the systems of control and monitoring were beginning to yield results. Genuine commercial trading in other commodities, such as cotton, oil seeds and pulses began. Unlike food grains, which had to be purchased on behalf of the government at a stipulated minimum price, MARKFED could trade in these other commodities as a free market operator. With a strong marketing team for processed products MARKFED was able to match the private sector.

The cotton-growing districts of southwest Punjab proved an ideal ground for MARKFED's bright young professionals, fresh with their MBA degrees. It was decided to entrust commercial trading in cotton to two raw young men, Mehmood Khan and Uday Pal Singh Gill, just 25 and 27 years in age, from India's top management institutes. I mention these two names in particular as Mehmood and Uday went on to excel in marketing at the international level. After 28 years at Unilever, Mehmood became the Head Global Innovation Strategy at the head office of the same conglomerate Unilever in London. Uday presently works in Jakarta, Indonesia, as Chief Executive of Indorama Ventures, a leading company in the world for manufacture and marketing of personal hygiene, automotive and lifestyle materials. Some of the young managers qualified in a central examination of the Union Public Service Commission to join prestigious central services such as the Indian Revenue Service. The young business executives groomed at MARKFED maintain that the experience they gained as independent managers at MARKFED was to pave the foundation of their success in their career.

Within a year of its advent, the Cotton Cell within MARKFED showed handsome commercial profit, which offset loss that accrued in other traditional operations. The newly empowered managers in the Cotton Cell attributed their success to several factors, namely, the adoption of scientific management information systems and the introduction of instant communication through a dedicated, secure wireless network. The use of these techniques was then novel in the cotton trade. They are now considered rudimentary ingredients in any form of professional marketing. Furthermore, in a process of decentralization of power, substantial authority to purchase and sell was delegated to the team.

From the year 1980, MARKFED began to export fresh vegetables grown in Punjab to countries of the Middle East

(United Arab Emirates, Bahrain, Kuwait and Saudi Arabia) and also to the United Kingdom. A commercially successful venture, this helped to diversify activities.

At MARKFED there was never a dull moment. Even as commercial marketing operations were proceeding successfully, some startling developments in the marketing of fertilizers rocked the institution. MARKFED supplied about 50 per cent of all chemical fertilizers (around 700,000 metric tonnes in gross weight) consumed in the state annually. During successive years MARKFED had been making losses in the marketing of fertilizers. My Monitoring Manager, a professional named D.K. Jain, who had earlier in his career worked for the public sector company Hindustan Zinc, brought to me some astounding figures to show that we were stocking huge quantities of stocks, which remained unsold over long periods. The fertilizers, which include imported stocks as well as some manufactured in the country, are to be kept in readiness for delivery to the consumer farmers in the season. As a measure of caution the Director of Agriculture insists that sufficient stocks are in hand with the cooperatives at all times to meet the coming demand. Jain informed me that MARKFED had been storing volumes of fertilisers that were much greater than were eventually sold. This had led to heavy costs of maintenance of inventory. In Punjab fertilisers are sold by the three categories of institutions, the cooperatives, some public sector agencies and private traders. The viability of fertilizer marketing is dependent on the carrying cost of inventory. The crucial ratio for profitability is the ratio of average monthly stocks in hand to average monthly sales. In the three years of Jain's study this ratio for MARKFED was respectively 2.62, 5.20 and 4.62. The same ratio for all other external agencies selling fertilisers in the state was just 1.21. If we carried such huge inventory, there was no way our operations could be viable. I was at pains to persuade the state government to allow MARKFED to reduce its inventory, for running its fertilizer marketing professionally.

Even as negotiations with the state government were in progress it happened that the Ministry of Agriculture, Government of India, decided to enhance the selling price of some fertilizers by as much as 35 per cent. As Managing Director, I was delighted at the decision. The entire inventory of stocks in hand with MARKFED would be up valued by 35 per cent. Overstocking could deliver a bonanza to MARKFED, so I reasoned. Alas! I had not bargained for the perfidy of my staff in the field. Despite clear orders on the new selling price of fertilizers, many field employees continued to bill the sold stocks on paper at old rates, while making actual sale at the new, higher rates, effectively pocketing the difference. This was a major scandal. The government was rightly perturbed. On receiving reports of the corrupt practice, I ordered multiple enquiries, which were entrusted to the most honest managers in the organization. Within a week we identified at least 45 employees who had indulged in transparent malpractice. Apparently, the recalcitrant field staff had not been clever enough to erase their footprints from the illegal transactions. The instances of petty larceny were bound to be found out. As the enquiries began, the defaulters approached every possible person in authority in the government in an attempt to save their skin. The evidence was so damaging that these were open and shut cases. The Chief Minister and the Cooperation Minister were presented a status report showing direct complicity of the offenders. It was agreed that a lenient view could be taken if any employee charged with defalcation admitted his guilt, and returned the amount wrongly pocketed. Leniency entailed that the employee would not be dismissed from service; he would be given a lesser punishment (stoppage of four increments in his service). In respect of employees who wished to contest their arraignment the enquiries would take their course.

The bungling was the work of amateurs. It was no surprise that almost every chargesheeted employee confessed guilt in writing and deposited the money illegally acquired in a MARKFED account. I was flabbergasted when some of the offenders approached me personally with the actual banknotes of ill-gotten wealth. Overall, it was a satisfactory resolution, but one that was possible only because the institution had become equipped with good systems and good enforcement personnel.

The ongoing tension with the elected members of the Board, led by the Vice Chairman, continued eventfully for almost two years. In the meantime, the press also stepped in, finding the prospect of juicy stories for filling the papers. Some of the aggressive members of the staff had links with the media and several marketing deals found their way into newspapers with sleazy headlines. I suggested to the Chief Minister that, since the differences between the Vice Chairman Mr Hero and me as Managing Director appeared to be irreconcilable, he could consider moving one of us away from the organization.

In the month of June 1982, Mr Harcharan Singh Hero had shifted his loyalty from the Akali party, and formally joined the Congress, which was the ruling party in the state of Punjab. The decision to admit Mr Hero in the ruling party had been taken by the political leadership of the Congress at the national level without consultation with Sardar Darbara Singh, the Chief Minister of the state. Having effectively deserted his original party, Mr Hero was now a member of the ruling party. The government promptly rewarded the turncoat by accepting his demand of elevation from the position of Vice Chairman to that of Chairman MARKFED. Orders were speedily issued, whereby Mr Hero replaced the earlier nominated Chairman. Immediately on this announcement, Mr Hero was welcomed in the office with garlands and sweets by some members of the union of employees. His first decision as Chairman was to occupy the office of the Managing Director and declare it as the Chairman's office. Some employees brought down the name plate of the Managing Director and trampled it underfoot, accompanied with cheers of their colleagues.

That, in the end, marked the conclusion of my tumultuous stay at MARKFED, which had lasted two years and ten months. The government issued orders transferring me to the Secretariat as the Joint Secretary in the Department of Irrigation and Power. To his credit, Mr Hero remarked, and this was conveyed to me, that while he had every respect for my honesty and integrity, I had stood in the way of his elevation to the position he felt he deserved.

PELF AND POWER

At the entrance to the Secretariat of the states of Punjab and Haryana in Chandigarh is an imposing brass plaque, inscribed in bold capital letters with the following words:

'The wise men of antiquity, when they wished to make the whole world peaceful and happy, first put their own states into proper order. Before putting their states into proper order, they regulated their own families. Before regulating their families, they regulated themselves; they tried to be sincere in their thoughts. Before being sincere in their thoughts, they tried to see things as they really were.' (Confucius)

Le Corbusier, the renowned French-Swiss architect of Chandigarh, had himself mounted the metal board at the time of inauguration of the building in the year 1953. The Civil Secretariat, where the plate is conspicuously installed, is the home of the Executive, one of the three organs of our democratic state. The etched quote from the ancient Chinese philosopher highlights the ideals of integrity and objectivity expected of those in authority. The words remind entrants to the portals that they must wield power with wisdom and care.

At its core, governance consists in appropriate exercise of power. For ministers, who are political leaders, the importance of every portfolio is measured by the level of power and patronage attached. Likewise, civil servants aspire to positions which are endowed with authority. When taking office, every leader swears an oath to use power entrusted to them for the public good.

A few months after my dramatic exit from the corporate sector, I found myself in an entirely different environment. I was attached, on my promotion as Secretary, to none other than the head of the State, the Governor of Punjab. My office was in the grand government house called Raj Bhavan. This was the seat of pomp and splendour of the state, though not of its executive power.

An Exalted Office

An appointee of the Government of India, the Governor is *numero uno*, protocol wise, within his state. His official privileges are defined. He resides in grandeur and opulence, but in normal times he enjoys no executive authority as such. At Raj Bhavan the Governor is feted and saluted by persons distinguished in public life. He receives callers of many hues, including political leaders, as well as activists from such diverse fields as social work and education, and even from institutions linked to the performing arts and sports. On important national occasions, such as Independence Day and Republic Day, he hosts a large gathering of distinguished guests from civil and military life, called 'At Home'. Invitations to certain official parties by holders of high office, like the President of India, the Governors of states etc. are titled, 'At Home'. The phrase signifies that the host would be at home at the appointed time to receive the invited guest. The title of the invitation presumably adds greater dignity, protocol wise, to the exalted office. He also administers the oath of office to constitutional dignitaries such as ministers and the Chief Justice of the High Court and to other statutory authorities. He is called upon to summon and address the house of legislature. All these chores are comfortable to accomplish.

The status of His Excellency (that honorific is still in use while addressing the august incumbent) is a continuum of a tradition from colonial India, the difference being that the (British) Government of India had invested the Governor with huge authority. The Government of India Act, 1935 had provided for elections to the national and state legislatures, but the elected leaders enjoyed little substantive authority. The Governor was then the final arbiter in most matters; he controlled the law and order machinery; he could, and did supersede many decisions of the elected representatives at the behest of the paramount ruler, the British Crown. He was an effective bulwark against any semblance of autonomy of local leaders in matters of administration. Under the Constitution of India, the Governor is now a figurehead. All business is conducted in his name, but it is the elected Council of Ministers, headed by the Chief Minister, that exercises administrative control. In exceptional circumstances, however, an elected government of a state can be suspended or dismissed. The Government of India can then, under Article 356 of the Constitution, take over the reins of the state government for some period of time. This is exactly what happened during the year that I worked as Secretary in Raj Bhavan. From being governor in just name he became de facto head of the state government overnight. I was witness to a remarkable transformation in his role.

The initial few months of my appointment in Raj Bhavan were a time of leisure. The incumbent Governor was Anant Prasad Sharma, a retired leader from the state of Bihar, who in his days had been a trade unionist. So long as he functioned purely as de jure head of state, my own duties as his Secretary were mainly fixing engagements for those who wished to call and arranging His Excellency's visits to institutions in various parts of the state. If the Governor is the democratic incarnation of a maharaja, the Raj Bhavan is akin to a princely palace, which functions like a well-oiled machine. A Comptroller of the Household attends to all aspects of hospitality, which are meticulously defined in the book. Two uniformed aides-de-camp (ADCs), young officers from the Indian army and the state police, attend on His Excellency at all times. On tour, the head of state is accompanied by an entourage of personnel charged with protocol, security and health.

For persons aspiring to luxury and ceremony without heavy responsibility, the position of a Governor is strongly recommended.

A Dream Cottage in the Hills

True to colonial tradition the Governor of Punjab has an official summer office in the hills, where he can repair to avoid the heat of the plains. For some part of the year he and his key staff can move officially to a well-appointed retreat called Hem Kunj (literally 'a nest in the hills') situated at a height of about 8000 feet (2500 metres) above sea level just 15 kilometres beyond Simla,[1] the capital of the state of Himachal Pradesh, which adjoins Punjab. In the reflected glory of our boss, the entire team and I considered this a paid holiday. Befittingly, the staff is housed in well-furnished cottages located in the campus of what is formally named Punjab Raj Bhavan (Camp Simla). The Governor's summer place is an ideal resort for nature lovers, who can freely trek the hill paths to their hearts content. Those fond of books can indulge their literary pursuits. Here I could enjoy luscious fruit from the gardens, including cherries and strawberries, rare luxuries for dwellers in the plains, and apples picked directly from the tree. The meticulously maintained gardens, including manicured lawns and a small orchard and vegetable patches on terraced slopes are a visual delight. Such is the skill of the gardeners at the estate, that over the years the Hem Kunj gardens have repeatedly been adjudged the most attractive among all competitors in a festival of horticulture in Shimla. Botanist Meena introduced several lovely species of flora to the children. For two months we

1 Simla is now named Shimla, meaning literally, the summit of a hill, or the conical top of a headdress, or turban.

dwelt in idyllic surroundings, atop a hill with a breathtaking view of the higher ranges of the Himalayas.

The abode was like a dream manor transported from the English countryside to nestle in the lower Himalayas. The original building, named Dane's Folly, had been imaginatively constructed more than a century earlier by one Louis Dane, a ranked British official. Dane had recreated in the tropical mountains the ambience of an English country house. His folly was his expectation that the town of Simla would grow around his mountain house, which it never did. My office and living quarters were in the original Dane's Folly building, a simple cottage of 19th century vintage, which merged seamlessly with the landscape. It was much later, in the 1970s, that modern architects created the present official residence of the Governor, called the House, as well as the adjoining cottages for the other aides. The new construction follows architecture typical of the city of Chandigarh. The layout of the House proper was lavish, as becoming the status of its regal occupant, but the grand design, inspired by Le Corbusier's creations, was perhaps not as adjusted to the conditions in the hills as my humbler annexe. The traditional sloping tin roof over my head was comparatively weather-proof. The elaborately modelled flat roofs of the House proper, on the other hand, often required attention of maintenance engineers after heavy rain and snow. There is something to be said for simplicity and environmental friendliness in architecture. Be that as it may, the head of the state of Punjab was served in his hill estate by a retinue of attendants, catering to every need. Wherever he travelled, to Simla town or other parts of the state, the administration of the state of Himachal Pradesh accorded him the ceremony and deference due to a visiting head of state.

Nostalgia

For me, the hill town of Simla evoked feelings of nostalgia. At the age of 12, I had spent the summer holidays with an aunt who taught in an industrial school in town. Some six years later, when my father was posted at Simla, and I was at the university, it was my home for every vacation. Now, as Governor's Secretary, I had enough time on my hands. I was familiar with all the haunts in and around town, and tried vainly to persuade the children to trek to such spots as the Glen, which was at the base of a steeply descending valley, and Annendale plateau, which then was a playing ground, and the Blessington tennis courts, which transformed into India's only ice skating rink in winter. Surprisingly, the children were happy to visit my erstwhile reading den, the Municipal Library, an imposing structure on top of Simla's most visible landmark, the Ridge. During my schooldays I had avidly consumed (gobbled up, as my aunt remarked) all the books in the children's section. The daily consumption then had been two books, the maximum number that I was permitted to borrow. I recall that I had been apologetic when I turned up every day to borrow a fresh quota of reading material. Now, after years, the shelves stacked with the books of adventure and humour were intact. I had begun my reading spree with

Tarzan's adventures; Richmal Crompton's schoolboy stories of William; the make-believe world of Enid Blyton; the volumes of Biggles, a fighter pilot during the Second World War and the classics of Dickens and Stevenson. All these familiar hardbound volumes lay exactly where they had been 30 years ago. The works of P.G. Wodehouse, my favourite from college days were ours for the borrowing. On enquiry, the librarian found that my membership of the year 1955 remained on record, since I had not withdrawn an amount of 15 rupees that had been charged as a security deposit almost 30 years earlier. The membership was restored and the children too became enthusiastic members. I could share their excitement.

During the month of June 1983, the Cricket World Cup was being played in England. Some matches featuring the Indian team were staged when we were at Simla, but we could not watch them on television, as the reception from the primitive TV network of the day was weak. My son Anurag was thrilled enough to hear the radio commentary describing the exploits of the Indian players, initially labelled by British sports writers as 'a rag tag bunch of amateurs'. He predicted that India's poorly regarded team would win. Miraculously, his prophesy came true. Back in Chandigarh, when I, along with the retinue had returned from the hills, we were able to watch the grainy images of the finals on a black and white TV set, the best technology that was accessible at the time.

The two-month paid holiday ended all too soon. The above digression is in stark contrast with what follows. From an unhurried existence in the salubrious mountain air, my boss was shortly to descend, or ascend, if you will, to the real world of hardcore governance in the plains. The summer holiday was followed by a period in which power and responsibility was unexpectedly thrust upon the Governor of Punjab, as the Government of India assumed direct control of the state's administration. During the spells of the President's Rule I worked as the Governor's Secretary for just a few months. In that brief period I saw first hand the focal point of power shift from the Secretariat to Raj Bhavan, even as my own responsibilities were enlarged overnight.

A Conflict Emerges

A storm of violence and bloodshed was to engulf the state of Punjab for a good part of a decade. For the period between the year 1983 and 1992, except for a two-year hiatus 1985–1987, the state of Punjab had no elected government. Inevitably, the political environment impacted administrative functioning. My focus in this book is the face of administration in diverse conditions and under various political dispensations. I mention briefly the unprecedented events that engulfed the population of the state at large.

Since its reorganization in the year 1966, Punjab had been ruled alternately by two political parties, the Indian National Congress (INC), a national party and the Shiromani Akali Dal (SAD), a regional party. Both parties were dominated by Sikh leaders. In the year 1973, the SAD party had adopted a resolution proposing redistribution of power between the

Centre and the states in India. This was called the Anandpur Sahib resolution, after the name of the small town of Punjab where the meeting was held. The demand for greater autonomy for the states did not emanate from Punjab alone. Similar demands had been voiced by several political parties from various parts of India. Amid an ongoing national debate on the centre–state relationship it transpired that some Sikh groups began to make allegations that the Central Government was discriminating against the state of Punjab, and in particular against the Sikh community. Some factional leaders went to the extent of raising an emotional demand for the creation of a separate Sikh homeland, which they gave the name of Khalistan (literally meaning 'land of the pure'). In pursuit of the idea of a nebulous homeland, some firebrand leaders even called for armed struggle. Initially this demand was not taken seriously even by the majority of the Sikh community, which had invariably participated actively in the normal election process. Around 60 per cent of the population of Punjab comprises the Sikh community. Throughout India the Sikhs are integrated in society. The Sikhs have distinguished themselves in numerous fields. As brave fighters they dominate the armed forces; as skilled farmers they have transformed Punjab into the bread basket of the country and one of the most prosperous of Indian states; with their noted spirit of enterprise, they excel in the business industry and many other fields.

Many writers, including objective observers and partisans, have written prolifically about the conflict in

Punjab. The original debate was basically about state autonomy within the constitutional framework. Some groups with militant leanings hijacked the political agenda, and gradually replaced it with a plan of armed struggle for an independent Sikh state. The resultant mayhem was to engulf many parts of Punjab. As the militants began to use terrorism as a weapon, they received, largely from abroad, clandestine support for their separatist agenda from elements hostile to India. The intelligence agencies had identified the groups, especially from neighbouring Pakistan, who were nurturing secessionist tendencies in Punjab.

Even as fiery speeches in the public arena became common, the government did not anticipate that any proponents would take to outright murder. The sectarian groups had a deep-rooted plan to create communal discord. Beginning from early 1983, there were selective attacks on persons from the Hindu community, and also on moderate Sikh leaders. The security forces, which were at the forefront, were also targeted in numerous violent incidents. The intention was to instil terror in the Hindu community within Punjab, in the expectation of a backlash against the Sikhs in other parts of the country. The design was to destroy the fabric of communal harmony, for Hindus to be driven out of the state and to create conditions in which Sikhs from other states might be compelled to return to Punjab. The objectives were blatantly secessionist.

The Centre Takes Command

The flash point, which compelled the Central Government to intervene, was the cold-blooded murder of some six passengers, all Hindus, of a night bus by a group of armed extremists on the Grand Trunk Road, which according to the old numbering system was India's National Highway 1, in the district of Kapurthala. A terrorist group, wedded to violence for attainment of the goal of an independent Sikh state, claimed responsibility for the heinous incident, which took place on 5 October 1983. The unprovoked killing of innocent people shook the entire nation. Days after the gruesome assassinations, the Governor of Punjab, Mr A.P. Sharma and the Chief Minister, Sardar Darbara Singh, were summoned to New Delhi. I was asked to accompany the Governor.

Late in the afternoon the Governor and Chief Minister flew together by the state plane from Chandigarh to reach the residence of the Prime Minister, where the Union Cabinet met to review the alarming situation. As the Chief Minster's Principal Secretary and I waited in an ante room, it was announced that the Cabinet had concluded that there was a breakdown of law and order. It was decided to immediately dismiss the elected government of Punjab, to dissolve the legislative assembly and to impose the President's rule in the state. The Government of India thus dismissed the government of a state (Punjab) that was ruled by its own party, the Indian National Congress. It was a unique decision for the Union Government to seize direct control of a state where it was itself in power. I recall vividly that after the cabinet meeting ended Mrs Indira Gandhi, the Prime Minister herself, walked past us casually. Clad in a traditional sari, she appeared a slight figure. There was no elaborate presence of security personnel around her.

The team that had travelled to Delhi returned immediately to Chandigarh. At that time the airport at Chandigarh was not equipped with night landing facility for aircraft. We therefore travelled by road. It was a gloomy atmosphere in which all of us left Delhi late in the evening to reach home by about 3 am.

The sensational developments had caught unaware the Chief Minister and also the Governor himself. With the proclamation of Central rule, the machinery of the state government headed by the Chief Secretary, took steps for conduct of official business in the changed circumstances. The Raj Bhavan hummed with activity as it might not have done for years. Within two days came an announcement that Punjab would have a new Governor. After having worked with Mr A.P. Sharma for a short time (eight months precisely) I now had a new boss, Mr Bhairab Dutt Pande, a distinguished former officer of the Indian Civil Service, ICS. Mr B.D. Pande had a reputation for efficient administration, having served as the Cabinet Secretary, the highest position in India for any civil servant. He was in fact already working as Governor in the state of West Bengal. In a lateral transfer the two top functionaries Mr A.P. Sharma and Mr Pande exchanged places. I worked with Mr Pande for about four months, before my transfer to the Secretariat.

BUSINESS, USUAL AND UNSUSUAL

How did civil administration perform during the stormy period when terrorism was at its peak? As the Administrative Secretary, one is in the core of the government's activities, both at the state headquarters and when touring the districts. This narrative does not chronicle the performance of individual government institutions. It seeks to provide a view of how the systems for governance functioned under a variety of conditions. Being a part of the management structure of the government, I could witness first-hand the impact of suspension of political activity in a democratic state. There was also opportunity to observe the behaviour of individual leaders in situations stressful and sedate. Surprisingly, even at a time when terror stalked the land, the machinery of administration proved resilient. The Secretariat was seen, in Shakespeare's phrase, to creep at its petty pace from day to day. In other words, it was business as usual.

The President Rules

When central rule began in 1983, the union government appointed four retired civil servants as Adviser to assist the Governor. The powers of the state council of ministers were now with a body called the Governor-in-Council, which consisted of the Governor, his advisers and the Chief Secretary. During the two spells of central rule (from 1983 to 1985 and from 1987 to 1992), the government frequently changed the Advisers, who enjoyed the status of ministers. Furthermore, during the decade there was a procession of as many as 10 Governors. Many felt that the incumbent heads of state were not given sufficient time to stand and deliver. In one important change in the year 1984, Mr K.D. Vasudeva, the Chief Secretary was replaced by Mr S.S. Dhanoa, an IAS officer from the Bihar cadre.[1]

The government did, of course, periodically move officers, including myself, from post to post, but civil administration functioned mostly in the same manner as it had learned to do under an elected authority. Amid the turmoil, the operations of the field agencies were seldom disrupted. During central rule, in the absence of elected ministers, the administrative secretaries had greater responsibility in decision making and execution. Certain codified rules of the government for allocation of business, and also delegation of powers, guided all authorities.

Under an elected government every minster is answerable to the council of ministers, headed by the Chief Minister. Every department has an established administrative apparatus for conduct of its duties. Most ministers are

---

1 S.S. Dhanoa worked as Chief Secretary, Punjab for less than two years (1983–85).

less interested in matters of strategic policy than in such mundane matters as postings, transfers and appointment of staff functionaries, including those in junior cadres. In India's democratic arrangement, local political leaders sponsor the pleas of staff for placement or promotion. The school education department, for example, has a cadre of teachers numbering around two lakhs. The minister is besieged with requests from teachers to be posted at stations convenient to them. The education minister spends an inordinate amount of time and energy in the process of such postings and transfers. Since there are many candidates vying for a limited number of positions that are considered 'desirable' or 'attractive' it is well-nigh impossible to accommodate every demand. The task is rendered more complex when the competing employees are backed by local leaders. At the same time, policy matters, such as improving the quality of instruction, are neglected. In the states, elected leaders are often compelled to give priority to the individual demands of their constituents.

During spells of the President's rule, the senior officers exercised greater authority than under an elected government. Along with power comes greater responsibility. Those at the helm needed to be carefully objective and unbiased, knowing that their decisions would be open for review by any incoming government. The Governor and his advisers accepted that the President's rule was a temporary arrangement, like a holding operation. In many important matters, they consciously avoided taking decisions, preferring to leave fresh initiatives for the elected leaders to take in due course. Central rule does not by itself make for speedier administrative decisions in government.

The empowered Governors did make efforts to secure better coordination at district level between the officers of the IAS and IPS, who worked as Deputy Commissioners and District Superintendents of Police respectively. Julio Ribeiro records that during his tenure as the DG of Police, Punjab, he specifically sought and received valuable inputs from the Deputy Commissioners of various districts, many of whom had an ear close to the ground. 'I knew that the DCs had more contact with the ordinary people than the police officers'.[2] In respect of public opinion in the villages and towns, he could obtain from the Deputy Commissioners certain information beyond what he received from the security agencies. In his book Ribeiro repeatedly stresses the importance of an integrated approach to governance, involving closely both the Deputy Commissioners and the district Superintendents of Police. He insisted[3] that Police Superintendents 'would continue to report to the DMs (District Magistrates) who were IAS officers'.

As part of my official duties, I toured various parts of the state extensively. For some time, Julio Ribeiro, who had been elevated as the Adviser to the Governor, was my immediate superior. Ribeiro felt that field visits of senior officers instilled in the public a sense of confidence. I recall one occasion

2 Julio Ribeiro, *My Life as a Police Officer*, Viking, 1998, p. 321.

3 Ibid., p. 321.

when I was to visit a technical institution in a little town, Sarhali, situated right on the international border in the district of Amritsar. On the day prior to my scheduled visit, terrorists had struck in the very town, killing some people. Ribeiro suggested that I go ahead with my planned tour, and so I did. Most senior government officials normally travelled without any accompanying security personnel for personal protection. In the border districts, however, the Deputy Commissioners insisted on deputing armed policemen to escort me in risk-prone areas. The three districts of Ferozepur, Amritsar and Gurdaspur abutting India's border with Pakistan were considered more 'disturbed' on account of terrorist activity. I was especially happy to visit Amritsar and Gurdaspur, since en route I could meet my parents, who were settled at Beas. The police provided armed escort to individuals in respect of whom they perceived some 'security threat'. These included personages such as the Governor and his Advisers, and some high-profile officials like the Chief Secretary and Home Secretary. Of course police officers on active duty were always protected, as also Deputy Commissioners heading the districts.

Reconstruction and After

Following Operation Blue Star[4] in June 1984, as the Administrative Secretary for the departments of the local

4 This was an operation led by the Indian army to dislodge armed militants who had taken control of the campus housing the Golden Temple, the holiest shrine of the Sikhs. Many commentators have written about the happenings, in which there were a number of deaths.

government, Housing and Urban Development, I was assigned two inter-related tasks in Amritsar city. Firstly, to mitigate huge human problems of many thousands of residents and shop owners, whose buildings in the periphery of the Golden Temple complex had recently been destroyed. All these families, who had lost their homes and livelihoods, had to be rehabilitated at the earliest. The second task was to improve the physical environment of the land surrounding the temple. This entailed removal of haphazardly constructed buildings, many of which were damaged or dilapidated, and the creation of a road (called a *galiara*, a street or corridor) all along the outer perimeter of the complex, to facilitate easy movement of traffic. As directed by the government, an integrated project to accomplish the twin objectives was prepared.

The Golden Temple complex is situated in the heart of the walled city of Amritsar. Over the years, hundreds of shops and congested houses had come up in narrow streets adjoining the temple. During the events concluding with Operation Blue Star most of the buildings in the immediate vicinity of the complex had been badly damaged or destroyed. All the shop owners and residents had wisely fled. These buildings, which were decaying and damaged, were in fact both a security hazard and an environmental blot. The SGPC,[5] as well as the government, had always wanted to

5 As explained in the previous chapter, Shiromani Gurdwara Prabandhak Committee (SGPC) is an elected, authorized institution for management of the Sikh temples, including the Golden Temple Complex, Amritsar.

create a corridor around the complex for free circulation of traffic and for convenience of pilgrims. They had baulked at displacing a large population, which would naturally oppose any move to dislodge it. The widespread damage to the properties during Operation Blue Star presented the window of an opportunity. Alongside the mopping up activities, the plan aimed 'to reconstruct, beautify and develop the entire area around the complex, including the damaged streets and buildings'.[6] It was noted that 'the deteriorating environment of the area surrounding the Golden Temple is a cause of alarm for the holy shrine itself'.[7]

I was fortunate to have as Housing Commissioner one of the most brilliant civil engineers in the state, a Chief Engineer by the name of N.S. Sodhi. Sodhi was imaginative, resourceful and scrupulously honest. He was a specialist in construction of buildings and roads. Sodhi had also worked for several years on an assignment in Iraq. In Iraq he had impressed a leader no less than the President, Saddam Hussain. With Sodhi's vital technical inputs a plan of action was presented to K.T. Satarawala, the new Governor in early July. This was a multi-disciplinary project. It entailed several parallel time-bound activities, for which formal involvement and consent of several different authorities under the various laws was necessary.

---

6 Project for Development of area surrounding Golden Temple Complex, Amritsar (1984) Government of Punjab, Departments of Town and Country Planning and Local Government.

7 Ibid.

These included:

1. The immediate compulsory acquisition of a substantial area of land under the Punjab Development of Damaged Areas Act, 1951. For this compensation was to be paid to each owner.
2. The demolition of structures deemed dangerous under the Punjab Municipal Act, 1976.
3. Re-establishment of business premises for all displaced persons. For this purpose, a new market for the displaced shopkeepers, 1800 in number, had to be developed. Within a month of the start of the project, the traders were firstly given temporary booths to begin sales. The same people were soon allotted permanent shops constructed by the Improvement Trust in an adjoining location. They could purchase the premises or take them on rent.
4. The construction of housing accommodation for 2400 families by N.S. Sodhi's Housing Board. The newly built houses and flats were offered for purchase to the concerned families. For this they used the monetary compensation received by them for the properties acquired by the state government.
5. The construction of a *galiara* (peripheral corridor) by the municipal corporation of Amritsar for free movement of traffic around the Golden Temple complex.

For the government, rehabilitating the displaced population was a matter of high priority. For the families ousted from the area, restoration of livelihood and housing was paramount. SGPC welcomed the initiative as it reduced congestion around the shrine.

It was no surprise that when we presented the project report to the Governor, he accorded approval on the spot. Two aspects of the integrated plan especially appealed to the Governor. Firstly, all activities were to be completed within a very short span in time of just 10 months. Secondly, direct financial liability of the government was minimal. Institutional finance was forthcoming for the householders and shopkeepers on easy commercial terms of loaning.

N.S. Sodhi, who was the key executor of the ambitious project, more than justified the faith that was reposed in him. He completed the construction activity within a span of nine months, that is, a month ahead of schedule. Likewise, the Municipal Corporation and the Improvement Trust adhered to their schedules. All owners of shops and houses moved to their new premises. The *galiara* corridor became functional, to the great relief of the visitors and the delight of the worshippers, who in the past had to struggle to reach the main entrance to the temple. SGPC was pleased too, that the vicinity of the shrine had been cleared of unsightly construction.

N.N. Vohra,[8] a senior IAS officer who was overseeing the project as the Home Secretary of the state government, heaped praise on Sodhi. The government is commonly notorious

---

8 N.N. Vohra was at that time Punjab Home Secretary. In due course he served as the Union Home Secretary and also distinguished himself as the Governor of the sensitive Jammu and Kashmir state.

for delays in execution and commissioning of its projects, which often results in overrun in terms of cost. That the project could be commissioned within the given framework of time and financial provision was considered remarkable. The promptitude and success of the project at Amritsar was possible because every stakeholder, be it the shop and house owners themselves, or the political and religious leaders, along with the government agencies involved, was equally determined to see its timely success. Not a single institution or individual tried to challenge the proceedings for demolition and land acquisition or the procedures for compensation. Even the terms of allotment of the properties were cheerfully accepted by the beneficiaries. N.S. Sodhi approached the project as a personal challenge and camped at Amritsar for weeks on end. All the main agencies involved being in my charge, I visited the sites of the work frequently, and reviewed the progress in the presence of representatives of the affected people. One lesson imbibed was that if all stakeholders are closely involved in the process of planning and execution, the pace of work can be accelerated. In a time crunch even the much maligned bureaucracy can rise to the occasion.

A Memorable Encounter

During the time I worked in the urban sector of the state, I had one wonderful elevating experience of an entirely different nature. This was an unexpected encounter in August 1984 with Mother Teresa of Calcutta,[9] the famous founder

9 The city of Calcutta is now known as Kolkata.

of the Missionaries of Charity. At that time, Mother Teresa was already revered for her charitable work in the slums of Calcutta. It was several years later that the Nobel Peace Prize and also the Bharat Ratna, India's highest honour, were to be conferred on her. After her death in 1997, the Roman Catholic Church was to anoint her as Saint Teresa of Calcutta.

I recall vividly that afternoon in my Secretariat office. As I was working on some routine files, my staff informed me that an important visitor, Mother Teresa herself, had come unannounced to meet me. I was so astounded at this unexpected visitor that I jumped out of my chair and literally ran out of my office to welcome the grand lady. I could hardly believe my eyes that here was the Mother in real life. She cut a shy, retiring image, clad in a rough white sari with her trademark navy blue border. She must have been just five feet in height. So tiny did she appear physically that I felt embarrassed to be seen to tower over her slight figure. I had to bend almost double to greet her as she offered to shake hands with me. What struck me most was a twinkle in her eyes. On observing my obvious discomfiture at her being required to wait outside my office, she wore an amused smile.

As we sat in my office, the Mother made a specific request for allotment of some land in the city of Jalandhar for her Mission to establish an orphanage. For her purpose, she had identified a small vacant plot belonging to the Improvement Trust of Jalandhar. The Trust authorities had rejected her request, as the rules did not permit it. She was now approaching me as my department controlled local urban institutions like the Jalandhar Improvement Trust. Mother Teresa appealed with utmost humility and innocence that she would be greatly obliged if I could assist her Mission. She had come from Calcutta specifically for this task, she said, for which she would stay for some days in Chandigarh if need be. She said that her organisation carried out purely charitable activities and might not be able to afford the market price of the land. She requested that the government might charge some concessional rate for giving land to the Mission. I immediately assured that I would call the papers from the Jalandhar office and then take a decision. She should be spared the odium of visiting government offices, I felt. I assured her that I would myself meet her at the place where she was staying in Chandigarh.

When I studied the papers, I found that the issue was not as straightforward as I had expected. The Trust in Jalandhar pointed out certain rules, which normally debarred permanent transfer of its properties located in certain areas of the city. As Secretary of the department, I was not empowered to allot the land that the mission wanted. On scrutinizing the rules, I discovered a clause whereby the government could relax the policy if the public interest so warranted. The power for relaxation lay with the minister of the department. Since there was no ministry at that time, the Governor could take a decision to relax the rules. By now I was determined that Mother Teresa's petty request must be granted. I immediately met the Governor to apprise him of the issue. What worthier cause could there be? So I reasoned. Her project promised vital relief to the downtrodden and distressed. As such the Mission was merely fulfilling the state's objective of social welfare. The Governor, Mr K.T. Satarawala, did not commit himself. He agreed, however, to meet Mother Teresa the next day to consider her request.

Thereafter, the matter took an interesting turn. Escorting the Mother to the Governor's office, I requested the great personality to join me in a harmless little conspiracy that I had hatched. I advised that she should plead with the Governor that I was not supporting her, and that I was, like bureaucrats, hidebound by the rules. My plan was that the Mother's plea might provoke a reaction with the Governor. In the process the Governor might be prepared to overrule me. I assured Mother Teresa that I would not mind being so overruled. I can never forget the hearty laugh that Mother Teresa had on hearing my proposition.

As we were ushered in to the Governor's office Mother Teresa departed from the unwritten text of the approach that I had suggested. 'The Secretary is trying his best!' she exclaimed, 'but he is afraid to take a decision.' I was stunned. She made no emotional plea, but left it to the Governor to decide. K.T. Satarawala closed the matter in a few seconds. 'Of course we will give you the land. And you don't have to pay for it.' Obviously the great lady understood men and matters far better than I did! As she left, the Mother left me a personal handwritten injunction on a chit of rough paper (that is all I could produce impromptu as an autograph book), which reads, 'Dear Rajan, God loves you. Love others as He loves you. God bless you. M Teresa mc 13.8.84'. That autograph on a scrap of the government's stationery is now a cherished possession. In the name of God, the Mother exhorted love and delivered selfless service to all.

A Leader in Hibernation

During the long stints of direct central rule in Punjab all political champions were perforce in a state of involuntary inactivity. Foremost among them was Sardar Parkash Singh Badal, the tallest leader of the Shiromani Akali Dal (SAD) party. Over the years, Mr Badal had stood in opposition to the policies and actions of the central government. On account of his critical views Mr Badal had spent several years in what was euphemistically termed 'preventive detention', that is, physical imprisonment that restricted his political activities. Evidently, the government of the day feared that Mr Badal might incite public disaffection. In the year 1975, when he strongly deprecated the imposition of a political emergency by the government of Mrs Indira Gandhi, Mr Badal had been jailed under the Maintenance of Internal Security Act. The emergency curtailed civil liberty. The two years that he spent in jail then had actually built up his public image as a fighter against oppression.

In the year 1985, although no longer in prison, Mr Badal did not join the short-lived coalition government (1985–87). The Chief Minister was Sardar Surjit Singh Barnala (1925–2017). Mr Barnala's term as Chief Minister of Punjab proved merely to be an interregnum in the prolonged period of central rule, which was resumed, and continued for another five years. It was a period of uneasy calm in an environment threatened by militancy. All the ministers were placed on the list of 'threatened' persons and were provided strong personal security. There was at that time a common joke in the public in regard to the visibility of ministers in the districts. If asked about the distance between, say, Chandigarh and Jalandhar, a pat answer would be 'two red lights!' For the uninitiated, this meant that along the 100-mile-long journey, a traveller was likely to encounter at least two convoys of ministers, whose official vehicles carried a red beacon, along with other conspicuous security cover. That so many ministers were bold enough to travel in the field would have reassured the common man that a visible government was well in control of administration.

Barnala is the name of Mr Surjit Singh's home town, and technically not his surname. In the same way, Mr Parkash Singh (born 1927) is a Dhillon, which is a sub-caste of the Jat Sikhs, but he is known by the name of his village Badal in the district of Muktsar. A common practice in Punjab is for leaders to append to their first name the name of their village or locality. Surnames often connote the social background. Since the time of the tenth Sikh Guru, many adherents to the faith do not mention the caste into which they were born. This tradition seeks to promote equality in the communities. Suave, soft spoken and moderate, Mr Badal is famed for never having lost his cool, despite gravest provocation. He has been honoured by the highest bodies of Sikh temporal power and by the Akali Dal party, which he headed as President for many years. In the year 2015, the Government of India bestowed on Mr Badal the Padma Vibhushan, the second highest award in the country.

In the year 1987, following some violent incidents of militancy, Mr Barnala's government was dismissed. When Mr Badal strongly condemned this decision, the Government again decided to isolate him as a prisoner in jail. Only this time he was not sent to regular prison, but was incarcerated in a government building, which was notified as a special jail.

Over his long political career Mr Badal occupied the chair of the Chief Minister of Punjab in five different terms between 1970 and 2017. In between, on the three occasions that his party lost elections to the state legislature (in the years 1983, 2002 and 2017) he functioned as leader of the opposition. He moved insouciantly from jail to assume the hyperactive duties of head of the state government. While I worked with him officially on many occasions, one unique encounter that I had with him dates to the autumn of 1988. Our meeting took place in unusual surroundings. He was at that time not the Chief Minister, but was undergoing one of his spells of preventive detention. My visit to Kadwapani (the Hindi word means literally 'bitter water') in a forest rest house in the heart of the expansive Rajaji National Park (a protected forest sanctuary) was fortuitous. It transpired that at that time, the District Magistrate of Dehradun, within whose administrative jurisdiction the rest house was located, was Vibha Puri, an IAS officer, who was my own sister-in-law. Vibha heeded my plea that I be allowed to meet the detained VIP. A stickler for propriety and protocol, Vibha verified from the rule book that a political detainee could receive personal visitors. Since I was one, she permitted my request.

At first glance, the premises resembled a holiday resort surrounded by the woods, not a detention centre for columnists who threatened peace and tranquility of the country. The police guard at the entrance nonchalantly waved in the flagged car of the DM. Mr Badal was astonished to find me in his secluded verdant retreat. He was effusive in praise of the DM, who controlled the so designated special jail. '*Biba* (an endearment in the Punjabi language for a young daughter) has given me every facility that I demanded,' he remarked. Vibha interjected that the demands of her VIP prisoner were petty, which were easily met. It seems that Mr Badal had merely requested to be given some implements for gardening operations and some fertilisers, to create a functional kitchen garden. Ironically, and fittingly too, the foremost leader of the most progressive agriculturists in India was manually toiling in a makeshift miniature farm. He proudly showed us the blooming patch of greens that he had personally developed. 'An ideal prisoner!' is what Vibha termed her distinguished guest. Apparently, vegetables from the garden were offered to the jailors (his security guards) for their consumption. When I remarked that Mr Badal was looking well, he came out with a startling observation, 'This prison suits me just fine. See, I have shed at least 15 pounds of body weight. Every morning and evening I play badminton with my guards.' Indeed, the palatial lawns boasted of an open-air badminton court. In parting, Mr Badal made an open offer to *Biba*. 'Please tell me if I can do anything for you, in this state or in the Government of India.'

As we headed back to Dehradun, it struck me that Mr Badal was considered his imprisonment an undisguised blessing. Here he was, enjoying his sojourn into practical horticulture and indulging his passion for physical fitness. Amidst the salubrious surroundings, he had come into his own. Earning future political capital from his temporary placement in the park would have been a fringe benefit. He was to emerge rejuvenated after the period of forced hibernation.

In the Citadel as a Player

I had worked earlier in the Raj Bhavan for one year as a member of the Governor's staff. Now, some three years later, I was welcomed as a frequent guest in the same premises. This transpired during the period between 1986 and 1989 when Siddhartha Shankar Ray was Governor of Punjab. In the prevailing security environment Raj Bhavan had become a fortified citadel. My privileged entry to the precincts was solely on account of Mr Ray's keen interest in the game of tennis.

Siddhartha Ray was a multifaceted personality. An aristocrat and one of India's top lawyers, Ray had served as

Chief Minister of the state of West Bengal. He had impressive lineage, being a grandson of Chittaranjan Das, the famous freedom fighter and nationalist. What distinguished Ray from his predecessors at Raj Bhavan was his avid interest in sports. In his university days Ray had been an outstanding footballer and cricketer. Here in Chandigarh, he decided to patronize the game of lawn tennis, in playing which he displayed flair even when he was well past 60 years in age. I happened to be among the few civil officers at Chandigarh who played the game regularly. I also happened to be the elected President of the local tennis association. Within months of coming to Chandigarh, Ray established quality grass courts over the expansive lawns right in front of the Governor's residential quarters. A number of other tennis enthusiasts were invited often to join the Governor for a few sets of friendly tennis matches in the late afternoon. As a serving officer, an invitation from the Governor was in the nature of an official command. The other players, whose profession was outside government, naturally considered it a rare honour to enter the Raj Bhavan.

Every evening, winter or summer, if he was in town, the Governor would receive us on the tennis lawns. The sojourn to the Raj Bhavan was a special social occasion as much as it was a sporting gathering. The players included teachers, officers from the defence services, civil servants like me and some judges of the High Court of Punjab and Haryana. Ray and his wife Maya were gracious hosts. They invited the spouses of the players too to join the garden party. On the sidelines of the sporting activity Mrs Maya Ray, whom we could address as Maya *di* looked after the guests with solicitude. Some young upstarts even began to address the Governor as Manu *da*. I myself never took any such liberty. In that setting I considered myself a government official on duty and scrupulously avoided any overt familiarity with the hosts. I think the Rays appreciated the correctness of my behaviour, and that of my wife Meena, who likewise looked up to Maya Ray as an esteemed senior, and never as an equal. The Rays were a highly sophisticated couple. Maya Ray had lived for many years in England and displayed social grace typical of British nobility. Every single guest received her personal attention, which endeared her to everyone.

During the first year of the Governorship of S.S. Ray, Surjit Singh Barnala's Akali government was in power. In May 1987, the tenure of Barnala was cut short, and the state of Punjab came again under the President's rule, which was to last for five years. Ray was now head of government also, with vastly increased responsibilities. Despite his official preoccupations the tennis evenings, crowned with great hospitality, continued. Many important political leaders were given appointments to meet the Governor on the Raj Bhavan lawns adjacent to the tennis court. I reckon that several crucial confabulations affecting the state, and even, perhaps, the country, were held within my vision, although out of my earshot. The interlocutors sat in chairs placed just a few meters from a corner of the tennis lawn where players might run to retrieve a deep forehand shot. This was Ray's adaptation of the phrase, 'The show must go on.' Only the show here was defined as was an evening of social tennis featuring the Governor's guests. Concurrently a more important, discreet, super show featuring the Governor and his political visitors was being conducted in secrecy under the open skies. The visitors included union ministers and foreign dignitaries too.

As one group of four players concluded their game, Ray would leave the VIPs (his very important political guests) to enjoy their cucumber sandwiches, and with his trademark direction, 'Come along!' urge his partner, a college lecturer named Subhash Marriya, to enter the arena with him. After playing one set of tennis, the Governor would return to his official engagement outside the open court, as it were. At times important persons linked to security, such as Lieutenant General P.N. Hoon, General Officer Commanding in Chief, Western Army Command and Julio Ribeiro, Director General Police, later Security Adviser, would take to the courts. The Governor's entourage of tennis players accompanied him to evenings in the headquarters of the Army Western Command and to the tennis courts of the High Court nearby.

Ray's tennis team of some 10 or 15 players travelled with him to various district towns in Punjab for playing a series of friendly matches with local adversaries. Unfazed by incidents of terrorism in some parts of Punjab, Ray would compete, with his team, in a series of doubles tennis matches with the opposing team, cheered by the wives of the players as spectators. Whichever town we visited, Patiala, Ludhiana, Jalandhar or Amritsar, we enjoyed hospitality worthy of friends of the Governor, our captain. During these tours it seemed to his team of players that Ray's primary interest was the game, and that he was managing to combine official work with sporting activity. Actually, he was adroitly using the platform of sport to reach out informally to many segments in society. After the sporting engagement ended, the Governor would confabulate separately with numerous delegations and individuals. Ray was endowed with great physical and mental energy.

I once took the liberty of inviting Mr and Mrs Ray home for lunch. The other invitees were mainly from the tennis group, and their spouses. The Governor's adviser, Julio Ribeiro, and his wife Melba also accepted our invitation. We faced some commotion at home before the guests arrived, as an elaborate security apparatus was brought in place to ensure foolproof security for the guest of honour. Every inch of our small house was meticulously combed by the security men, who even had sniffer dogs as part of their regimen. Seeing the house teeming with uniformed policemen was a new experience for our children. When we sat with our guests in our little lawn the team of snoopers had miraculously disappeared. During their mission the security personnel had intruded on the privacy of my home, but the security cover that protected our guests was unobtrusive.

I had to delicately balance my position as an officer of the Punjab government with my membership of the inner circle of the head of state and government. My colleagues were somewhat surprised that despite my being the Governor's tennis partner, the work he entrusted to me was comparatively low profile. During Ray's time, I was Secretary for Science, Technology and Environment, an assignment that I found interesting and challenging, although it did not confer on me significant authority or patronage. There was never even a murmur in the corridors that my proximity to Ray had earned me any official privileges. Rather, in all official dealings, I was hard put to deliberately maintain a discreet distance from the Governor.

Decentralisation under Central Rule

During the last two years of the President's rule, that is, from 1990 to 1992, the government adopted a strategy to systematically empower elected institutions at district, block and village level to plan and execute smaller development projects locally. In towns the municipal local bodies, and in rural areas, the elected institutions in the three-tier structure of 'Panchayat Raj'[10] were accorded unprecedented authority and responsibility. As much as one-third of the annual

10 Panchayats in India have existed from ancient times. Each 'panchayat' was traditionally a body of five village leaders, chosen to manage affairs of immediate concern to the population of the respective village. The number of members of a panchayat is now not limited to five persons. In Punjab there is a panchayat for every village, and the size of this executive body is determined by the population of the village. The Constitution of India enshrines a commitment to a strong three-tier system of Gram Panchayat in the village, Panchayat Samiti in a development block and a Zila Parishad in every district. 'Panchayat Raj' connotes governance by the locally elected institutions in the rural areas of the country.

development budget was placed at the disposal of the elected local bodies in towns and villages. An institutional arrangement authorized local self-governing bodies to plan and execute small development projects of primary concern to them, without reference to the departmental authorities at the state headquarters. At a time when political activity was in limbo, the government was anxious to involve grassroot leadership in development activity. The measure was expected to energise elected leaders in villages and towns alike. The district administration, under the respective Deputy Commissioner played a major role in the process.

It was Ray's successor, Nirmal Kumar Mukherji, a former ICS officer, who appointed me as Secretary for Rural Development and Panchayats, a position that gave me insight into the working of village institutions in Punjab. Unlike Ray, who was a flamboyant personality, Mukherji maintained a low profile in his short (six month) stay as Governor, Punjab. Mukherji's focus was on building up democracy at the lowest, grassroot or village level. I had occasion to meet Mukherji just once, and that too for a few minutes only. He told me that, in my appointment, he expected me to bring into the mainstream of governance all the elected village institutions in the state. During the financial year 1990–91, an amount of Rs 320 crores, that is, more than one-third of the total plan budget of Rs 900 crores, had been allocated for expenditure on what was called decentralized planning. Mukherji's plan was that while the state was under central rule, the rural population should be reassured that it was directly administering all government-funded development activity.

Every department of government is obviously delighted if large funds in the state's budget are formally allocated to it. It was clear that the substantial amount of money placed at my disposal did not constitute largesse for discretionary spending. For me as Secretary for the department of Rural Development and Panchayats, it presented a major challenge. It meant creating systems for the village institutions to objectively determine and plan their immediate needs. Equally important was establishing a transparent mechanism for appraisal of every project, and also providing effective safeguards to check possible fraud and misuse of funds. In the existing arrangement the panchayats (numbering more than 12,000 in the state) enjoyed little authority to plan or execute work. Officials of the Rural Development department were used to preparing projects at the behest of their superiors in the state capital. It was the Minister who decided how available funds were distributed within the state. It was the headquarters that determined which district or development block or village would be favoured even in such petty matters as the paving of streets or construction of storm water drains. Most importantly, the sanctioned works were constructed by government engineers. The engineering code has standard operating procedures for all construction activity. All projects are undertaken by selected private contractors; the government engineers are merely supervisors, the cost of supervision being inbuilt into the project estimates. In practice, small projects executed on government contract cost substantially more than if these were to be handled by an individual or a local institution.

Fortunately, I held charge of the department of Science and Technology along with that of Rural Development. Integrating the skills of the staff from both departments, we managed to develop Management Information Systems (MIS) for each individual project. According to the guidelines of the department of Planning and the department of Rural Development, all panchayats were authorized to spend up to five lakh rupees for each individual work. For larger projects the authority was with the next higher tiers in the panchayat hierarchy, the Block Samiti, or the Zila Parishad. The role of engineers of the rural department was to prepare the technical project. The village panchayat concerned carried out construction on its own, with technical guidance of the engineers. In order to involve the entire community, the project was to be approved by the general body of the population of the village, called the Gram Sabha, while the executive body, that is, the panchayat carried out the actual construction. The progress of the works was monitored by the MIS reports that the panchayat submitted periodically. A coloured wooden board at the site of every minor work announced to the passerby such details as the name of the *sarpanch* (village headman), the date of commencement and progress every day and even the number of labourers engaged. This boosted the morale of the village body.

Considering that the set of procedures was uniformly adopted in hundreds of village projects in all districts of the state, it was a mammoth accomplishment that the entire budget allocated was spent expeditiously. This is obviously not the place to make a technical evaluation of the experiment. The Deputy Commissioners, who monitored the progress within their districts, reported that the village communities were enthusiastic that they themselves were deciding on what the villages wanted and were even more delighted to take responsibility for actual execution of the task. The economy and the promptness with which the work in the villages was accomplished were astonishing. For example, an amount of Rs 99,000 was given to a panchayat for construction of a three-room primary school. With local labour, paid and voluntary, the village panchayat completed the construction at two-thirds of the cost and that too within a period of three months. The government engineers usually took more than two years for commissioning such buildings, and demanded additional money to meet any overrun on cost. Likewise, minor projects like construction of little bridges over rivulets and the paving of streets and providing drains for waste water were done at low cost, as the villagers offered voluntary labour. Any village body saving money allocated to it could use the surplus for other small schemes of its choice.

It was a vision of Governor N.K. Mukherji that fired the state's initiative to empower the local communities. At the outset there were apprehensions by many, especially the engineers, that entrusting authority to the village community would lead to widespread financial bungling, and to poor quality of execution. When the accounts were audited no defalcation came to light. The engineers themselves agreed that by and large the quality of construction too was satisfactory. In June 1990 Mukherji had already left his position as Governor. He was not there to observe the results of his initiative.

It was expected that any elected government would take forward the successful attempt at decentralization. Sadly, such expectation was belied. I happened to work as the Finance Secretary, in 1992, with the Congress government led by Sardar Beant Singh and again in 1998 with the Akali led government of Sardar Parkash Singh Badal. As political adversaries the two governments differed with each other on many matters of policy, but both were unanimous in discarding Mukherji's experiment with decentralization. During the two years 1990–92 every district Planning Board that approved village projects consisted of more than 60 heads of panchayats selected from all the development blocks in the respective district. The elected government dismantled the panchayat dominated boards, and replaced them with committees with Members of Parliament and Members of the Legislative Assembly. The reasons why the state government has been less than enthusiastic about decentralisation and delegation of authority are not far to seek.

Wielding the Reins of Power

A democracy rides on effective governance at three levels, at the centre, in the states and by the local community. Nations such as the USA and UK derive their strength from grassroots institutions, variously termed as counties, city councils or boroughs. These elected local bodies in towns and villages wield authority for taxation, development and regulation, police administration and even adjudication in respect of local laws. After the tragic events in the USA of 11 September 2001 the world witnessed the astounding sight of Rudy Guiliani, mayor of New York City commanding emergency relief measures from centre stage, even as President Bush stood meekly by in the background. It was clear that within the jurisdiction of the local body concerned, the elected Mayor of the city and not the President of the most powerful nation on earth called the shots.

In India, by contrast, the organs of local self-government, municipal councils in towns, and panchayats in rural areas, are the weakest of the three tiers of government. Inspired by Mahatma Gandhi's concept of the village as a republic, Panchayat Raj has been accorded much lip service in India, but in most states, including Punjab, panchayats have few financial or administrative powers. They function as poor handmaidens of state political leaders.

Many states plead for autonomy in relation to the national government, but stoutly resist decentralization from state to village. The unwritten approach has been 'state powers good, village powers bad'. In the states, many elected panchayats are suspended, under government orders, on some ground or other. Suspension of an elected local body, and placing it under some small government functionary, is akin to imposition of the President's Rule in a state. Public perception is that the real authority lies at the state headquarters. Consequently, there is hardly a murmur of protest when hundreds of panchayat secretaries, who are technically employees of panchayats, are recruited, not by the panchayats, but under orders of the state government.

For decades 'Panchayat Raj' has remained merely a national slogan. The year 1992 saw the government legislate the 73rd amendment to the Constitution of India to strengthen and empower the panchayat bodies, then numbering 496 Zila Parishads, 5905 Block Samitis and 230762 village panchayats. For effective empowerment, the states were expected to enact appropriate state laws, and to implement them. The states have shown little alacrity in this regard. The reform measures have so far been mainly cosmetic. These include the reservation of leadership in the village institutions for women and members of the scheduled castes, the establishment of State Election Commissions to conduct panchayat elections and the setting up of State Finance Commissions to improve the finances.

There is still no substantial devolution of financial and administrative power to the local bodies. Village folk are concerned primarily with issues of schooling, healthcare, welfare and services for their day-to-day existence. The key functionaries that can help to fulfil these basic needs, such as school teachers, medical and veterinary staff, rural water supply officials, agriculture inspectors and even engineers engaged in rural projects continue to be answerable to their departmental superiors. In the absence of control of elected bodies at district and village level, absenteeism of government employees is rife. The local panchayat, for example, has no institutional link with the village school or with service departments.

Authority at state level is self-perpetuating. Departmental heads and lower staff prefer to report to bosses who are removed from the field. Their accountability would improve if their performance were to be appraised in the field by legally chosen democratic bodies. A common argument against empowerment of panchayats is that village leaders are unskilled and untrustworthy. It is wrong to doubt the competence and integrity of local bodies without affording them an opportunity to perform. Graft is less likely when members of the community, who are in the immediate vicinity, are themselves vigilant.

My exciting assignment in the rural sector lasted two years. In early 1992 the newly elected government of Sardar Beant Singh gave me responsibility to manage the finances of the state.

The World of Tennis

Alongside official duties, I became busy with sports management. For many years, starting 1986, I worked as President of Chandigarh Lawn Tennis Association (CLTA).

This honorary position, to which I was elected unanimously, presented an opportunity. In January, 1987 the Chandigarh administration allotted on lease with CLTA a tennis stadium complex that was ideal for tennis related activities. A team of trained coaches, led initially by Wing Commander Beyant Singh, a former tennis champion from the armed forces, established a good training scheme for young boys and girls. As per a project of International Tennis Federation, training began when the children were as young as four or five years in age. There were soon as many as 400 enthusiastic children on the rolls. As this was a non-profit organization, the training charges were kept low.

Tennis in India was traditionally regarded as an elite sport, limited to children of well-to-do families. As an experiment in social equity, it was decided to admit children from poorer sections of society in the programme. A residential facility, called Chandigarh Academy for Rural Tennis (CHART) was set up within the campus for a small group of children from low-income families, for whom the association bore the entire cost of board, lodging, training and schooling. The source of recruitment was an untapped reservoir of raw talent, namely the villages of Punjab and Haryana. Selection was made primarily on attributes of physique, fitness and aptitude as per internationally accepted parameters for young athletes. Starting from scratch, the faculty worked to mould and groom these recruits to attain their potential as tennis players. These prize children lived in dormitories in the stadium premises and adhered to a strict regimen of training and fitness. To begin with, CHART admitted every year six to eight boys (after some years girls too joined). With the very first batch, there were some unexpected problems. The boys were physically gifted, no doubt, but were unused to the discipline and unfamiliar surroundings of a hostel in a city. One of the boys from Ferozepur district of Punjab, who had probably never slept in a cosy room in his life, could not cope with the rigours at school and in the hostel. One evening, to the dismay of the hostel warden, he was found missing from the dormitory. Thankfully, with the help of the police, he was traced from his village. Within a few years, the experiment in social engineering in sports began to show visible results. Two of the boys, Robin Dhingra and Birbal Wadhera, who were the sons of simple gardeners, became champions at the junior level. Robin was crowned Asian Junior champion. He qualified as a trained coach, and is presently training players in Melbourne, Australia. Birbal works as a lecturer in the sports department of Panjab University, Chandigarh. A far cry from their humble beginnings!

After some time, the Indian Army's Western Command sent a dozen children of soldiers for training. The academy acquired an international dimension when Commonwealth Youth Centre requested admission for selected children from nine countries in the region. The success of the tennis projects was guided by a brilliant trainer by the name of Kawaljeet Singh, who was persuaded to relocate in Chandigarh as Chief Coach, from the distant state of Assam, where he worked. Kawaljeet was on the panel of Tutors of International Tennis Federation. He was so highly regarded in tennis circles that the association agreed to pay him the substantial level of emoluments that he could command in the market. This expenditure justified itself soon enough. The most spectacular results of Kawaljeet's training methods were seen in the year 1999. That year, at the age of 16, Sunil Kumar, a village boy from Kapurthala in Punjab was crowned the youngest ever national grass court champion in the open, senior category. Sunil had joined CHART in the year 1993, at the age of nine years. The same year Kawaljeet's trainees bagged the national titles in the age groups of 18 years and 16 years too, making it a hat-trick of winners from the city.

Over the years, CLTA conducted in Chandigarh numerous international events, including three ties of the Davis Cup. We have many friends and associates from the sports fraternity. The association is linked with several sports institutions abroad. But the most notable has been the partnership with several Spanish sports institutions for training the promising children from Chandigarh at centres in Spain. CLTA's honorary international adviser from Spain, Javier Sansierra, coordinates the collaborations.

I was fortunate to be involved in the management of the game at Chandigarh for more than 30 years, as President, as Chairman and as an adviser. I am also a Vice President of the national body, All India Tennis Association. My link with tennis has continued even after I retired from the government service.

REVOLVING CHAIRS

As officials in a state rise in seniority, they could occupy the position of an administrative secretary. Since a number of individuals attain this rank, the state government, at its pleasure, moves the civil servants from one position to another. For an observer, the shuffling of officers is amusingly like that of guests around a dining table at a mad tea party described in the novel, *Alice in Wonderland*. In the fantasy, every quaint character unquestioningly occupies the chair allotted. In the real life of governance too, every government functionary must handle the portfolio allotted to him or her. For 21 years that I worked as a Secretary to the state government, I was moving around the administrative table.

The assignments with the government entailed diverse tasks. At home, one could count numerous blessings, especially a cheerful household. Sir John Bowring, the British political economist had observed, 'A happy family is but an earlier heaven.' Being based in the city of Chandigarh was convenient. Meena was settled at her teaching job in the city, which meant that her salary augmented the family income. Certain vicissitudes struck our family, as they do any other.

Thus there was an anxious time in the year 1984, during which Meena suffered from breast cancer and its effects. Fortunately, she recovered well, bravely not missing her college even as she endured drastic treatment measures. At this stage, we could watch the grown-up children progressing through life. Bini managed to secure a good first division at all levels in school and college, and she was even the university topper in the examination for Master of Business Administration. She also played basketball for the university team and persisted with her training in music. At the age of 22, she was married in a simple ceremony at Beas. It was my mother who arranged the match with Shivinder, a professional dentist in the UK. The bridegroom's party consisted of just two dozen guests. In 1991, shortly after the wedding, she moved abroad.

As for my son, Anurag, he faced a happy choice after completing high school. He was selected to join the Indian army as a cadet in National Defence Academy and he also secured admission in an engineering institution in Chandigarh. He preferred the engineering course. While at college, he was struck with a passion for sports in a manner that caused us anxiety. His captaining the university tennis team was of course a matter of pride. His certification under the regulations of International Tennis Federation as a qualified coach was equally welcome. As conservative parents however, we drew the line when he declared that he wished to become a professional tennis coach. To this day, he has not forgiven us for dissuading him at that early stage of life from his preferred vocation. After earning degrees in engineering and an MBA, he worked in the corporate sector for close to 15 years, rising to be the Vice President of a reputed company, but his heart was never in business. Against our wishes, which no longer counted, he threw up his attractive job in Delhi to set up an NGO. He is now happy to be working quietly for the welfare of rag pickers and slum dwellers, helping them with livelihood, and also in the field of healthcare.

As the rest of the family was busy with their interests, there was plenty of variety and excitement in my own vocation as an official of government.

Flitting in the Corridors

With years I found myself among the senior-most officers in the country. At that time fresh entrants to the IAS had to be between 21 and 24 years old. I had turned 21 just two days before the date stipulated as minimum for eligibility. I was possibly the youngest ever in history to join the service. In the year 1998, the age of retirement too was raised from 58 years to 60. With this, I was to serve the government for a period of more than 38 years. My own batchmates, as well as many colleagues who joined service several years later than I, retired before I did. Despite this apparent advantage of age, I was destined to occupy the post of Chief Secretary for just a few months. This was at the end of my days as a civil servant. For six years, some officers, lower in the gradation list, held that coveted position ahead of me, despite my service record being equally good. The consolation was that I received the emoluments of the top post from the day my lower-ranked colleagues did, although I was not formally seated at the head of the table.

One low-profile department that I handled was linked with science, technology and environment. The job was futuristic in its orientation. It offered scope for some innovation and creative activity. There was an opportunity to establish from scratch several institutions in important scientific disciplines. While the government promoted them, these bodies were designed, by their memoranda of association, to function autonomously. It is necessary to insulate highly qualified technocrats, who manage scientific institutions from extraneous influences, especially of government functionaries. Powerful leaders are tempted to foist and support persons of comparatively low merit on public institutions. Such organisations needed to be nurtured with care. One such body was the Punjab State Council for Science and Technology, which cultivated a scientific temper by promoting suitable projects in the state. Another, the Punjab Energy Development Agency (PEDA) was charged with development and adoption of new and renewable energies. Internationally, there is a growing emphasis on environmental sustainability of economic development. In consonance with India's national policy, PEDA became a fulcrum for projects of generation of solar energy and for conversion of wastes into energy. A world-class science museum displaying modern exhibits was established in

Kapurthala for scientific orientation of the youth. This was the Pushpa Gujral Science City, an initiative of Inder Kumar Gujral, then India's Prime Minister. Then there was the state Pollution Control Board, which had to be energized for fair and effective regulation.

It transpired that when I was assigned some so-called 'powerful' posts I often happened to have differences with my superiors, the ministers. The administrative secretary handling self-governing bodies for towns and villages, or institutions in the cooperative sector has authority of control over many cadres of personnel and also large financial resources. Likewise, ministers covet portfolios such as irrigation and power, and health and education for their considerable scope for patronage. These politically sensitive assignments hold the seeds of discord between the minister and the secretary. Where disagreement between civil servant and political superior persists, the government discreetly, or unceremoniously, as one could regard it, shifts the officer concerned to another charge. Such lateral movement is deemed a 'hazard' of the profession.

For resolving conflict between civil servant and minister, the standing rules for conduct of government provide for the Chief Minister to intervene. Technically, the secretary concerned is allowed to refer any intractable issues to the Chief Minister, through the Chief Secretary. In practice this is an option of last resort. Most officers and ministers establish a form of mutual understanding; tensions do not always come to a head. The popular television series *Yes*

Minister satirically captures the essence of the relationship between ministers and bureaucrats in the realm of the British government. Similar cut and thrust is common in the functioning of governments in India. Both partners in the power equation, the minister and the secretary, are continually competing for space. On some rare occasions I was compelled to appeal for the Chief Minister's intervention to resolve the internal conflicts. The Chief Minister of the day usually decided such issues in favour of the minister, except where the stand of the minister appeared to be patently unfair or illegal. In a situation where the minister concerned does not enjoy complete backing of the Chief Minister or is seen as a threat to the hegemony of the latter, the secretary's position is upheld. Such a denouement, upholding the bureaucrat's position, is rare, usually engendering a simmering tension. In most cases the Chief Minister adroitly transfers charge of the department to another colleague, with whom the minster is happier to work. For the officer concerned, a high profile portfolio, and one designated, in colloquial Punjabi, as a *khudda line* (meaning 'sidelined') job carries the same emoluments. In my case, the question whether I had been kicked upstairs or downstairs was a matter of public perception. It was a gentleman's game, played usually without public exhibition of acrimony. Working amid such tensions requires a civil servant to maintain a degree of detachment. He also needs to subdue the human frailty of egoism. In the power game the Chief Minister of the day is sometimes pleased to watch some officers and their ministers squirming, being at loggerheads with one another.

It transpired then that the two hugely contrasting portfolios that I handled for longish periods (each more than five years) were of Science, Technology and Environment on one side and Finance on the other. The former position offered limited authority in terms of management of men and money; the incumbent performs away from the limelight. The Finance Secretary of a state, on the other hand, is a visible symbol of government's authority; he commands awe and grudging respect within the state and outside. As a critical pillar of the establishment, he carries a burden of great responsibility.

Professor A.P.J. Abdul Kalam: A Giant who Breathed Science

I worked in the sector of Science and Technology (S&T) for more than six years, an unusually long period, in three separate stints. Engagement with S&T activities accorded one stupendous opportunity. In the year 2000, I was privileged to meet and interact frequently with Dr A.P.J. Abdul Kalam, who was at that time the Scientific Adviser to the Prime Minister of India. Dr Kalam had earlier carried out pioneering work in missile systems as Chairman of the Indian Space Research Organisation (ISRO) and in the development of India's nuclear weapons. As I was involved with several projects of scientific research and development in the state, I made a request to meet him in his office. His office fixed an appointment quite promptly. The duration of my time slot, so his secretary conveyed, was 15 minutes. I had drawn up a list of items for Dr Kalam's guidance and support. He was pleased that I had prepared well for the meeting; the matters interested him. Our first meeting lasted 75 minutes, five times longer than scheduled.

He was all by himself when I entered his room in the Vigyan Bhawan complex on Maulana Azad Road in New Delhi. A man of less than medium height (he was probably five feet and five inches tall), he sported long locks of salt and pepper hair. He was wearing a full sleeved navy blue shirt and cream trousers. This was the apparel he chose to wear always, even later during the five years from 2002 to 2007, when he was to serve as President of India. True to Professor Kalam's own ideals of Gandhian austerity, the office was spartan in terms of furniture: a writing desk with no clutter of papers or files and a sofa set discreetly placed in a corner. This was the turf of a giant of India's scientific community! He called in his aide, introducing me to him with a smile, 'Meet another Rajan.' His colleague was Professor Y.S. Rajan, a tall, bearded and bespectacled scientist. Rajan had assisted Dr Kalam in many of his projects, and they had together co-authored some books. As I began to speak, Professor Kalam interjected that he had carefully read the background note sent to his office in advance. I apprised Dr Kalam that a major concern for the state of Punjab was that, despite comparative prosperity of the farming community, the living conditions in rural areas continued to be poor. Could scientific application help in upgrading the quality of life and infrastructure in the villages? In a happy coincidence, this was exactly an area on which Dr Kalam was focused at that time. Dr Rajan informed me that Dr Kalam had submitted to the Government of India a document detailing his vision for India of the year 2020. His model aimed at establishing communication and infrastructure in villages that could match the facilities in good towns. He was confident that the Prime Minster would agree to his suggestions for systematically transforming the rural landscape at least in some parts of India. It was a most stimulating discussion. As the meeting extended beyond its schedule Dr Kalam waved aside his harried personal secretary, who pleaded that the next visitor was waiting.

This was the first in a series of interactions that I was privileged to have with the great man, who was ordained shortly to be India's Head of State. Dr Kalam promised to visit Punjab and even to be the honorary Patron of the Science City project in Kapurthala district that the state government was establishing. Some months later, Dr Kalam even met Sardar Parkash Singh Badal, who was then Chief Minister of Punjab to present his vision for the state as it could be in the year 2020. I was summoned from Chandigarh to join the Chief Minister at Kapurthala House, New Delhi, where Dr Kalam and Dr Rajan made a presentation for the state of Punjab. After reviewing the economic potential of the state, a specific proposal emerged. If Mr Badal so wished, Dr Kalam was prepared to design and install an institutional framework based on application of science and technology to overhaul the rural infrastructure in the state. Dr Kalam even suggested that the Government of India could give financial support for the visionary project. It is my lasting lament that Mr Badal did not seize the glorious offer of Dr Kalam on his model of rural development for Punjab. As it was, Mr Badal became preoccupied with the forthcoming state elections. In early 2002, he was no longer the Chief Minister. Eventually Dr Kalam's ambitious plan for the state could not take off. At the same point in time, he was unexpectedly catapulted to the position of President of India. The blueprint of rural India's transformation with the application of modern technology in the span of 20 years remained on the shelves of the Planning Commission of India.

The state government did try to establish some village projects in line with Dr Kalam's vision. On my request, Professor Kalam visited Kapurthala to see the Science City project. There he spent a full day to study the plans, and gave us a perception of science and its application. His total involvement in the discussions with young scientists on a single project of S&T was something beyond our imagination. Dr Kalam lived and breathed science. No detail was too trivial for his attention. He suggested that the Science City should have a section on the development of armaments in India. We were astonished to learn from him that the first military leader of the world to develop and use rockets was Tipu Sultan in his battle against the British in Seringapatam,

Mysore, in 1799. Tipu Sultan had in fact established a rocket corps as part of his war effort. Tipu's technology was adapted by the victorious East India Company for further research and development in Britain, so Dr Kalam explained.

In regard to India's defense and nuclear programmes, Dr Kalam was conspicuously reticent. About his days at ISRO, he refused to comment altogether. Between the lines, one could read that, for India's top defence scientist, those past days were over and hence irrelevant. He would never allow any mention of his own contribution to India's defence projects. He preferred to live in the present, and to speak rather about the development of the scientific temper among children. He suggested several projects for popularising science through exhibits in the Science City, and for refinement of the curriculum for teaching science in schools. It was a privilege to be in the exclusive company of Dr Kalam for more than a day. For four hours we travelled together by car from Chandigarh to Kapurthala (a distance of about 200 kilometers). I learnt that Kalam was a strict vegetarian and teetotaler. 'My brahmin friend (YS Rajan who was also in our car) is a non-vegetarian,' he observed smilingly. Dr Kalam was quite happy to speak about his childhood in a fishing village near Rameshwaram on the Coromandel Coast in Tamil Nadu. He even agreed to allow the Science City to display snippets from his schooldays as exhibits.

It was an honour that Dr Kalam accepted me as a keen learner of his ideas of scientific development. He called me by my first name, and was invariably informal and friendly.

Had I dreamed that the scientist with whom I was sharing a *tête-à-tête* would be the next President of India, I might have been ostentatiously deferential. Observing his demeanour, and his speeches, though, it was obvious that Dr Kalam valued his role as a scientific mentor over that of a deified Head of State. In the year 2003, I boldly sought permission to make a courtesy call on His Excellency A.P.J. Abdul Kalam, the President of the Republic of India. Astonishingly, the President found time to meet me and my wife Meena for as long as 40 minutes in his office in Rashtrapati Bhavan, New Delhi.

With his characteristic memory Kalam had remembered that Meena, whom he had met during a visit to Punjab, was a botanist. We were both overwhelmed that during our call, he personally took us on a computer-projected tour of the gardens of the President's vast estate, highlighting several exotic herbal plants that he had himself introduced. At no time did Dr Kalam consider his entry into India's presidential palace as an ascent to a higher station. For him it meant merely a temporary transfer from the role of a teacher-researcher to a symbol of the nation's authority. He was as humble and self-effacing as ever and quite as warm and friendly as when he had discussed science education in the state of Punjab three years earlier.

From the Future to the Present

The assignment of Finance Secretary in the Government of Punjab is a form of importance that was, in Shakespeare's phrase, 'thrust' upon me. In the year 1992, after a long spell of the President's rule, an elected government, headed by a bold and popular leader of the Congress party, Sardar Beant Singh, assumed office. The new government ordered changes in the placement of a number of civil servants at key positions in the state. The new Chief Secretary, Ajit Singh Chattha directed that I should take charge of the department of finance immediately. This was a surprise. During the 27 years of my service I had not worked in the field of Finance which for me was an esoteric subject. Observing my apparent diffidence, the Chief Secretary conveyed that the Chief Minister had personally decided to entrust to me the portfolio, considered as critical for the state government.

Within the government the position of Finance Secretary is regarded as prestigious. The incumbent enjoys a certain form of patronage and power, as he controls the purse strings. The hackneyed saying, 'Money makes the mare go,' is only too true in respect of government functioning. All departments of the government have perforce to approach the finance department. Since important matters before the council of ministers involve financial implications, the Finance Secretary has to sit in on these official deliberations. Even ministers treat the Finance Secretary with some deference. At that time, the highly graded assignment was viewed by the bureaucracy as a crown of thorns, as the coffers of the state were severely depleted. The Finance Department (FD) was then engaged in perpetual firefighting to sustain the flow of funds. During the recent long period of central rule the government had been chary of levying any form of additional tax. The central government had wished to avoid creating any perception that it was squeezing the population of the state. For years it had steadfastly evaded any unpopular decisions. Public expenditure, on the other hand, was burgeoning. The consequence was an impoverished exchequer. To begin with, it was necessary to call on Dr Kewal Krishan, the Finance Minister and also on Mr Beant Singh, the Chief Minister.

In political circles Dr Kewal Krishan was regarded as a sincere, diligent public leader. He belonged to the old school of nationalists from the Congress party, the individuals who had in their youth been involved in the freedom struggle against British colonial rule. He continued to wear in public the traditional white-coloured *khadi* 'Gandhi' cap. One of the senior-most members of the cabinet of ministers, Kewal Krishan had worked earlier too as Finance Minister, and also as elected Speaker of the state legislative assembly (the Vidhan Sabha). Comparatively senior in age—he would have been over 70 years at that time—he was a popular grassroots leader from Mukerian, a small town in the district of Hoshiarpur in the foothills of the Himalayas. At a time when most of his peers were immersed in politics as a full-time occupation, Kewal Krishan engaged in his successful medical practice of the traditional Indian discipline of Ayurveda. On joining the ministry, he took a sabbatical from the medical profession. The doctor was highly regarded for his commitment to the downtrodden, whom he was known to treat free of charge. He had a formidable background as a seasoned, idealistic administrator.

My first encounter with Dr Kewal Krishan was distinctly frosty. Rather than beginning with pleasantries, the minister greeted me with a curt observation; he noted that I did not have experience of working in the financial sector. Taken aback, I could merely mumble that he was factually correct; my experience was in other functions of government. I went so far as to say that I was not aware why I had been given this important charge. I even ventured to suggest that the Finance Minister himself would have approved my appointment. This little exchange probably left him nonplussed, as it did me. I came away with the impression that I was not the minister's choice for the assignment. Could it be that the Chief Minister had ordered the appointment without consulting his minister in charge? Departing from his office after a meeting lasting 10 minutes, I assured my minister that I would try to do justice to the job.

I admit I was bewildered at the chilly start of the new innings in my career. Over my years with the government, I had sometimes been in conflict with ministers. Since Dr Kewal Krishan had never met me earlier I could not fathom the reason for the apparent impasse. I hoped that my second port of call, the Chief Minister himself, would elicit a warmer reception. And here I was not disappointed. It was almost as if I was dealing with a different genre within government.

Democracy in Action

A strange sight greeted me as I walked along the corridor leading to the CM's office. A sea of humanity, bobbing with a variety of turbans and ubiquitous caps, clothed mostly in the typical garb of the farmers' community of Punjab, seemed to have descended on the second floor of the Secretariat, where the Chief Minister's office is housed. It was as if hundreds of village folk had gathered in a fair. I realized that many of the groups had merely come to catch a glimpse of their popular leader in his seat of power. The common thinking among people in the hinterland of the state went something like this. During the almost 10-year-long period of the President's Rule, the administration had been in the hands of persons external to the sons of the soil, aloof from the common man. With the revival of democratic rule in the state, they wished to personally greet the newly anointed head of government as one of their own. The Chief Minister and other leaders had, expectedly, begun to tour various districts in the state. The practice with ministers is to spend at least two or three days at weekends in their constituencies, where they interact closely with their electors. The weekdays are kept for official work at the state headquarters, Chandigarh. Punjab being a small state, every district can be conveniently accessed by road within a short travelling time of four or five hours. The thronging crowd here in Chandigarh obviously included many whom the Chief Minster had not been able to meet personally during his travel to the districts during a customary victory lap after the recent elections.

Systems of regulation of entry of visitors into the Chief Minister's office wing were not yet in place. In due course, as the new government settled in, more strict security arrangements were established. Visible right then was a spontaneous flush of enthusiasm at the revival of popular government. The euphoria of an uninhibited interaction between a democratic leader and his voters was, for a spectator, quite overpowering. Among the visitors were, inevitably, numerous supplicants with personal grievances and demands.

Since I had a prior official appointment, the Chief Minister's attendants enabled me to wade smoothly through the gathered crowd. The interior of the Chief Minister's room was slightly better organized than the corridor outside, but the spacious office room too was chock-a-block with visitors. It could best be described as a small amphitheater, where the principal personage of the drama sat behind a large desk, surrounded on all sides by a passionate audience. The Chief Minister himself was a tall and graceful Sikh gentleman, clothed from top to toe in spotless white. His turban was slightly dishevelled, possibly in the jostling at the hands of a mob of his own admirers. He was quite unfazed with the massive surge of visitors; rather he seemed to be enjoying the wanton display of public affection. Speaking to each group and individual in the typical language of rustic Punjab, interspersed with lively wit and humour, Sardar Beant Singh was totally at home amidst the groups surrounding him, which included unlettered farmers. The numerous written applications placed before him were passed on to the official staff, with an assurance to the applicants concerned that they would be attended to. I had learnt that the Sardar was a law graduate from Lahore, a town that had been the centre of higher education of the undivided Punjab before the partition of the country in 1947. At this stage of his momentous career, he was charged to deliver good governance to the people of his soil. Unfortunately, after just three years in office, his life was to be tragically cut short by his assassination at the entrance of the very Secretariat that was his seat of power. Later in this chapter, I will say more about that momentous event.

The moment my entry was announced Mr Beant Singh directed his personal staff to guide me to an anteroom. As I moved from corridor to office to anteroom, there was a progressive degree of orderliness in the precincts. Inside the anteroom were seated some retired officers of the armed forces; the staff had offered them tea as they awaited their appointment with the head of state. Brushing past the citizens milling around his office table, the Chief Minister entered the smaller cubicle to attend to me. He politely requested the distinguished military officers to withdraw. On this, my first encounter with the CM, I found that he could instantly switch himself away from the crowds of well-wishers outside. He was focused on what he had to say to me, totally oblivious to the cacophony outside. He even apologized for what he admitted was an unruly gathering. 'We politicians have to live with this,' he smiled disarmingly.

In my years in administration I followed a methodical practice of planning every word that I would need to utter in any discussion, especially with important officials. For the present crucial meeting I had come prepared to make three statements before the Chief Minster. One, that I could not boast of special skills in the field of public finance, my new charge, and that my minister himself had commented on this; two, that I would do my best to tackle the financial problems of the state as I understood them; and three, that I would heed all special directions from the CM. As I began with my careful litany of submissions, the Chief Minister cut me short, remarking that he was fully acquainted with my background. Following my brusque treatment at the hands of the Finance Minister, I hesitantly apologized that I was not a seasoned financial expert. Once again, he interrupted, in a tone of finality, 'It is my decision to give you this charge.' Mr Beant Singh added, for good measure, that he was conscious of the financial distress facing the state. In a kinder tone he assured that he would give me all support in my efforts.

If the interview with my Finance Minister had lasted 10 minutes, that with the Chief Minster took all of five minutes. Here was a man of few words; a decisive person who expected performance above all things.

What remained unsaid by the CM was more vital than the words he uttered. The CM expected me to perform in the man-sized job, and he had assured me of his full support. It was a lesson in brevity, and in astute motivation. No crisper directions could have been emerged from a head of government.

The next call was on Mr Ajit Singh Chattha, the Chief Secretary. In a state, the supreme executive authority is the council of ministers. Every minister functions through the Secretary and other officials in a hierarchy. The Chief Secretary is the effective head of the entire bureaucracy. While he does not concern himself with the day to day functioning of individual departments, he coordinates important matters, pushing through initiatives of policy. He acts as the eyes and ears of the executive. As the official secretary to the council of ministers, his position in the state is analogous to that of the Cabinet Secretary in the government of India. Expectedly, the meeting with the Chief Secretary was businesslike. A short statured dapper Sikh gentleman, Ajit Chattha exuded great poise and self-confidence. In years he was some eight years older to me, but just two years higher in seniority. It transpired that he took the civil services exam at a much later age than most others. At the time of partition of the country in the year 1947, his family had been uprooted from western Punjab, which became a part of Pakistan, and had to migrate to eastern Punjab, on the Indian side. According to an official dispensation young men and women whose academic studies happened to have been disrupted in the events of 1947 were allowed what was termed 'refugee concession' in terms of the maximum age for taking the examination for entry into the civil services. Consequently, Ajit Chattha had entered service at the age of about 29 years. By academic training Chattha was an electrical engineer. He had even taught in an engineering college before entering the IAS. At the time I was Managing Director of MARKFED, and Chattha had been my immediate superior. He was respected as a sharp, clear-headed administrator, with a strong scientific bent of mind. At once a technocrat and a bureaucrat, he was extremely friendly and outgoing. He encouraged practical measures for financial improvement.

Chattha conveyed that the Chief Minister assigned high priority to financial management; he now expected explicit steps to manage the crisis. 'I would have to study and understand the situation before suggesting any specific remedies,' I said guardedly. Chattha put me totally at ease. He understood that, for financial sector reform, unpopular decisions were required; reform was imperative. For this, he assured that we would together carry the entire government machinery with us. It was obvious that Chattha enjoyed the total trust of Beant Singh, the Chief Minister. Here then I was another style of motivation.

The ball was now squarely in my court.

Desperate Balancing

'Annual income 20 pounds, annual expenditure, 19 (pounds) 19 (shillings) and six (pence), result happiness. Annual income 20 pounds, annual expenditure 20 pounds ought and six, result misery.'

(Mr Micawber in *David Copperfield*).

The senior functionaries of the department include officers of the IAS and the state civil service, as well as experts in various disciplines linked with finance. In my very first meeting with them, I took recourse to this reference in the famous novel of Charles Dickens. As a student of literature, I found that the basic horse sense of the fictional Mr Micawber could colourfully guide the department on the rudiments of practical budgeting, viz. that the state must subsist within its means. Accepting that our efforts to control expenditure were likely to displease a number of institutions and individuals, I mentioned the story of the leading female character in the well-known long poem of Alexander Pope, *The Rape of the Lock*. The said lady, Belinda, a coquette in high society, would cheerfully flirt with suitors, but warded off most of them tactfully,

'Oft she rejects, but never once offends.'

Could FD follow a similar line? Could we say 'No!' with a smile? The financial specialists might have been startled at the use of literary allusions in hardcore finance. The hard-boiled FD men did, however, carry a smile as they left the meeting.

Poetic quotes from great writers might make an impact on stage. Managing the finances of a state requires a different, prosaic form of grind. This came home in stark relief when observing the huge difference, technically termed the revenue deficit, or the balance from current revenues, between the expenditure being undertaken and the receipts available for funding the same. The figures with the Finance Department showed that during the year 1992–93, the state would face a revenue deficit of at least one thousand crore rupees (one hundred billion rupees), which constituted at that time about half of the state's annual budget. A state can finance its expenditure by taxes or by borrowing. During the years of direct central rule, the Punjab government had avoided the painful recourse to raise taxes. Successive governors of the state had been pleading with the centre for any form of support. The Government of India had looked askance at what it considered as profligacy of the state government, conveniently forgetting that during the President's rule the central government was itself controlling the state government. Rather than sanctioning outright grants to redress the financial imbalance, the central government had been offering what were euphemistically termed 'special term loans'. It transpired that in availing of the dispensation the state fell deeper and deeper into a debt trap. With the restoration of popular rule, the proverbial chickens came to roost. Only the perch for the chickens had now shifted from the national capital to Chandigarh. Recourse to loaning instead of substantive taxation in preceding years obliged Beant Singh's government to bear the impact of the decade-long dissipation wrought by the national government. Since every single loan so raised had to be repaid, the red column in the books depicted ever increasing liabilities. In order to restore a semblance of normalcy in its financial management the state would clearly have to levy taxes of a substantial magnitude.

The precarious situation was explained in a meeting of the Council of Ministers. Ajit Chattha, the Chief Secretary, apprehended that the elected political leaders would not impose additional taxes with any enthusiasm. It was decided that I would blandly describe the impact that the government's insolvent situation was having on the lives of the public. In my very first appearance before the cabinet of ministers I found myself narrating an unembellished horror story of the prevailing symptoms of financial illness. The amounts essential for running the normal business of government were not being released to the departments, thus stymieing the work of development. The employees of the government were not receiving their salaries on time; even the benefits due to retiring personnel were being delayed for months on end. The petrol stations refused to extend further credit to government agencies for POL (petrol, oil, lubricants), so many official vehicles were off the road. An immobile police force meant that the security of the common man was compromised.

The moneys of the state government are drawn from its own accounts with its banks. The banks permit the state to overdraw a limited amount for a few days. As our state was persistently living beyond its means, it frequently exhausted its overdraft facility and turned to the central government for succour. In order to bail out a stricken state, the central government offers it what is euphemistically termed a 'ways and means advance', on which interest is charged. In the event of the state defaulting in repayment the Reserve Bank of India directs that the accounts of the state government in the banks be frozen. For many months the state had been defaulting in repaying these short term advances. For good measure, the cabinet note listed the repeated occasions on which the government's treasuries were closed. Bankruptcy was becoming a matter of public shame for the government.

It was explained to the ministers that the Chief Minister had himself written to the Prime Minister of India, and had also met the Union Finance Minister to stress that the state of Punjab had fallen in what was technically a debt trap, a stage of collapse when it needed to borrow for serving its daily needs. The CM had argued that the state should be absolved of repaying the outstanding special term loans. These had been used by the state on behalf of the union government to finance the national war on insurgency. Before the cabinet I submitted, somewhat melodramatically, that the role of the Finance Department was reduced to polishing a begging bowl to present before the central government. In the dire situation we requested that all departments should on their own raise financial resources. It came as a surprise that the distressing picture of the crisis left the ministers cold and unmoved. The focus of the gathering was more on the sumptuous tea and snacks being served, than on remedies to tackle the desperate situation.

Catching the bull by the horns, Chief Secretary Chattha decided that every department would determine what revenues it could generate and also cut unnecessary expenditure. The finance department convened a meeting every Saturday, where individual administrative secretaries found themselves on the mat, as it were. This plan of action was resented by the senior officers. Not only were they deprived of a holiday (offices being a closed on Saturdays); they were required to begin unpopular steps affecting the agencies in their charge. FD endured many snide remarks by senior officers, who found that their leisure time was being curtailed. Many found that some important preplanned activities, such as a session of playing golf, were being rudely shattered by the whims of a loathsome finance department. Chattha was firm that the comprehensive exercise must be completed. The watchwords were financial discipline and resource generation. During two months of acute diagnosis, the financial entrails of every single department had been virtually exposed in scrutiny. A rudimentary path for mobilisation of resources for the state was charted.

'Steps to meet the financial crisis' was listed for discussion in a meeting of the Council of Ministers, which in Punjab is held every Wednesday. As is usual, most of the ministers had not read the explanatory note, which detailed the potential of enhancing taxes and non-tax revenues, as they were called. The Finance Minister had cursorily seen the paper, but realised its implications after the paper had already been circulated. Dr Kewal Krishan informally asked the Chief Minister to postpone discussion, as he had some reservations. The CM declined this request, so the item came up for discussion as scheduled.

In the cabinet meeting the proposals for taxation caused a grand furore. The ministers were unanimous that the suggestions of the finance department be rejected; some milder members suggested a face saver that the Finance Minister be directed to present more reasonable suggestions. Some outspoken ministers maintained that the tax measures would severely dent their standing with the voters. The image of the government, they feared, would be impaired, thereby ruining their chances of success in forthcoming elections. One minister went so far as to warn that the fury of the people would be so great that the ministers would not dare to enter the villages of even their sworn supporters. The majority of the members of the Council voiced the view that the proposed taxation was a recipe for political disaster. As the diatribe was at its pitch, I sat mute in a corner, trying to hide my head as author of what was dubbed a politically suicidal plan. 'The most unkindest cut of all' was when Dr Kewal Krishan, the Finance Minister himself, cast his lot with the dissident majority and pleaded for reconsideration.

It was apparent that a hornet's nest had wittingly been stirred. With even the Finance Minister demurring, the Finance Secretary could well be dubbed as the villain of the piece. The cabinet waited with bated breath for the reaction of the Chief Minister. Astonishingly, he had been observing the onslaught with quiet composure. When all the ministers had had their say, Sardar Beant Singh spoke. His observations lasted at most two minutes. 'I appreciate your misgivings,' he began, 'but we have to take some tough decisions.' The Chief Minister did not utter a word to counter the apprehensions that his colleagues had articulated so loudly. He began, 'We have heard every one present here.' He continued further, with a chuckle, 'You know, we have with us our *sarkari munim* (an official accountant, meaning the Finance Secretary, referring personally to me).' Smiling mischievously, he concluded, 'Why not try out the plan that our *munim* has prepared?' The conference room was stunned into pin drop silence. 'Mr Chief Secretary, let us pass on to the next item.' It was time for tea and snacks, which were relished in an atmosphere of bonhomie.

The minutes of the meeting recorded, baldly, 'The note of the Finance Department was considered and approved.' At a stroke, an amount of 1850 crores of rupees had been approved for imposition of taxes during the year by various departments of the Government of Punjab. This could help to counterbalance the deficit during the year. The Chief Minster had disarmed the critics; he had shrewdly overruled even the Finance Minister, by a splash of humour. It was astonishing how a skilful leader with fundamental understanding of issues can use political capital to tackle a crisis. In accepting the drastic steps Beant Singh had relied on horse sense; he had owned the appraisal of the finance department. It was not deemed necessary to explain the intricacies of taxation to the vociferous members of the cabinet of ministers. The Chief Secretary Ajit Chattha would obviously have briefed him in advance. Beant Singh was clearly his own man, not easily swayed by contrary views. This might have been the highest dose of taxes approved in a single cabinet meeting. As always the Bard had an apt choice of words for the ground situation in my state:

'Diseases desperate grown,
By desperate appliance are relieved,
Or not at all.'

(*Hamlet*, 4.3.9–11)

Unlike the wavering protagonist in Shakespeare's play, the CM had stood firm and decisive. On vital matters like taxation the buck stopped at his door. By this bold decision Beant Singh had brought back the state from the brink of financial collapse. Most fellow bureaucrats were as blissfully unaware of the magnitude of the accomplishment as the ministers who had witnessed the dramatic anti-climax in the cabinet room that day.

The misgivings of the ministers about public outcry against the unprecedented decisions on taxation proved to be unfounded; the adverse public reaction was insignificant. While the tax proposals had been based on facts and figures and technical analysis, Beant Singh had his hand on the pulse of the people. He had gauged correctly that the affected people would understand the compulsions of the government and accept the bitter medicine. The farmers' community even accepted a huge enhancement in the charges for supply of irrigation water for agriculture. Hitherto they were paying a nominal amount for delivery of precious water for their fields, which covered only a fraction of the expenditure that the government incurred on the service. The amount that the Government of Punjab could recover annually as additional 'water rate' was still much less than it spent on the cost of collection. It is another matter that several years later the next government led by Mr Parkash Singh Badal took the disastrous step of abolishing the water charges for agriculture altogether. That is, however, another story.

A political fall out of the episode was that one of the senior ministers Mr Harcharan Singh Brar resigned from the cabinet as a mark of protest. Brar held the important portfolio of Irrigation and Power. Coming from a wealthy farming family from the Moga-Muktsar region of southwest Punjab, Brar was highly sophisticated and well-educated. Esteemed as an aristocrat among politicians, he had been an aspirant for the top post of Chief Minister, but his party had instead preferred Beant Singh for his earthy grassroots popularity. Brar seized upon what he felt was an opportunity to cement his base in the community of farmers that dominated political space in Punjab. He projected his resignation as an act of self-denial on behalf of his electors. If Harcharan Brar expected that his protest would cause his own stock to rise, he would have been disappointed. His resignation left his party leadership cold. He was destined to wait a couple of years before his life ambition of occupying the Chief Minister's chair could be fulfilled. As it transpired, his elevation to the top position came in tragic circumstances, the calamitous event of assassination of Beant Singh, Brar's close friend of years.

The Pains of Reform

Even as the tax drive narrated above began, I took a step that might confound straitjacketed bureaucrats even today. Shortly after joining the Finance Department I wrote a personal letter to Dr Manmohan Singh, who was at that time Union Finance Minister, seeking an appointment to discuss reform in financial management in the state of Punjab. It was unknown for a small time official of a state government to thus approach directly the most important minister of the Government of India. In my enthusiasm I did not realize at the outset that, in short circuiting normal channels of communication between a state and the centre, there was a contravention of bureaucratic propriety. The government could well have ostracized the move, since the Finance Minister was not taken into confidence. Fortunately, the faux pas went unnoticed. Rather, it opened a door to a more professional approach to financial management in the state.

Just a year earlier, in a bid to obviate imminent bankruptcy the Government of India had launched momentous reforms to liberalise the economy.

Dr Manmohan Singh was hailed internationally as a reformer who had salvaged India's economy. He quickly removed debilitating controls that had shackled enterprise and stunted economic growth over many decades. The path breaking initiatives of the national government of Prime Minister P.V. Narasimha Rao, with Manmohan Singh at the helm of the Finance Ministry, were rapidly transforming the stifled economy. Where would a state seeking to undertake financial reform find a better guide than Dr Manmohan Singh? This was a moot question. Surprisingly, within a week Dr Manmohan Singh invited me to meet him in his office in the North Block of the Secretariat in New Delhi.

Punctual to the minute, the Union Finance Minster received me warmly. It was a relief that he did not chide the breaking of official protocol. Rather, he seemed to welcome my unusual enterprise. As we spoke I forgot that I was in the company of a powerful controller of India's economic destiny. His manner was that of a learned Oxbridge don, suave and measured in word. Indeed Manmohan Singh had earned his doctorate in Economics at University of Cambridge, UK, after graduating from Panjab University, Chandigarh and securing a Master's degree from the Delhi School of Economics. He had worked as the Governor of the Reserve Bank of India and also as the Chairman of the University Grants Commission. It was an imaginative master stroke of India's Prime Minister to bring an economist of such distinction to head the critical Ministry of Finance.

Dr Manmohan Singh was sporting his customary impeccable white *khadi* and a sky blue turban. He introduced me to a short, scholarly looking gentleman. I judged from his accented English that he hailed from a state of south India. This was Professor Raja J. Chelliah, Chairman of National Institute of Public Finance and Policy (NIPFP), India's foremost institution for research in Public Finance. After a few preliminaries, the die was cast. The Finance

Minister directed that NIPFP would study and appraise the financial problems of Punjab and suggest practical reform measures. From the Ministry of Finance Professor Chelliah and I were motoring to his office in Qutab Institutional Area in south Delhi. Dr Chelliah introduced me to his team of Dr M Govinda Rao and Tapas K. Sen, India's top economists. We discussed the contours of the engagement of NIPFP with the Government of Punjab. The academics, as I considered them, enthusiastically accepted the task of conducting a comprehensive study, eventually titled, 'Management of Public Finances in Punjab'. In the very first meeting it was agreed that a team from NIPFP would visit Chandigarh within a fortnight to settle the terms of reference of the technical study. Dr Chelliah was assured that the key functionaries of the state government would work with the experts. It was decided that the specialists would present their recommendations within a few months.

It was clear that Dr Manmohan Singh was not merely an economist formulating national policy. He was a determined and practical administrator, who was prepared to step in personally to support states at the operational level. Accepting that the government of Punjab was serious about financial restructuring, he had promptly involved India's leading economists in the line in the exercise. The eminent academicians and the state's administrators would work in tandem. Dr Chelliah was venerated as an economist internationally. The state government was fortunate to have his guidance.

It was at this stage that I apprised my minister and the Chief Secretary about the study. Dr Kewal Krishan was a staid administrator, who stood for maintenance of the status quo, chary of unconventional initiatives. Over the last few months we had built a working relationship. Apprehensive that he might oppose the project I mentioned casually that Dr Manmohan Singh himself had introduced NIPFP to us. As it turned out, Kewal Krishan was quite casual about the idea; he considered that this would be merely a theoretical exercise. Ajit Chattha, on the other hand, was quite delighted to secure for the state the association of an institution as reputed as NIPFP. Immersed as the government was at that time in the plans for raising revenues, Chattha agreed that the suggestions of specialists would only strengthen our drive. Consequently, when Govinda Rao and Tapan Sen came to Chandigarh, the concerned officials of the state government worked closely with them.

The enhancement of revenues approved by the cabinet of ministers had been a limited expedient to tide over the immediate crisis of the revenue deficit during the year. Chelliah's team went much further to propose a comprehensive financial restructuring. They bluntly termed the fiscal situation in the state as 'critical'. They studied in depth such matters as non-productive expenditures, the viability of the various public enterprises of the state, the level and nature of user charges and subsidies on services provided by the state and the efficacy of the tax structure. For the team of the state government involved in the exercise, this was a learning experience. The status of financial management of our state was compared with that in the rest of the country. We had a glimpse of best practices in financial management within and outside India.

Dr Chelliah and his experts duly presented their first report in February 1993. They observed that despite the fact that the annual per capita income of the state was at that time the highest among all the states in the country, the government of Punjab was in a precipitous fiscal decline. The annual rate of growth of the economy of Punjab was lower than in the country as a whole. Punjab was thus sliding from its pre-eminent position in the country. NIPFP noted that the negative revenue balance was growing alarmingly, which meant that less and less money was available to fund its development schemes. Expenditure on day to day items of administration, including salaries and pensions was rising, whereas revenue income was stagnating. It was no consolation that other states in India were facing similar fiscal distress. There is no magic wand that can transform deficits into surpluses, that was soon understood. The Report suggested a number of remedial steps for attaining financial stability. Noting that as much as 62 per cent of the revenues was committed to the payment of salaries and pensions, NIPFP proposed a ban on fresh recruitment of government employees. The employees in Punjab were the highest paid in the country, their scales being even higher than those of their counterparts in the central government. The Report advised that the scales in Punjab be brought on par with those at the centre. Likewise the charges for delivery of services needed to be hiked; loss making public enterprises deserved to be closed. There were suggestions for reform in the structure of the police force, to make it leaner and more professional. The study also suggested greater oversight on performance of departments and public sector undertakings, and an overhaul of the tax structure. Basically the experts suggested higher generation of resources of higher magnitude and also wiser utilization of the funds. Expectedly, Kewal Krishan did not give his countenance such ideas, no matter how well reasoned.

When Dr Chelliah called on the Chief Minister, Beant Singh asked him for his impression. Chelliah replied with a memorable one liner, 'Punjab is an economically progressive state,' he volunteered, 'but financially backward.' Shorn of technical jargon, it meant that that the hard working and enterprising people of the state had built up the state to a level of prosperity, but that the successive governments had let down the state by deficient financial management. Fiscal profligacy had continued apace for over 20 years.

There are three basic components of the annual budget of a government. These are: a review of the financial situation, the plans of the government for development and the provision of funds for the execution of the plans. One of the tasks of the Finance Secretary is to draft the speech of the Finance Minister incorporating these three features of financial management. In the central government the budget proposes taxation measures for balancing income and expenditure. In the states, on the other hand, the presentation of the budget is viewed as an occasion for pleasing all sections of the electorate. The document indulges unashamedly in populism. Playing to the gallery, the Minister announces many high sounding measures for economic development and welfare; the government projects itself as a champion of the poor and needy. As the Finance Secretary, I served both a Congress government and one that was led by the Shiromani Akali Dal. Notwithstanding the differing political complexion, the respective Finance Ministers scrupulously avoided any imposition of new taxes. No matter which party he represented, the Finance Minister proudly proclaimed, 'I have the honour to present a tax-free budget.' This would occasion a thumping of desks by the legislators of the ruling party, and silence by the opposition. The entire process was an exercise in self-delusion. The fiscal deficit could at times constitute an amount as large as one-third of the expenditure envisioned during the financial year. The Minister would airily announce, 'The resources for bridging the deficit would be raised during the course of the year!' Amazingly neither the treasury benches, nor the opposition, would challenge this transparent sleight of hand. The media would lap up the subterfuge, and news headlines would read, 'A tax free budget for Punjab.'

The balance sheets do not lie. Over the years, the state government was cavalier in promising such facilities as new roads, hospitals and schools, and schemes for removal of poverty and inequality and unemployment; it was conveniently remiss in providing money to fund the works. After the legislature approved the expenditure, the year would be spent in desperate steps to keep the state afloat, financially. If the government lacked the guts to impose taxes at the start of the year, it was futile to expect a surge in political confidence during the course of the year. Expenditure on salaries and on establishment, including the perquisites for all organs of the state, the executive, the judiciary and the legislature is a given. If resources are short, the government is compelled to cut the allotments for development schemes.

The Chief Secretary, Ajit Chattha observed that no matter how justified, fiscal reform would be a painful option for the political leaders. In the current scenario, the state could at best try out some reform gradually and piece meal. The timid approach found some support in the famous observation of the French philosopher Voltaire, 'The best is the enemy of the good.' In any system of governance, the economic and political strands are closely entwined. Great political courage and sagacity is required to push through tough decisions for the long term benefit of the state. Beant Singh had courageously raised some revenues, but the yawning mismatch between resources and liabilities was continuing.

After an initial burst of enthusiasm for fiscal discipline, for government it was business as usual. Such reform measures that began proceeded at a snail's pace. Many of Chelliah's recommendations were discarded altogether. For compressing administrative expenditure, he had proposed that the number of administrative divisions be reduced; that police districts that had proliferated be abolished, so that civil districts and police districts become coterminous, as they were earlier; that vacant posts should be abolished, and new recruitment of unskilled staff banned. Bowing to political considerations and to pressures from unions of employees, the government took contrary decisions. Instead of reducing the number of police districts, fresh civil districts and sub-divisional offices were created, which necessitated fresh recruitment of departmental field officers and supporting clerical staff, even for vacant posts that had been considered redundant.

How difficult the process of cutting down wasteful expenditure can be was brought home when in early 1993, when the Government of India set up, with some fanfare, a national committee on austerity. The Planning Commission of India, which was headed by the Prime Minister himself, and included the Chief Ministers of the states, circulated a paper explaining how unproductive expenditure could be curtailed. Every state was asked to effect economies in its expenditure. In Punjab the department of finance was detailed to prepare a policy paper. Enthusiasm for the task was short lived. A week before the important event was to be convened in New Delhi the entire exercise was called off. The committee was given an unceremonious burial, never to be resuscitated. It was clear that for all its pious enjoinments on fiscal discipline the government of India had chickened out. The essence of the approach in the national policy note was a well-coordinated tightening of belts by the centre and the states. When it came to the crunch, the national government was as timid in biting the bullet as the states.

Meanwhile the state lurched from crisis to crisis. At the macro level it could be argued that in regard to finances, the relationship between the central, federal government and the states is skewed. The major portion of the revenues generated in the country is retained by the centre. Every five years the Finance Commission of India reviews the ratio and nature of distribution of finances between the centre and the states. The history of successive Finance Commissions shows that the states have always felt that the formulae employed to determine their share discriminates against the states. The purse strings are with the centre. The states enjoy limited powers of taxation. On their part, the states are financially irresponsible. They are perpetually looking behind their shoulder at a looming election for the state legislative assembly. The ruling party and the opposition are engaged in competitive populism. In the unlikely event of the ruling party daring to burden the electorate with taxes, the opposition is waiting to pounce. For the Finance Secretary concerned, there is never a dull moment, nor a comfortable one in office. He is perpetually dousing the flames of a threatening insolvency.

In all my years in finance I could never remove the deficit in the budget that I was tasked to frame. Such a position can be quite agonizing.

In a scenario where the legitimate demands of departments, including for budgeted expenditure cannot be served, the department of finance earns the reputation of a tyrant. As this little happening illustrates, we did try to take some steps to present FD's human face. At one time it was discovered that on account of a never-ending cash crunch, many retiring employees had to wait for months before their pension and other dues were paid to them. The Minister ordered that every retiring employee would be paid his or her dues on the very date of retirement. The beneficiaries were pleased. Even the staff of the finance department was enthusiastic. Almost excessively enthusiastic, it transpired, as the following painful incident demonstrates.

Shortly after the government's decision to facilitate the release of dues to retirees, it happened that a dear colleague met a sudden, untimely death, at a young age, when he was at the peak of his career. This was Rajinder Singh, my batch-mate and a close friend. We had in fact spent an academic year together at Cambridge, UK. At the *bhog* ceremony, a service to commemorate the departed soul, friends and relatives and even ministers of the government had congregated. Amid the people present, I recognised a mid-level functionary of the Finance Department. I became suspicious to observe a large handbag that he was carrying. On questioning, the man stated proudly that he was carrying in cash the entire benefits to which the wife of the departed officer had become entitled after the sad demise of her husband. The FD's representative felt that he was displaying due compassion, in terms of the recent policy decision, to deliver the dues in public. It was truly crass to place wads of bank notes before the bereaved widow on such a solemn occasion. Fortunately, a callous faux pas was averted and my dear friend, Agya, Rajinder's wife, was saved public embarrassment. There was an unexpected lesson from this morbid episode. How difficult it is for an institution to mend its image of a tyrant, and suddenly present a humane side!

A Tragic Departure

In India's democracy, a state government displays willingness to take decisions viewed as unpopular largely in the first two years of its inception. During the latter part of its tenure the elected leaders have their eye fixed on the next election, due in the coming two years or so. The approach of Beant Singh's government was in line with the trend. At the start of his term of office Beant Singh displayed rare courage in tackling the two major problems of terrorism and financial instability. It was clear that the battle against insurgency was proving successful; most violent terror groups had been eliminated, and within just two years there was peace in the countryside and in the towns. On the financial side too there was improvement, although reform was still a work in progress. Around the middle of the year 1995 the government decided to switch from reform mode to election mode. Decisions to placate sections of the population came on the anvil. One such proposal was to supply wheat flour and lentils at highly subsidized rates to the poorer sections of the population in the state. In true bureaucratic style, the Finance Department vehemently opposed the '*atta daal* (rice-lentil) scheme', as it came to be labelled. The Finance Department prepared a note stoutly resisting the idea. Some other states in India had delivered such doles, which were expected to serve as sops in advance of the elections scheduled in 1997. The Finance Minister Kewal Krishan fully supported the strategic proposal for supply of subsidized food, disregarding the inability of the state to afford such substantial unproductive expenditure. A typical hiatus between a civil servant and a political leader!

For settling the issue the Chief Minister Beant Singh had fixed a meeting with the Finance Minister, with me in attendance in his office room at 5 pm on a particular day. That very day, 31 August 1995, was to prove fateful, for Beant Singh himself, and for the state of Punjab. Just half an hour before the scheduled start, the CM's office informed me that the meeting stood postponed to another date. At around half past five, when I was still in my office on the eighth floor of the secretarial building, I heard the sound of an almighty explosion. The glass windows in the entire building were rattling. There was chaos all around. Around 6 pm it was announced that the explosion had taken place at the entrance of the Secretariat building. An hour later, it was disclosed that the Chief Minister himself, along with a number of members of his staff, had been killed in a bomb attack. The CM's office is located on the second floor of the Civil Secretariat. The bomb exploded as the Chief Minister was about to enter his waiting car. The police investigation later reported that the bombing was the work of a suicide bomber, who had blown himself up along with the Chief Minister and more than a dozen members of his staff who were accompanying Beant Singh at the end of his day at the office.

Having worked directly with Beant Singh, I had come to admire him for his personal courage and his compassion. His passing was for me a personal tragedy. I had come to look up to him for resolving intricate administrative matters. He was invariably cool and unruffled, even as he would have been aware that his own existence was hanging by a thread. He paid with his life for taking terrorism head-on. The target was obviously the Chief Minister himself. Fate had ordained that so many innocent persons should die along with the assassinated leader. It occurred to me that had my meeting with the Chief Minister taken place as programmed, some other persons, including myself, might have been close to the CM at the time of the tragic event.

In the somber atmosphere, a new Chief Minister from the same political party, Harcharan Singh Brar replaced Beant Singh. Brar would hardly have been pleased to take the reins of power in such sad circumstances. He too was to occupy the chair for a little over a year. For a short period of three months, November, 1996 to February 1997 Mrs Rajinder Kaur Bhattal, also from the Congress party followed Brar as Chief Minister. The veteran of the Akali party, Parkash Singh Badal led the government for the next term 1997–2002.

With Beant Singh's successors fiscal reform was no longer a priority.

When a civil servant is required to serve two successive governments that are strongly opposed to each other, he is sometimes placed in a piquant situation. I had worked as Finance Secretary for almost five years with the Congress governments. In 1998 Chief Minister Badal recalled me to the same post, now upgraded to be at par with the Chief Secretary. The new Finance Minister, Captain Kanwaljit Singh happened to be an old friend and class fellow from my schooldays. In drafting the budget speech of Kanwaljit Singh, I found myself duty bound to record, 'Our government is unfortunate to have inherited an empty treasury. The responsibility for mismanagement of the finances lies at the doors of my predecessor government, and the incompetent officials who mishandled the finances over a long period of five years.' This testimonial could, ironically, serve as just dessert for a career bureaucrat.

Was the above assessment accurate and true, I sometimes wonder! I regret that never in my years in finance was I able to balance the state's budget, except on paper. This earned me opprobrium at home. When the matter of handling the family budget came up, my daughter Bini, who had studied economics, was openly contemptuous of my abilities. Likewise my son Anurag, an engineer and an MBA by academic training, was convinced that, given my track record with the government, I was incompetent to handle crucial family finances and accounts. The majority of members of my little family decided that my wife Meena, a botanist, was a fitter candidate in the field of budgeting and finance. My protestations that for years the government continued to entrust me with thousands of crores of rupees were dismissed out of hand. I had to acquiesce meekly. In the event I was denied the authority of control over funds. Happily I stood divested of responsibility for managing the family's accounts too.

The Finance Department grows upon you. If working as official financial helmsman is a trying proposition, moving out from the straitjacket of official sanctions and refusals can be a bitter sweet event. At the time of my departures I felt relief at leaving a hot seat. The relief was tinged with feelings of regret, somewhat like those expressed by the famous Prisoner of Chillon, when he moved from years of bondage in a prison to freedom outside:

'*My very chains and I grew friends,*
So much a long communion tends
To make us what we are:—even I
Regain'd my freedom with a sigh'.

('The Prisoner of Chillon', Lord Byron)

A VIEW AT TWILIGHT

For a civil servant to hold the highest civil appointment in the state is, in the famous line of the Bard, 'a consummation devoutly to be desired'. The position of Chief Secretary in the state had for long proved elusive. I finally did serve at the top post, albeit for a mere three months.

My first meeting with the administrative secretaries was virtually a farewell event. In my address, I mentioned that I had queried my wife Meena, who was a botanist, if she could name any species of the plant kingdom that are sown early in the season, have a long period of gestation, but which flower very briefly. The officers understood the obvious context of the biological allusion. The buzz in the corridors was that despite logging the longest ever term in history as an officer (a duration spanning a record 38 years and one month), I would have the shortest ever run (three months in time) as Chief Secretary of the state. Such a career graph was considered uncommon. I could not resist quoting a short poem of the 16th century English playwright Ben Jonson, who lived for years in the shadow of his more celebrated contemporary, William Shakespeare:

'It is not growing like a tree
In bulk, doth make Man better be:
Or standing long an oak, three hundred year,
To fall a log at last, dry, bald and sere.
A daisy of a day
Is fairer far in May:
Although it fall and die that night,
It was the plant and flower of light.
In small proportions we just beauties see,
And in short measures, life may perfect be.'

The words couched a conviction that, even in a short period, one could make some meaningful contribution. I voiced some pious platitudes on the duties and responsibilities of public servants, and the need for the bureaucracy to maintain punctuality and discipline. In the context of the state's struggle with terrorism, the members of the IAS and the IPS must publicly stand shoulder to shoulder. Under no circumstances should the state be threatened by a return to the dark days of insurgency.

A Storm in a Teacup

How seriously would the government officials take a leader who was scheduled to depart so soon after his arrival? A rude answer arrived all too soon. This was in the form of a bewildering reaction of the IAS Officers' Association.

Protocol requires the state Chief Secretary to make courtesy calls on the Governor of the state, the Chief Justice of the High Court, the Speaker of the state legislature, and on the counterpart Chief Secretary of Haryana state, also based in the city. In conformity with etiquette, I duly met these eminent persons in Chandigarh, and also called on the Union Cabinet Secretary and the Union Home Secretary, both IAS officers, in New Delhi. Kamal Pande, the Cabinet Secretary was my batch-mate and the Union Home Secretary was a year junior in service. Even Dr A.P.J. Abdul Kalam, the President of India, kindly granted me an audience, a rare honour. For good measure, I also visited Mr M.S. Bhullar, the Director General of Police, in his office.

Imagine my consternation when I learnt from reports in the media that certain colleagues from the IAS had condemned my initial actions as Chief Secretary of the state! The criticism related to my address to senior officers, and to meetings with important functionaries. The President of the Punjab IAS Officers Association was quoted as complaining that the Chief Secretary had brought great disrepute to the Indian Administrative Service and also to the state of Punjab. The contents and tone of a resolution that the Association had announced was puzzling, to say the least.

Like other colleagues, I had been a member of the state IAS Officers' Association, being closely involved even with its cultural and sports activities. For years, I had been the captain of a cricket team comprising officers of the IAS and the IPS. Along with enthusiastic sporting officers of various ages, we played friendly matches periodically. Considering the existing bonhomie among officers, the reported statement was astonishing. It was unprecedented for the representatives of a service to condemn the conduct of a civil servant heading the state administration, especially on matters of protocol.

The signatories to the critical observations adduced two grounds for their umbrage. Firstly, they took exception to remarks in an official meeting that, for inculcating discipline, officers should themselves observe punctuality in office. The resolution asserted that the IAS officers were being treated like 'schoolboys' (the exact word used in the resolution). Secondly, it was averred that, for the Chief Secretary, an IAS officer, to visit the Director General of Police, an IPS officer, the status of the IAS had been impaired. In regard to self-discipline, I had, admittedly, urged that senior officers must set an example for the entire officialdom in the state. The adverse reaction imputed that the very invocation had humiliated the fraternity of IAS officers. In a craftily drafted sentence the Association concluded, 'An officer enjoying a short term presence in the highest post of Chief Secretary should not be permitted to cause long term damage to the administration in the state.'

Expectedly, the outburst of the Association representing IAS officers formed the grist of media comment. Perhaps to the dismay of its authors, their very indictment itself was condemned in the papers. Some commentators wrote that in feeling piqued by enjoinment on discipline, the IAS officers were exhibiting arrogance. The press criticized the service for what it perceived as egotism. A question was raised as to why any IAS officer should be considered 'heaven born' (a pejorative term employed by some journalists), and above the normal rules of conduct for public servants. The journalists were gleeful at the opportunity to pin a label of elitism on the IAS. In regard to my call on the Director General of Police, most newspapers considered it an act of grace. Some papers commented that the IAS displayed wanton airs of superiority vis-à-vis other government services. Apparently, some ill-chosen words seemed to have boomeranged on those who voiced them.

I recalled the words of the English playwright Oscar Wilde, 'There is only one thing in the world worse than being talked about, and that is not being talked about'. The event brought me, inadvertently, into the limelight.

The episode created a piquant situation. The unseemly comments of a body claiming to represent the service had to ignored, even as the individual cooperation of the members of the same service, the IAS, had to be secured.

The little storm blew over soon.

Red Lights and Pomp

It was while handling protocol that I realized the importance that persons within government and outside it attach to visible symbols of status. The Chief Minister was hard put to entertain numerous requests by many public figures for permitting the use of a beacon atop their vehicles. The symbol proclaims loudly that the occupant is entitled to special respect. According to the 'blue book' of official guidelines, the dignitaries blessed to display the emblem comprise a complex hierarchy of individuals. The list includes the President of India, the Prime Minister and his cabinet, and Judges of the Supreme Court and High Courts, Governors of States, the chiefs of the armed forces and many others. These VIPs can flash the distinguishing red light in any part of India. Cabinet ministers in the states have to content themselves by merely displaying the red symbol within the limits of their respective states. Humbler still are junior ministers, Lieutenant Generals and equivalent in the armed forces, and Chief Secretaries of states, who may display, but not flash the red light. District Judges, Collectors and Police Superintendents stand lower still on this splendid ladder of opulent dignity, for they can only flaunt a beacon of the colour amber, a hue that pales before the grandiose ruby red.

Near the turn of the century, some policemen had the temerity to demand proof of authority of some persons, who happened to be judges, to display red beacons on their cars. When the Honorable High Court discovered that the Central Motor Vehicle Rules did not authorise the use of red lights, it decreed that red lights were essential to uphold the dignity of judges occupying an exalted position. All the state governments dutifully notified a larger list of entitled persons. In the process, the states cleverly added, on their own, the names of additional personages that they considered as worthy of the honour. Any VIP worth his salt must necessarily be accompanied by security guards. Inevitably, the beacon adorned vehicles began to figuratively stumble over one another. The proliferation of beaconed cars had added to traffic congestion.

Pandering to the ordained red light holders was, inevitably, at the cost of such emergency services as hospital ambulances and the police, which were entitled to display beacons of blue. The priority in right of way to blue beaconed vehicles providing emergency services stood superseded in the face of red beacons displayed by status conscious VIPs.

Thankfully, around the year 2015, the Supreme Court of India stepped in, arraigned the governments, and directed that the use of beacons should be drastically restricted, remarking, 'Status is enhanced not by travelling in red beacon vehicles but by work done by them (the designated persons).' The Court could well have perceived an altogether different common connotation of the term 'red light'. Localities bearing that description are not considered the most wholesome places for dignified persons to visit.

Sadly, much time and energy of the government was spent in symbolically certifying the dignity of many individuals.

One other insignia of high standing in India is the size of the house that a person inhabits. Within government, it is understandable that the hierarchical standing of the occupant should determine the size of an office, and its furnishings. It is ironical, that in younger days, when an official has growing children at home, the government allots to the individual a modest housing facility. In course of time, when the children have moved out and less space is required, large bungalows serve as habitat for those near the top of the official ladder. Bungalows provide space for seating an attendant, who is charged with answering telephone calls and the like. A minority of officials decline official housing, being happy to live in a house they might have built, or, like me, have inherited. Small houses have no space for seating a telephone attendant, or for security guards. Around the year 2000, when there was little mobile telephony, communication was only done by landline telephones. Many callers were surprised that some officers took telephone calls directly, and did not route them through attendants.

On one occasion, the old-fashioned telephone was providential in averting major loss of life and property. It was midnight when the phone at home rang. It was a panic-stricken citizen from the township of Mohali, adjoining Chandigarh, who reported that a huge conflagration of flames had gutted a factory manufacturing medicinal drugs. The fire was spreading, unabated, to adjoining houses, among which was the caller's own dwelling. Irritated at being thus disturbed, I curtly advised the man on the line to approach the fire brigade. The desperate caller said that there were many fire engines on the spot, but the firemen could not control the flames caused by potent chemicals; their water cannon only fanned the blaze. On impulse, I spoke on the phone to the station commander of Chandigarh's air force station. This happened to be Air Vice-Marshal D.S. Guram, whom I happened to know personally. Guram acted swiftly. Well after midnight, his fire-fighting unit was able to control the inferno with a kind of chemical foam, which the air force had found efficacious in controlling fires caused by crash landing aircraft. The deadly chemically fired flames were doused. Mohali should be beholden to the Indian Air Force for preventing a greater tragedy.

Reaching to the Ground

What exactly is the role of the Chief Secretary in the state's administration? The machinery of government is well oiled and functional. Provided that the incumbent is cool, diligent and impartial, the institution of Chief Secretary runs smoothly on auto pilot, which is the momentum of a long established tradition. As leader, he is expected to resolve inter departmental conflicts, and be a friend, philosopher and guide for the various institutions, each engaged in its own sphere of activities. As the Secretary of the council of ministers, the Chief Secretary is privy to important policy decisions. He assists the ministry in the implementation of policies by the concerned institutions, without himself interfering in their day to day work. He can be a bridge between the bureaucracy and the elected executive. He also represents the state government in interaction with the Government of India. As per protocol, the Chief Secretary interacts with constitutional authorities and also with foreign delegations. The incumbent having worked in a variety of sectors, these tasks are not onerous, nor should he find difficulty in managing diverse affairs of state.

With a view to focus on district administration, I decided to tour the state. The idea was to meet the field officers to motivate them. Being at the cutting edge of decentralized governance, the district officers are the face of the authority of the state. The common man looks to them as a dispenser of public service as well. Traditionally, the administrative heads of the districts, the Deputy Commissioners, are bright young IAS officers. The Chief Minister valued close coordination between the Deputy Commissioner, who functions also as District Magistrate (DM) in respect of law and order, and the Senior Superintendent of Police (SSP of the district). Both civil and police officers were accordingly invited to meetings arranged at Jalandhar, Patiala and Ferozepur, the three divisional headquarters. The top brass of the police, including Mr M.S. Bhullar, the Director General of Police, joined the meetings. The agenda was thus a review of development work and delivery of public services in the state and also matters concerning law and order and security. The meetings conveyed government's clear message that the District Magistrates and the SSPs must work in unison. In their published books[1] both Mr J.F. Ribeiro and Mr K.P.S. Gill, the stalwarts in the successful fight against terrorism in Punjab, had especially acknowledged the imperative of close rapport between the DMs and SSPs in the field.

Everyone understood the nature of the working relationship of the DMs and SSPs. While the SSP controls

---

1 Julio Ribeiro, *My Life as a Police Officer*, Viking, 1998; and K.P.S. Gill, *The Knights of Falsehood*, Har Anand Publications, 1997.

police administration in his district, he consults the DM on law and order issues, especially in times of crisis. Under the rules the DM has overall responsibility for maintenance of public order. In extreme situations, where public order and tranquility are threatened, the DM has to take decisions on the use of force as necessary. Both the DMs and the SSPs were happy that the Chief Secretary was meeting them jointly. Perhaps the interaction would have strengthened camaraderie.

One area of coordination at district level was in regard to the administration of criminal justice. The High Court and the state government have constituted a standing committee of the District and Sessions Judge, the DM and the SSP, which is expected to review the progress of criminal judicial matters in every district once every three months. Official notifications, some from as long ago as the year 1930 when the colonial British government was in power, laid down the role of the district panel. The guidelines issued almost a century back, with certain refinements, are in force even today. The District and Sessions Judge chairs the meetings, which are convened by the District Magistrate. Building on the sacrosanct principle that the judiciary is independent of the executive, the forum appraises the prosecution and disposal of criminal cases in the courts. The effectiveness of the prosecuting agency is reviewed.

It was no secret that some DMs were diffident in convening the important district meetings regularly. For this reluctance there were, possibly, two reasons, both apparently contrary to each other. Firstly, an erroneous impression that in protocol the DM is equal in status with the District Judge; and secondly, the awe in which some civil and police officers, held the judiciary, which was the arbiter of criminal justice. In actuality, the judiciary is a constitutional authority, whereas civil officers, no matter what their emoluments might be, are public servants working for the elected executive, which is the Council of Ministers in the state. In order of precedence, the District Judge is undeniably an authority superior to the DM and the SSP. During discussion, the Chief Justice of the High Court had whole heartedly agreed that the DMs and SSPs should regularly apprise the District Judges as per the standing directions. The instructions in regard to coordination had the tacit approval of the Chief Justice of the High Court. The original author of the instructions, who would have been the Chief Justice of Punjab High Court in the year 1930, had presided over a vast Punjab state that then comprised the states of Punjab, Haryana and Himachal Pradesh of the present day, besides West Punjab, which is the largest and most important province of today's Pakistan. The deliberations would have helped to invigorate the panel of the three crucial authorities at the district level.

The Chief Minister expressed satisfaction with the feedback from the districts that was reported to him.

A View from the Top

Captain Amarinder Singh, the Chief Minister, did not hold the title of Maharaja that his father had, as all erstwhile princely states had vanished soon after India became independent. As a political leader, he was happy to be addressed as Captain, a rank that he had earned in the army. This cultivated his image as one among the common people, and downplayed his aristocratic lineage. The captain deported himself in the dress of the farmers in the countryside. He was a rare example of a prince by birth being democratically elected to the office of head of a state government.

Captain Amarinder knew me from my years in the service, and also as an active member of the Board of Governors of Yadavindra Public School, Patiala (YPS), of which he was the Patron. The school, which is one of India's reputed institutions, had been founded by his father, the Maharaja of Patiala, Yadavindra Singh. Several meetings of the Board of Governors of YPS were held in the premises of his personal residence at Patiala, called New Motibagh, Patiala, which continued to be called the Maharaja's palace. The last Maharaja of Patiala had in fact transferred his original palace, Moti Bagh (literally 'pearl gardens') to the Government of India. It serves as a vast campus of the prestigious National Institute of Sports. Captain Singh invited the school board, of which I was a member, to meet in a grand hall that served as a library. The library itself was a sight for sore eyes. Elegantly and tastefully designed, all four walls of the huge room are stacked to the ceiling with a collection of hardbound books. Considering that the ceiling of the library is close to 25 feet high, the number of books in the collection would run into tens of thousands. The host informed us that he had designed a raised platform on which the interested reader could climb to access the highest shelves. Even as school administration was being discussed, I purveyed the shelves from afar. There were original leather bound volumes from the Victorian age, when colonial power would have been at its zenith, and even from earlier centuries. Many of the priceless books would be collectors' items. One wall is mounted with volumes of writings in the Persian script. The remarkable collection would obviously have been assembled by several generations of princes in the line. The successive Maharajas of Patiala were clearly Catholic in their taste. While there were books of many a genre, the Captain's own passion lies in the field of military history. Captain Amarinder is an avid reader, and has authored several books especially on Sikh military exploits. How he finds time to pursue his abiding interest amid the commitments to politics is indeed a wonder. Visitors ogle with awe the paintings adorning the corridors and the artifacts aesthetically placed in the rooms.

Located close to New Motibagh is a unique museum of coins and medals, perhaps the only one of its kind in the world. The collection was first seen in London by Captain Amarinder's grandfather, Maharaja Bhupinder Singh. The Maharaja spent a small fortune to purchase the entire collection for his state. The exhibits include coins and tablets from ancient civilisations, and also medals for bravery and distinction awarded in military campaigns over several centuries. The value of the collection is beyond imagination. The house of Patiala has handed over possession to the state government, but for want of assured security of the priceless items the government has not yet been able to open the museum to the public. Only a few visitors, after through screening, can enter the museum. Truly, the princes had an eye for art and a sense of history.

Among the variety of skills of Captain Amarinder is that of a horseman. Polo is acknowledged to be a dangerous sport, demanding agility and prowess. Even at an age close to 60 years, he played polo matches alongside India's champion team of the army. I witnessed some polo matches, where he held his own against the professionals much younger in age. Captain Amarinder graciously allowed my daughter Bini, who was for some time producing television programmes in the UK, to interview him for the small screen. A bonus for Bini was that she could feature the captain's mother Mohinder Kaur, and his wife Preneet, in the picturesque backdrop of New Motibagh. Both ladies had a distinguished political record, although they were affiliated with opposing parties. Rajmata Mohinder Kaur, as she was addressed, was a former Member of Parliament. After the carnage witnessed at the time of India's partition in the year 1947, she had devoted years to the rehabilitation of thousands of unfortunate women who had suffered indignity and worse. Preneet is the sitting member of parliament from Patiala. Needless to say, Bini's telecast, which featured erstwhile royalty, was a hit in the UK.

Captain Amarinder continues the famed tradition of hospitality of the house of Patiala. Among his remarkable accomplishments is that of a chef. I recall an occasion when he urged me to try a dainty vegetarian dish, carrying an exotic name *paneer lababdar patialvi*, I think, which he had personally cooked for me earlier in the day, knowing that I was a vegetarian. It was embarrassing when the Chief Minister apologized that I could not enjoy his other culinary creations, which were meat-based. If the cosy ambience of a luncheon inside the dining room was an event in itself, a banquet to greet Prince Charles of Wales, the heir to the British throne, and the Duchess, Camilla, was a truly memorable occasion. With a dress code prescribed, the guests, numbering about 150, were out in their finery. Affluent men of the business world and film stars are known to entertain lavishly. It is doubtful, however, if any glittering party in Delhi or Mumbai could match the finesse and personal touch that we, as guests, enjoyed that evening on the lawns of New Motibagh. Not everyone could sit at the high table with the visiting dignitaries from Britain, but the Captain personally introduced every single guest to the royal couple. The party displayed not a vestige of the distant colonial relationship; only a return to the noble civility of old.

True to the tradition of governance that he would have imbibed from the administration of the old state of Patiala, as Chief Minister the Captain delegated authority and responsibility to his senior administrators. Such empowerment was as per the book, but at times local political leaders were not pleased that some of their recommendations regarding posting of civil officers of their choice were overlooked by the Chief Minister. Any Chief Minister has often to bow to the wishes of many public leaders in regard to individual personnel matters. It is gainsaid that several political bigwigs resented the preference that the bureaucracy seemed to enjoy. On official matters he usually went by the advice of his key ministers and officers. Once convinced about the integrity and competence of officials in key positions, he would support them to the hilt. His approach would have been conditioned by his early career as a young officer in the Indian army and by his regal upbringing. In administration of the state, he blended the system of hierarchy and command imbibed in the armed forces with the requirements of politics.

As an example of the Chief Minister's handling of appointments in the districts, I recall one dramatic case, from around the year 2003, that of a young IAS officer by the name of Krishan Kumar. It is common for leaders of opposing political parties to favour their own candidates from the civil service for appointment in their respective districts. In respect of Krishan Kumar, who was posted as the Deputy Commissioner, Nawanshahar, all the Members of the Legislative Assembly (MLAs) hailing from the district urged the Chief Minister to transfer the officer from their small district. The Chief Minister was surprised that the MLAs belonging to both the ruling party and the opposition, who would normally be at loggerheads on most issues, were jointly demanding ouster of the officer. Neither group had any complaint about the officer's honesty and performance. They respected him for his integrity and accepted that Krishan worked like a dedicated missionary, who was popular with the public at large. The charge of the MLAs appeared comical; they were dissatisfied with the officer since he had reduced the role of the elected representatives in district administration.

It transpired that Krishan Kumar had established a system, based on information technology, for prompt delivery of services and for redressing public grievances in his office. Traditionally, the local leaders enjoyed patronage for their ability in helping their constituents with their petty problems, such as obtaining copies of land records, certificates and the like, and also in pursuing their complaints of corruption and delay in various district offices. For many matters the MLAs were used to interceding with the district administration on behalf of their voters. Most of the problems faced by the common public were now attended to automatically in a Suvidha Centre (centre for facilities) set up by the Deputy Commissioner. In these arrangements, intervention by the MLAs in these matters was no longer essential. The elected representatives felt that their role was becoming redundant. By adopting information technology in government appraisal, touted later as e-governance, Krishan Kumar was ahead of his time. The innovative management information system (MIS) had endeared Krishan Kumar to the common man. It was viewed apprehensively by the elected representatives, who felt it impaired their local standing.

Despite vociferous demands, Captain Amarinder stood his ground, and retained Krishan Kumar in his post. The successful IT-based arrangement was dubbed by the media as the 'Nawanshahar model'. It was gradually extended to all districts in the state. Krishan was eventually moved to more important positions in the state, and later to the Government of India, where he was to work in the office of the Prime Minister. This episode is an account of a typical transition of administration from primitive systems to a technology driven model of service.

This book is not intended to be a chronicle of important happenings that transpired during a time frame, or a political commentary on contemporary developments. Nor does it seek to pronounce value judgment on the different governments. The attempt is to present the flavour of the environment of officialdom through the eyes of a person who happened to be among the dramatis personae.

Captain Amarinder Singh had a national vision on policies. During his visits to the national capital, we were required to set up a series of discussions for him with several ministers of the Government of India, as well as with noted economists and captains of industry. Many of the discussions would be over dinner, which the Chief Minister graciously hosted in New Delhi. With customary hospitality, he would invite for dinner even the Finance Minister Arun Jaitley, who belonged to the Bharatiya Janata Party (BJP), the then ruling party at the centre, which was politically opposed to the Congress, Captain Amarinder's party. Captain Amarinder enjoyed easy rapport with leaders across the political spectrum. The dinner parties were conducted with great flair. Matters of state were discussed in an informal atmosphere; politicians and domain experts alike interacted freely. It was for the attendant bureaucrats to pursue the deliberations officially on behalf of the state government.

On matters concerning the interest of the state of Punjab, Captain Amarinder Singh did not stand on ceremony; he was prepared to defy protocol when called for. In the year 2002–3 the state government wished to engage Fali S. Nariman, one of India's most revered lawyers, to defend the state in a dispute before the Supreme Court of India on the sharing of river waters between Punjab and the neighbouring states. The matter was crucially important for Punjab state, as water from the rivers, transmitted to farmlands via an intricate system of irrigation canals, was a lifeline for the agricultural community in Punjab. The other states locked in the dispute, Haryana and Rajasthan, were eager as well to have Mr Nariman as their counsel in the proceedings before the Supreme Court. Captain Amarinder Singh personally visited Mr Nariman at his house, with me in attendance. He thought nothing of having to wait a short while in the office of the redoubtable lawyer. When discussion began, Mr Nariman was bowled over by the Chief Minister's earnestness; he accepted the brief on the spot. The business of the day was settled in a minute; exchange of pleasantries over tea took half an hour. Matters of detail were entrusted to me, in my then position of Principal Secretary, Irrigation and Power. Mr Nariman defended the state of Punjab adroitly in the Supreme Court. Eventually, with a view to protect the rights of the state to the quantity of the shared river water, the state government boldly rescinded an earlier inter-state agreement. Till date the legal issues are still unresolved. It is not necessary here to go into the complexities of the dispute between the states. During the episode, what was most striking was the nonchalance with which the Captain disarmed the legal luminary, and secured his commitment to the state.

A Maharaja as a Commoner

Surprisingly, it was only near the close of my official career that I was able to know closely Brigadier Sukhjit Singh (retired), a prince from Kapurthala. During early childhood, one could only gape open-eyed at the palatial retreats of their Highnesses, as the common public addressed the princes and their kin. Like other former princes, the Brigadier inherited an estate from his father and grandfather, but not the title of Maharaja, since the nomenclature stood abolished. Brigadier Sukhjit Singh approached the Chief Minister with a plea to restore the glory of Kali Bein (meaning 'black rivulet'), a tributary of the river Beas that passes Kapurthala town to merge into the river in Amritsar district. On the bank of the *bein*, just 15 miles from Kapurthala, is located the small township of Sultanpur Lodhi, where Guru Nanak Dev, the founder of the Sikh faith, spent 13 years of his childhood and youth with his elder sister Nanaki and her husband. According to Sikh tradition, the young Nanak received spiritual enlightenment as he took a dip in the small rivulet touching Sultanpur Lodhi. The residents of Kapurthala and Sultanpur Lodhi were dismayed that over the last 20 or 30 years the holy *bein* was drying up for want of water in the stream. It was also becoming choked with garbage and waste. Traditionally, a historical gurdwara at Sultanpur Lodhi, which is dedicated to the Great Guru, received thousands of devotees. Now no visitor could take a dip. The flow of water was diminished and it was polluted. Brigadier Sukhjit pleaded with the Chief Minister for rejuvenating the dying rivulet.

The CM summoned me to join the discussion, as I was then Secretary for Irrigation and Power. The Brigadier had not come merely with a complaint. He had obviously studied the problem in depth. The root of the problem was that flow into the rivulet had been blocked upstream at a place called Mukerian in the adjoining district, for a hydroelectricity project. Some water, which was stored in a reservoir for power generation, was being discharged into another rivulet, which also flowed into the river Beas, but via a different route. The diversion had reduced the flow into the Kali Bein. Brigadier Sukhjit suggested that additional water be released for the *bein* from the constriction point at Mukerian. The power engineers were prepared to release water in adequate quantity for the *bein*, but the irrigation engineers were wary, so that it became a matter of conflict between two agencies of the state government. The distribution of waters from the five rivers flowing through India into Pakistan is subject to an international treaty, to which both countries are signatory. India was constrained from drawing any water more than its allotted share. The irrigation engineers feared that the plan might infringe the treaty. Brigadier Sukhjit countered that the international river treaty limited the utilization of water (for irrigation purposes, etc.); it did not debar any rerouting of water flow, provided that Pakistan continued to receive its stipulated share. The CM directed that I should find a solution. It transpired that the issue was not intractable. After a series of discussions of all the engineers and domain specialists, it was agreed that an additional quantity of 50 cusecs (50 cubic metres per second) be released into the holy *bein*. The perseverance of one Maharaja (of Kapurthala) for a social cause, and the decisiveness of another Maharaja (of Patiala) ensured that the rivulet was rejuvenated, and that too at a nominal cost. On his part, a bureaucrat, in this case the author of this book, had managed to read the fine print. The treaty stipulated the quantity of water that India could consume. Any additional water released into the *bein* continued to flow across the border to Pakistan, as it did heretofore, but followed a different route. The downstream users did not suffer in any manner. The pilgrims at Sultanpur Lodhi could enjoy the pristine flowing water that they revered.

There was a lesson from the episode. The glory of the old kingdoms might have vanished, but long after they had parted with their crowns, some princes at least contributed significantly to public welfare.

This was the beginning of a belated friendship between Brigadier Sukhjit, the grandson of Maharaja Jagatjit Singh of Kapurthala and myself, the grandson of Bharpur Singh, who was a secretary to the then Maharaja. It was a privilege to be welcomed by Brigadier Sukhjit at his residence, The Villa, which is built on the left bank of *Kali Bein*, and also to enjoy his hospitality at his summer place, The Chateau, in the hills of Mussoorie. The only regret was that the grand buildings of yore could not possibly be maintained as in their prime. The charge was now with a person who could take legitimate pride in his martial accomplishment but could hardly employ a retinue as his grandfather did.

Like his illustrious counterpart from Patiala, Brigadier Sukhjit was a professional soldier of the Indian Army. Captain Amarinder had to secure early release from the military after just three years as a commissioned officer, to attend to family affairs. Brigadier Sukhjit, on the other hand, had a full, distinguished career in the army. During India's war with Pakistan of 1971, for his conspicuous bravery as the commander of an armoured battalion of battle tanks, he was awarded the Mahavir Chakra, India's second highest recognition for gallantry. After his retirement in the rank of Brigadier, he has been engaged in charitable and philanthropic activity. Unlike Captain Amarinder, the

Brigadier eschewed politics and worked with passion for preserving the rich heritage of his erstwhile state. As a highly decorated military man, he remains closely involved in many activities of his former army regiment.

Shearing the Tape

The conclusion of my long career with the government witnessed no momentous events. The IAS Officers' Association invited me to a farewell tea party, as is the custom for retiring officers. Some colleagues spoke in adulatory terms, pleasing to the ear, about qualities that I was not aware I possessed. Appreciating the accolades, I announced that, on freedom from bureaucratic bondage, I did not intend to fade into idleness. In the new chapter of life, I proposed to indulge my interests in sports and social causes. I recited a sonnet, titled '*Vanaprasta*' (retirement), which I had composed for the occasion. The theme appeared to fit the occasion.

I had been playing tennis regularly from college days. Throughout my service career, I had managed to find time for the game, which was a passion with me. Since my last day in service fell on a Sunday, an off day at office, the formal transfer of charge took place in the tennis stadium in Sector 10, Chandigarh. The venue selected for change of guard was unusual, but apposite. Jai Singh Gill, my successor in office, and I had been friends and tennis partners. Over a period of 30 years, we had both been representing the state of Punjab in tournaments. I happened also to be the president of the local tennis association. We were conducting specialized training programmes for young players in the very stadium.

The occasion of retirement was celebrated by organizing a voluntary blood donation camp in the Civil Secretariat, where I was the first donor. On the adjacent bed, my son Anurag also donated blood. As a regular blood donor I was happy to be engaged, post retirement, in honorary work in a blood bank. For many years I was able, in an honorary capacity, to work for two organisations, one a sports body dedicated to build champions from amongst the youth, and the other a non-government organization for collecting and supplying life-saving blood to the needy.

The icing on the cake was a grand farewell hosted by Captain Amarinder Singh. Meena and I were guests of honour at a banquet. The Chief Minister had invited distinguished persons from public life, as well as members of the judiciary, and of course officers of the IAS and the IPS. The ceremonies were marked by grace and elegance, as becoming of the host. We were left speechless when the Chief Minister personally escorted us to the hotel exit. For the head of government to open the door of my car for Meena to enter was a moment that was as poignant as it was embarrassing.

Vanaprasta,[2] or 'Breaking Free'

Forward we moved, great challenges in hand;
Crusaders all, pledged to solemnly change
Wasting systems in a long stifled land;
Against poverty and oppression ranged.
The battles rolled in frenzied years; some work
Half done; travails and triumphs both the same;
Before the adverse tide we never shirked:
Played fair a winning or a losing game.
The balance sheet? Let's write it square and fair:
Trained to prove that black is almost white,
Great deeds can well be plucked from thinnest air.
Was it indeed our role to paint all bright?
Pondering long over, now's time to act;
Sail on regardless; a new goal's intact.

---

2 In the Indian tradition, the five ages of man are *Bachpan* (childhood), *Bhramcharya* (celibacy in youth), *Grihasta* (householding), *Vanaprasta* (retirement) and *Samadhi* (return to the Creator).

TIME FOR CHEER

Truly, retirement is a great teacher. It compels you to learn new things, and relearn what you knew already. As the customary trappings of office vanish, how you wish that you had learnt to type fluently. 'Never too late to start!' you convince yourself.

The dust-laden computer beckons. The steering wheel of the car responds, reluctantly, to your tentative handling, and you to the wife's uncomplimentary backseat driving. The city's streets and markets are strangely unfamiliar, you observe on your maiden drive as a retiree. Suddenly, it seems, all parking spaces are occupied. More motor cars imply an enlarged middle class, so goes your economic logic. Over the years, the class of car owners has also become much younger, you notice, as your bid to back into an inviting spot is thwarted by an outflanking movement by a dashing teenager in a bright red sports car. His 'Sorry Uncle!' is more a cry of triumph than an apology, a remark that rubs in the factor of your age.

No office hours to maintain, you console yourself, so there's plenty of time to do it all yourself! Just a few bills to pay, and bank accounts to settle, that is the listed business for the day. Surely an enjoyable morning's enterprise is in the offing. 'Will be back home in an hour,' you announce cheerily as you enjoin the wife to have lunch ready for your return. As you move from office to office, accosting sundry bank tellers, club accountants and surly receipt clerks, the magnitude of the unfamiliar task sinks in. Several home visits intersperse your odyssey, as you have perforce to retrieve your election voting card, your pension payment order and the like, for production before the authorities.

The tempting repast of lunch is delayed. The afternoon siesta is cancelled on account of 'unforeseen circumstances'. If you anticipated retirement as a period of comfortable languor and 'honeyed indolence' celebrated by the English poet Keats, you are sadly mistaken. A retired life is a deadly serious, time consuming business.

Retirement is, fortunately, not all drudgery. This is demonstrated vividly on the first Saturday of the month. It's the day when retired officers of the Indian Administrative Service (IAS) in town meet over high tea. This monthly meeting, conducted with unfailing regularity and punctuality, is marked with a degree of diligence.

Gone are the intra service and interstate rivalries, the race for coveted assignments, the currying of favour with the high and powerful. Forgotten is the weight of hierarchy, for all retirees are now equal. A rare camaraderie pervades the environment. The evening is replete with good humour, as aged bureaucrats let down their hair. Unsuspected gifts of creativity are on display, as hidden artists, musicians and writers emerge. On the agenda is discussion on revised pension, but such financial issues are considered of marginal interest. Of greater value to the company are the spontaneous witticisms, the banter and repartee. It is a delicious irony when the erstwhile pillars of the establishment, the constituents of the steel frame, rail against the oppressive red tape of the day. On one thing there is unanimity. 'Grow old along with me', the members echo the famous poet, for 'The best is yet to be.' Retirement can be great fun. It can be gainful too.

Fortunately, while yet in service, the state government had not foisted on me the paraphernalia of personal security guards, nor had I resided in an official bungalow. In the absence of obtrusive elements, one's privacy remained intact. The transition from a rung of high office to that of a common citizen was comparatively seamless. Post superannuation, as the event is officially dubbed, there were ample avenues for occupying spare time, of which there was now a surfeit. Over many years, I had been donating blood regularly. After demitting office, I volunteered to join a NGO engaged in blood management. In India the health sector has a loose linkage between the government and voluntary agencies. What better use could a former official make of time and energy than in a non-profit NGO? Especially challenging was the task of building up a new institution from its roots. The novel experience is described hereafter.

At the same time, for some years I had been engaged, in an honorary capacity, as president, and later chairman of the local tennis association. Sports administration entailed running a training institute on professional and scientific lines. No longer saddled with office work, one could bicycle early every morning, enjoy playing a couple of sets of tennis, and also observe the coaching being imparted to promising young boys and girls.

It was the game of tennis that occasioned a memorable visit in the year 2004 across the border from India's Punjab to that of Pakistan.

The Grass is as Green[1]

Three not-so-young enthusiasts, namely, Surinder Mohan Sharma, a serving police officer, Dr Jasjit Singh, a medical heart specialist, who worked as physician to the Governor of Punjab, and I had sent our entries to play the Veterans' National Tennis Championship at Lahore, Pakistan. In a sense, we were exhilarated to embark on the adventurous journey. Our wives too were bold enough to accompany us to a country with which we had had strained relations for years. The distance between Amritsar and Lahore is less than 40 miles, Wagah Border outpost being the middle point, where Indian travellers leave their cars, to walk across the line, to be received by their hosts from Lahore. On account of restrictive procedures that apparently delight the bureaucracy in both countries, only persons aged over 60 years, or those travelling in a reputed group, are allowed to

1 Some part of this is drawn from an article written by the author for *The Tribune* in the year 2004.

take the route by road. Even residents of Amritsar must travel 350 miles south to Delhi to catch a plane, or a ramshackle train, to reach Lahore. As we were lucky enough to have permission to cross the border on foot, we managed to reach Lahore after just a five-hour car journey from Chandigarh.

In 1947, the two countries had marked the line of demarcation through the state of Punjab.

A hedge it was. Neighbours on both sides had nurtured it assiduously over a period of 50 years. The barrier now concealed from us in the East the greens that were fabled to exist across the frontier. Never having ventured beyond, my own picture of the alien West had been coloured by the exotic hues created by others who had viewed the landscape decades earlier. Around the year 1938, my father had graduated from Forman Christian College, and my mother from Kinnaird College, both in Lahore. These were among the foremost educational institutions of the undivided country. Similarly, Jasjit's father, Dr Amarjit Singh Ahluwalia, who was several years younger than my parents, had begun his medical studies at King Edward Medical College, Lahore, just when India was declared independent. Amid the turmoil that accompanied the transfer of population on communal lines, Dr Ahluwalia, along with many Hindu and Sikh families, had to suddenly leave Lahore in a passenger train bound for Amritsar. The refugees were fleeing from communal riots that gripped the towns in the west. Dr Ahluwalia himself witnessed the massacre of several Hindu and Sikh passengers who were travelling in the same train from Pakistan to India.

Unlike Dr Ahluwalia, who underwent a traumatic experience, my parents, like many others of their generation, had pleasant and vivid memories of a youth spent in a wondrous city. Before the country was partitioned, Lahore was the most vibrant metropolis of undivided India, an unmatched centre of culture and education. The elders never tired of narrating the glory of Lahore, the capital city of a capital state, the original Punjab. Many writers have described the social environment of the time, which was modern, open and interactive. It inspired art, music, films and sports. During the early part of the twentieth century many young men and women blessed with talent or ambition, gravitated to Lahore, so we were told. We were regaled with the memories of our seniors: of colleges set in sylvan surroundings; of eating places serving a myriad and heady mix of cuisine; of sports extravaganzas witnessed by knowledgeable lovers of the game. Even as it pleasingly combined the traditional and the modern, Lahore was an established nodal point for organised protest against the oppressive colonial regime. The Punjab of that day had fashioned pacifists and revolutionaries alike. Lahore was home to freedom fighters and to distinguished jurists who defended them in court, at risk of political reprisal at the hands of the entrenched rulers.

So massive was the migration of people of various communities across the new international border in 1947 that almost every family in Punjab carried certain indelible memories of the times spent on the other side. Over the years, the new generation, at least in the east, developed a curious form of vicarious collective nostalgia for the environment famed to exist in the West. This fascination, and longing, was fanned not a little by armed hostilities that broke out periodically between the two sides. The visit to Pakistan, in the month of April 2004 (it was followed two years later by another, also thanks to the tennis connection) was tinged with great expectancy. 'How would we be received?' we wondered apprehensively, alive to the recurrent political tensions between the two nations. Furthermore, how real was that wonderful world so fondly remembered by the last generation?

Our trepidation was unfounded, as it transpired. In sight, sound and ambience, as also in the style and behaviour of the people we met, the other Punjab proved so similar to ours. With the affable hospitality that we were to enjoy, it was like a homecoming. The absolute anti-climax experienced on transportation across the line was no different from that of the boy in the childhood ditty who ran away from England expecting to see a spectacularly different world in the next-door Scotland:

'There was a naughty boy
And a naughty boy was he,
He ran away to Scotland
The people for to see–
Then he found
That the ground
Was as hard,

That a yard
Was as long,
That a song
Was as merry,
That a cherry
Was as red–
That lead
Was as weighty,
That fourscore
Was as eighty,
That a door
Was as wooden
As in England–
So he stood in his shoes
And he wondered,
He wondered,
He stood in his shoes
And he wondered.'

('The Naughty Boy', John Keats)

My 'wonderment' too, was at seeing the sameness of the two Punjabs. The Pakistani Rangers, gruff and jovial, who escorted us from the line, differed only in the style of their uniform from the amiable BSF officers who delivered us. Money-changers pursued us to exchange our Indian rupees (which commanded a premium, we happily realised) for Pakistan currency. On the roadside cattle and goats munched as carefree as their owners lolling on cots outside nondescript dung-plastered huts. The spoken word was Punjabi, with

Urdu (like our native Hindustani) being preferred for formal discourse. Entering the city of Lahore, chaotic traffic greeted us. Donkey carts and cyclists cut across the path of brand-new Japanese cars driven by well-heeled young businessmen. Amritsar's scooter rickshaws were replaced by the equally overloaded Gingze (pronounced 'Chinchi')—a breed of a three-wheeler imported from China adapted to local conditions. The traffic police seemed inured to the prevalent laissez faire. Foreign-made motorcycles took the place of our indigenous scooters, but the drivers did not bother to use the mandatory helmets, many preferring to carry the uncomfortable headgear in their hands, as youngsters still do in some Indian towns.

One important landmark in the town of Lahore is the Aitchison College, actually a world-class boarding school for boys from the gentry. Established in the year 1886 as an elite institution, it was appropriately named the Chiefs College, as students were all sons of rulers of princely states of the original colonial India. Among the distinguished alumni from the school were a number of Pakistan's political leaders and military officers, and also those who excelled in industry, education and social activity. I was anxious to visit Aitchison, as it was the parent institution of Yadavindra Public School, Patiala (YPS), which was my alma mater in India. I was also a member of the Board of Governors of YPS, which maintained its link with the parent body at Lahore. At the time of partition of the country in 1947, Maharaja Yadavindra Singh, a former student, had set up the school at Patiala to rehabilitate those Hindu and Sikh boys who had to leave Lahore midstream of their studies. At the time of our visit, the principal of Aitchison was Mr Shamim Saidullah Khan, an urbane, highly sophisticated Western-oriented educationist, who admitted, hesitantly, that he was a British citizen. He had been invited by a powerful board of school governors to return to Pakistan to head the school. Equally distinguished was his deputy, a gentleman named Ifteqar Ahmed Malik, who held the position of Bursar. Mr Malik happened to be a former chairman of one of the country's leading business houses. As the Principal and Bursar conducted our party through the huge campus spread over an area of more than 200 acres in the heart of town, we learnt about their unique status in Pakistan's society. Political leaders, military officers and executives in the top business houses of the country vie to have their sons admitted at Aitchison, as well they might, for the school serves as a nursery for the next generation of leaders in most important fields that dominate the country. Just 140 students, from among 10,000 or so applicants, are selected annually to enter the portals. It is small wonder that the management of Aitchison enjoys vast powers of patronage. On completion of schooling, many young men from Aitchison secure admission to foreign universities, particularly Oxford and Cambridge in the UK. They return home to begin chosen careers.

Our visit gave us a glimpse of the opulent ways of the Maharajas and Nawabs of yore. While the boys of that generation lived in lavish dormitories, scores of their attendants, including the tenders of their horses, were housed in well-appointed outhouses. After all, no prince at that time could venture without his retinue. Mr Khan, the Principal, narrated what he swore was a true story from the 1930s. At that time, the school found itself short of pupils; it catered exclusively to the sons of Chiefs, and would not admit any from outside the aristocracy. His desperate plea to Maharaja Bhupinder Singh of Patiala for augmenting the number of students evoked immediate response. The Maharaja offered to send at least two dozen of his own sons from Patiala for admission in the school in Lahore. The Maharaja was reputed to have had as many as 365 wives and female companions. Aitchison survived the crisis, thanks to the munificence of one prince. My own former school at Patiala was of course a far humbler version of a public school, quite unrecognisable from its parent. It was a feast to view the history of the princes as they would have lived in childhood. We were invited to lunch. Sadly, three members of our group could not do justice to the hospitality on offer. The repast included many exotic dishes, but they were all meat-based items, which the vegetarians could not enjoy. We were hard put to play down our host's embarrassment.

A dual economy stared us in the face in Lahore, much as it might in a Ludhiana or a Batala. A few shopping arcades livened up localities such as 'Gulberg' or 'Liberty'. Here modern architecture had spawned some high-rise buildings for the corporates. Complete orderliness prevailed in the cantonment, and in Model Town, where manicured public parks vied with stylish private lawns. The aristocracy was clearly alive and well. Large landowners had invested wisely, combining enterprise in farm and commerce alike. Most owners of larger bungalows had their own private guards for security.

The landmarks of the old Lahore described by my parents were intact. Anarkali Market, with its streets so narrow that the upper floors of its buildings almost blocked out the sunlight, the strong lighting creating a daytime atmosphere even at midnight, not least on account of heat emitted from the lamps. The shopkeepers haggled, as they would in Mai Hiraṇ, Jalandhar. They were visibly delighted to receive Indian visitors. They enquired with great curiosity about the bazaars where their parents had once traded—in Patiala, Jalandhar or Amritsar.

Food Street was a gourmet's paradise. Cheek by jowl with Western-style pizza parlours were humble *kulfi*-sellers and *kebab-wallas*[2] displaying meats exposed to the elements, as to vermin. Diverse retailers, travel agents, homoeopaths, and wonder of wonders, palmists and astrologers flourished in adjoining booths. No cause for homesickness for any in our party! Incongruities abounded. Right on the bank of an open waste-water drain on the outskirts of Lahore stood the dignified government office of Director, Land Reclamation. An accurate parallel would be the office of the State Pollution Control Board astride the Hudiara drain

---

2 *Kulfi* is a home-made ice cream; *kebab*: a barbecued meat delicacy; *walla* refers to the roadside seller.

that carried untreated sullage from Amritsar, ironically into Pakistan territory.

Poverty was visible in the streets of Lahore. Many slums, we learnt, had been relocated by the state government recently, the encroachments and hazards removed. The locals took great pride in their city. The Government College, citadel of higher education, had become a deemed University. The Forman Christian College (my father had insisted I must see his old hostel in Ewing Hall) was still revered, along with Kinnaird College for Women, as an institution of academic excellence. Some famous names had been changed, as in India. The name of Lawrence Gardens, where our tennis matches were played, had been changed to Bagh-e-Jinnah. In fact, we moved on foot casually from our hotel to the venue. Unescorted as we were, we caught the flavour of the daily life of ordinary citizens in a way that important guests could never enjoy. Anonymity helps to view the ground reality of an alien society. At most places we were taken as Pakistanis. It was only Meena's bindi and Jasjit's turban that distinguished them as Indians. As at the Taj Mahal in Agra, foreigners entering monuments had to pay a higher entry fee than the locals.

History was kept alive in Lahore. According to the official guide book, the city proclaimed its lineage as the ancient dominion of legendary Luv, the son of Sri Ramchandra, the ideal Hindu king. Lahore Fort was a protected national monument, preserving, to some extent the 'Diwan-e-Aam' (open house for supplicants), the 'Diwan-e-Khas' (exclusive chamber for judicial appeals) and the harems constructed by the Mughal Emperors who later occupied the fort at the height of their power. The fort housed evidence of the decadence of the Mughal Empire—some poetic manuscripts of the tragic last emperor Bahadur Shah Zafar (who was exiled to Burma in the year 1857), along with priceless 19th century murals from the era of Maharaja Ranjit Singh. Indeed Maharaja Ranjit Singh was highly regarded as a brave historical figure, whose Sikh empire dared the rising might of colonial Britain.

Thanks to an official connection, we were allowed to see the tomb of Anarkali, the legendary court dancer, dalliance with whom created a romantic image for Prince Salim, later the Emperor Jahangir. It was confounding that access to Anarkali's tomb was restricted, since it was located within the official archives, in a government building. Considering the size of the tombstone, Anarkali must have been a tiny woman! The secretary of the Department of Archives was Mr Bhullar, a Muslim Jat. Mr Bhullar had that typical 'Hail fellow, well met!' approach of the extrovert landed gentry. He enquired from us about the Bhullars in Eastern Punjab, with whom he claimed kinship. Mr Bhullar was delighted to learn that his kin flourished as progressive farmers, and also distinguished themselves in the professions, especially in the military and the police. Our host was Major Iftikhar Ahmed Rao, a Secretary in the Punjab Government, who was also President of Punjab Tennis Association. He arranged our visits to the landmarks in town, and also to some offices of the state government. Being from Punjab, we were struck with the fact that many of the officials we met bore the same surnames that were common among the community of farmers in north India. The first names were, of course Muslim, but the officials had no hesitation in accepting that their earlier generations were from among Hindus and Sikhs, who had converted to Islam.

I was to develop a good friendship with Iftekhar Rao, who was related to some Rao families in the state of Haryana. A few years after our Lahore visit, Iftekhar led a team of veteran tennis players from Lahore to play friendly matches in our stadium in Chandigarh. M. Ramsekhar, the secretary of our tennis association at Chandigarh, was at the time handling the Transport department in Haryana state. He arranged transport by coach for the Pakistani visitors from Amritsar to Chandigarh. In the alternative, the group from Pakistan would have had to undertake a tedious, circuitous journey from Lahore to Delhi to Chandigarh. While at Chandigarh, Iftekhar confided to me that driving through rural Punjab was a unique experience. He was highly impressed with the bustling little towns through which their luxury bus travelled. While motoring from Amritsar to Chandigarh, one is always irritated with chaotic traffic encountered in such settlements as Banga, Nawanshahar and Ropar en route. On the contrary, the Pakistani visitors, who took the same route, were struck with the signs of a booming middle class, such as numerous offices of travel agents, and busy markets for all the daily necessities, establishments that we take for granted. The perceptions of our foreign friends were a testimony to the success of India's democratic model of economic development.

Indians citizens were given visas that confined their stay to a specific town. Our travel documents did not permit us to venture out of the city of Lahore. Thanks to Iftekhar Rao, the state government gave us special permission to travel to Islamabad, located about 200 miles in the West. Impressive is the quality and management of the Grand Trunk Road, as it takes off from Lahore to reach Islamabad, Pakistan's national capital that now dominates its twin city, the traditional Rawalpindi. The GT Road, then listed as India's National Highway 1, stretches from Calcutta to Amritsar. The same highway, bearing the very name, moves on from Lahore to Rawalpindi. This major arterial road had been built in the sixteenth century by Sher Shah Suri, a ruler who had ousted the second Mughal Emperor Humayun, only to be overthrown by the Mughal after a few years on the throne at Delhi. We found the traffic on GT Road in Pakistan extremely orderly, controlled as it was by a highly visible National Highway Patrol, whose members pounced on any traffic violators. My driver Mehboob pointed at a bank van that was following the police vehicle. The function of the bank van, he explained, was to deposit all traffic fines imposed by the patrol, insulating the offenders against exploitation by the police officials. A charming innovation of the day to tackle a malady common in our country!

The Pakistan stretch of the GT Road traverses the three rivers of Punjab, Ravi, Chenab and Jhelum. We accomplished our return journey from Islamabad to Lahore, and thence to Amritsar and thereon to the home destination in Chandigarh within a space of two days. We would boast of a rare distinction of crossing, in a driving time of 11 hours, all the five rivers of Punjab, three in Pakistan, and two, Beas and Sutlej in India. Some years later, Dr Manmohan Singh, India's Prime Minister was to share his dream of free movement between India and Pakistan, which would allow citizens to breakfast in Islamabad, lunch in Amritsar, and dine in New Delhi. When that vision would fructify is to be seen, but our motoring feat was singular in its own right.

A parallel superhighway between Lahore and Peshawar had been commissioned shortly before we travelled. That road could, in quality of construction, as also the fluidity of traffic movement, liken to any motorway in Europe. It scarcely seemed the same country as typified by the good old Lahore that had been left behind. Sadly, hardly any motor traffic is visible on this marvellous road link. Somewhat cynically, I dubbed it a vehicle free motorway. Travellers were required to pay some toll tax for travel, but such levy could not have been the reason for dissuading users. Simplistically, the lack of a sufficient number of users could be attributed to the comparative absence of a booming middle class in the country. The old GT Road passed through several small towns, but nowhere en route did we see the ubiquitous *dhaba*s, small eating joints, nor the roadside fruit sellers that dot the highways in north India. Perhaps there was limited clientele, as the middle class, which constitutes the customers for goods in India, was then a missing commodity in Pakistan. The smaller towns would have been poor cousins of the grand city of Lahore. The only restaurant on the super highway where we could stop was run by the government. We were the sole customers who had stopped there; there was not much that the kitchen could offer that day, apart from toast, butter and tea.

If the town of Lahore was a study in contrasts, the city of Islamabad, perched on the edge of the state of Punjab, transported you to a fairy tale world. Modern architecture, stylish and innovative, had created the marvel of a city of immaculate streets, shaded drives, modern shopping malls and high-tech application, befitting a prestigious national capital. A showpiece for foreign visitors, Islamabad could be pictured as a grander Chandigarh transposed to an international stage. The most visible difference from Chandigarh was in respect of strict regulation of urban laws. Islamabad is situated at the base of a mountain range, as Chandigarh is, but the city had not so far succumbed to the pressures common to a developing economy in the third world. Legislation was obviously enforced, we found; encroachers on public land, and slums, were non-existent. Islamabad is spread over an undulating area measuring 900 square kilometres, of which 220 square kilometres serves as parks, with 460 square kilometres preserved in the original rural setting. The urbanised portion covers just 220 square kilometres. An ideal green city!

Even as we gaped breathlessly at this picture-postcard of a utopia, the hotel porter brought us rudely down to earth. 'What attractions could there be for Indian visitors?' he questioned innocently, unimpressed with the regulation and compliance of urban laws. 'Nothing special to see in Islamabad,' he averred. What really excited him were cricketers from India and Hindi films. It was the fantasy of a foreign land brought alive by the medium of television that was for him the ultimate reality, not his own elite city. Truly, distance had lent enchantment to the view, at least to a young man like he.

At Lahore, casual conversation frequently led the locals to launch a general diatribe against authority, represented by the politician, the petty civil servant, and amazingly, even the military. Governance was a major issue. Dissatisfaction with the quality of public service was articulated by the porter, the taxi-driver, the cloth retailer, the phone-booth attendant. The man in the street seemed fairly apathetic to the form of administration at the very top, be it military rule or a variation of democracy. Most people seemed fascinated with the functioning of Indian democracy, to learn about an environment novel and alien to them. There was grudging admiration for the system of elections that were shortly due in India. The common people we met were somewhat reassured when we intoned about similar visible ills of the system in India—the partisanship, the venality, the divisiveness of public figures. Pakistanis talk openly of the weekly charges: it's called '*hafta*' as in India-levied by petty police constables. They gripe at a deteriorating system of education that has created numerous inefficient school boards whose writ, absurdly, is limited to single districts in the state of Punjab. We noted resentment among the traders as well as the farmers with regard to a decision of the government to regulate the movement of wheat grain district-wise (shades of similar state barriers established in the 1960s in India!).

With General Parvez Musharraf as President, the country was then being ruled by the military, as it had been for the major period since its independence. During the visit I met several serving and retired officers from the civil service and also from the armed forces. I was keen to elicit their views on administration in Pakistan. Surprisingly, many people that we met informally were uninhibited in commenting critically on political affairs. These included some new friends on the tennis court. At the time of independence both India and Pakistan had inherited the same form of civil service. The Civil Service of Pakistan (CSP) was the successor to the Indian Civil Service as the IAS was in India. I gathered in cursory discussions that during the long phases when Pakistan was directly managed by the military, the status of the top civil service had been considerably undermined. Over the years, military officers were inducted laterally into CSP, and began to dominate the original civil service. At the same time, many serving military officers were directly assigned responsibility for civil administration at critical levels. It was common for army officers to work as Deputy Commissioner and Police Superintendent in the districts. A former Group Captain of the Pakistan Air Force enquired if it was true that the Army Chief in India saluted the Prime Minister of India. He was dumbfounded to learn that, as per the protocol in our democracy, all the service chiefs saluted the Defence Minister too. I was at pains to clarify that this positioning of the political leadership did not compromise the operational autonomy of the armed forces.

At that point in time Pakistan was toying with a form of administrative reform at district level. It was proposing to establish a cadre of Nazims (empowered administrators) that would be the cutting edge of government at the district level. Some civil servants feared that if unelected Nazims were drawn arbitrarily from the traditional feudal class of landowners, it would impair administration within government.

For the record, our doubles pair reached the semi- finals of the veteran doubles event, no mean achievement in a national tournament. After the match, we were accosted at the venue by some news correspondents. They asked several searching questions, which related to every subject except tennis. The scribes were curious to know about the Indian economy, about the search for peace between India and Pakistan and especially about the forthcoming national elections in India. They were delighted when we commended the hospitality that we received, which made us feel totally at home, and not in a foreign country. It was no hyperbole for me to declare that the affection showered on us would remain long in memory.

As in India, it was not uncommon for men in the street to be voicing dissatisfaction with the government of the day. When we heard people railing against the establishment, we were transported back to our own noisy democracy. Both states across the international border are called Punjab, a name derived from the five waters that are effectively divided between the neighbouring nations. We returned home with a conviction that more things bound together the people of the two Punjabs than separated them. In government parlance, the authority in Pakistan was invariably labelled 'Government of the Punjab'—note the nomenclature, the term 'Punjab' being akin to a common noun, connoting a body of land. In India, we grandly call it 'Government of Punjab', by so doing giving Punjab the attribute of a living, superior object. And that's one difference between their Punjab and ours!

Engaged in the City

The sojourn in Pakistan was an exciting interlude in the post-retirement occupations in Chandigarh. At the tennis academy, some children, who had been inducted at as young an age as five years, were beginning to perform well in tournaments for their respective age groups. On conclusion of my tenure as Chairman, the association was headed by my colleague and tennis partner, Jai Singh Gill, who also happened to be my successor in office as Chief Secretary of the Government of Punjab. I remained a patron of the association. For a number of years, the flagship scheme for village children from low-income families, Chandigarh Academy for Rural Tennis (CHART) had to be supported by the tennis association out of its limited resources. Around the year 2011, it was the Chief Minister of the state of Haryana, Bhupinder Singh Hooda, himself a keen tennis player, who decided that his government would sponsor children from villages in his state for specialized training in CHART. Players from Haryana were excelling at the national level in several sports disciplines. Partnership with a state government was a great opportunity for CHART to nurture and develop gifted boys and girls to their potential as tennis champions. Twenty boys and girls from the villages of Haryana were inducted in the residential academy at the age of nine years for imparting scientific training. These prize pupils also received international exposure in the form of travel to Spain as part of an agreement between the association in Chandigarh and its counterpart in Madrid. The project of CHART was immensely satisfying, both for the tennis association and the government of Haryana. At centre stage, of course, were the young trainees themselves, who were enabled to build a career, as players and even as professional tennis coaches.

There was opportunity to return to the periphery of the academic world, as one visited the Panjab University Chandigarh, my alma mater, to be sometimes invited as a guest speaker. It was stimulating too, to be on the panel of the Mahatma Gandhi State Institute for Public Administration for some events, to speak to groups of younger officers assembled for training.

A Service of Love

It was Meena who introduced me to her group of women volunteers, mainly housewives, who had organized themselves into a society for an inspiring social activity. This was the Chandigarh Blood Bank Society (BBS), which was dedicated to the movement for safe blood, collected exclusively from voluntary donors. The society was led by Mrs Kanata Saroop Krishen, who had in the year 1963 established collaboration with the Post Graduate Institute of Medical Education and Research, Chandigarh (PGI), one of India's leading medical institutions. She had devoted 40 years of her life to this cause. In its early years, the role of BBS was to identify and motivate donors to contribute to a great social cause that helped to save precious lives. PGI, on its part, was happy that voluntary donors were at hand to deliver blood for medical procedures that demanded transfusion. In developed countries, the source of supply of precious life-saving blood was voluntary donation. In countries like India, due to reasons of ignorance and poverty, volunteers were in those early days hard to find. Furthermore, professional blood donors were systematically offering their blood for sale. BBS, on the other hand, determined that every single unit delivered by it to hospitals came from healthy volunteers. BBS had been at the forefront of a struggle against the pernicious practice of sale of blood. The blood offered by such sellers, mainly poverty driven, was often unsafe. The dehumanizing practice endangered the health of the desperate sellers themselves. During times of crisis, as when soldiers were wounded in war, the public was fired by patriotic fervour; donation came unsolicited. BBS was working to create and sustain a culture of volunteered donation of blood. In recognition of her efforts in a noble cause, the President of India had in the year 1971 had conferred on Kanta Saroop Krishen the prestigious national award of Padma Shri. I had first met Kanta and her team of volunteers in the wake of the war with Pakistan. The army was then in dire need of blood to treat wounded soldiers. At Ropar, where I worked as Deputy Commissioner, hundreds of donors had gathered spontaneously. The quantity offered far exceeded expectations. My first donation at Ropar was the beginning of a lifelong affair; over the years, it was a privilege to contribute whenever an occasion arose.

While working as a volunteer in BBS, Meena saw at first hand the passion with which Kanta had built up her society as one on India' s foremost institutions in the field. As a part of a motivational drive, every morning the women, packed uncomfortably together in a modest van, would set out to visit educational and social institutions in the city and its suburbs. At that point in time, the scourge of AIDS was threatening all sections of society. It was noted that AIDS could be transmitted by HIV carriers, and also by unsafe sex practices. In accordance with the national policy, National Aids Control Organisation (NACO) had enjoined all state governments to involve reputed NGOs in spreading awareness about sexually transmitted diseases as a major cause of proliferation of AIDS. It took much courage for the women volunteers, of whom Meena was one, to speak openly to audiences comprising both males and females on matters like sex and the use of condoms, topics which were taboo in a conservative society. Kanta's own enthusiasm for the cause was infectious. Most of the group was more than 20 years younger than she, but tried gamely to emulate her in spirit and energy. Since its inception, the Blood Bank Society had come far. Kanta was personally responsible for moving the highest judicial authority, the Supreme Court of India, with a plea to ban the sale of blood. In her inimitable way, she persuaded a like-minded institution in New Delhi, called Common Cause to take up litigation free of cost. She similarly persuaded H.D. Shourie, a leading advocate to represent her society and some others, again gratis, in court. Kanata's obduracy finally bore fruit when, in the year 1996, the Supreme Court decreed that sale of blood be banned throughout the country.

By a happy coincidence, I had retired from government at the very time that BBS, in partnership with the Rotary Club of Chandigarh, decided to establish its own full-fledged blood bank. The Rotary and Blood Bank Society Resource Centre, as it was christened, offered me the privilege of heading the managing committee, a key administrative position, which entailed considerable interaction with diverse individuals and institutions. In the terminology of blood management, this was a 'Stand Alone Blood Bank', which was authorized to collect blood, and process its components for delivery to hospitals and nursing homes use in transfusion. While in government, one deals with policies and regulation. In this new position, one could now appreciate at first hand the ground realities in which a NGO works. This challenging assignment, which I held for twelve years, taught many lessons, not least the virtues of humility and compassion, which the founder Kanta was naturally imbued with. While BBS volunteers were responsible for arranging adequate supplies from volunteers, it was the growing credibility of the blood bank alone that determined the demand from user hospitals. Since this was a non-profit organization, the blood could be supplied at rates approved by the Drug Controller General of India, the regulatory agency. Fortunately, skills in finance and marketing were available in house, so a multi-disciplinary practical approach to scientific blood management emerged.

At the blood bank, there is never a dull moment. It works around the clock, assuring delivery of blood and its components within an hour of its requisition. It is almost always an emergency that brings patients and attendants to a blood bank. Prompt delivery of blood at midnight, or in the wee hours of the morning created an image of efficiency and dedication. At the same time, tremendous goodwill built up by its mentors, BBS and the Rotary Club, attracted substantial donations in cash and kind from the social and corporate sector, which funded the expenditure on procuring and replacement of sophisticated equipment. The governing council (the general body) continues to be headed by Mr R.K. Saboo, a doyen of the Rotary movement, who has been President of Rotary International. Along with other members, I could capitalize on goodwill generated with many public institutions over many decades. A fair amount of public dealing was involved. All in all, the hands on activities went far beyond what I had done while with the government. To be engaged in an activity that saves lives was a reward in itself.

When I had entered government service, Kanta's husband, Saroop Krishen was one of India's senior most officers of the Indian Civil Service. He served as a Secretary with the Government of India, and also as Chief Secretary of Haryana state. It was remarkable how comfortably Saroop Krishen had submerged his own entity, which was formidable, to be proudly acclaimed as Kanta's husband, a man behind a successful woman. Every year, on his birthday, he would send to the Blood Centre a handsome cheque as his cash donation. The grand couple showed extraordinary concern for the environment. I recall one occasion when Saroop Krishen wrote to the central and state governments, pointing out that the government was wasting huge amounts in notifying in newspapers lists of individuals owning thousands of pieces of land, which were to be acquired for projects. He had calculated that the wasteful expenditure during a single year by the governments of Punjab and Haryana alone amounted to several crores of rupees. As a sworn environmentalist, he had also estimated how many trees would have been cut to provide the newsprint used. On her part Kanta would try to recycle every scrap of material she could access. As an instance, she would collect used paper cups, and redesign them as attractive flower pots. The ultimate demonstration of environmental commitment must be the pledge by both Mr and Mrs Saroop Krishen for their bodies to be donated, after death, to the PGI. They felt that even the human body itself deserved to be recycled.For them, donation began with the commodity of blood and money; it culminated in donation of the body. Sadly, in the year 2006, when Mr Saroop Krishen died at the age of 93, there could be no funeral rites where we admirers could pay homage. Of such stuff are donors made.

Now 94 years old, Kanta Saroop Krishen has withdrawn from day-to-day activities of the blood bank, but her verve remains undiminished. In the year 2021, amid the pandemic caused by the corona virus, she learnt that a Delhi based NGO of my son Anurag was engaged in rehabilitating ragpicking women, who had been trained to convert waste material into items of utility. She immediately asked to meet Anurag, and on the spot donated an amount of 50,000 rupees for the eco-friendly project.

The Bench

Just two years after I had left the bureaus of officialdom, I was unexpectedly recalled from comparative leisure to occupy the bench of a quasi-judicial authority. In the beginning of October, 2005, I was surprised to receive a telephone call from Sardar Parkash Singh Badal, a three time former Chief Minister of Punjab, who was at that time the leader of the opposition in the state legislature. Mr Badal informed me that he had that very moment approved a proposal of the then Chief Minister, Captain Amarinder Singh to appoint me as State Chief Information Commissioner, Punjab. While thanking Mr Badal, who had always been kind to me during my service days, I scoured the internet to understand what the assignment entailed. It transpired that the Government of India had promulgated a new legislation, The Right to Information Act, 2005 (RTI Act), to empower citizens to obtain information from all the organs of the state, the executive, the legislature and the judiciary, both at the national level, and in all the states. With effect from 5 October 2005, the central government was required to establish a statutory Central Information Commission, and the state governments to similarly set up State Information Commissions. These Commissions were statutory bodies, armed with judicial powers for regulating the free flow of information in the public interest. It took time to sink in that I would be functioning as a judicial authority. On reading the RTI Act, I learnt that the Central Chief Information Commissioner (CIC) enjoyed the status and salary of the Chief Justice of the Supreme Court of India, and the State CIC that of a judge of the Supreme Court. The Act laid down that the Chief Minister and the leader of the opposition, along with another minister, should appoint a state CIC from among persons with suitable qualifications and experience. The incumbent could serve in the position until he attained the age of 65 years. I would thus be sitting on the bench for almost three years. It was gratifying to learn that the top political leaders, who might have different views on many matters, had agreed on my name for such an important position.

The Information Commissioners appointed at the centre and in the states came from diverse backgrounds. They included former civil servants such as the gifted Wajahat Habibullah, who was central CIC, along with some former Chief Justices of High Courts and also some academics and journalists. I had been propelled from comparative anonymity to a platform of high visibility. My Commission was empowered to compel all authorities in the state of Punjab to divulge items of information specifically demanded by any citizen of India. The enactment resonated with the media, which were now entitled to observe, especially, vital official records. I recalled the famous words of the 19th century Irish playwright, Oscar Wilde, 'the public have an insatiable curiosity to know everything, except what is worth knowing. Journalism, conscious of this—supplies their demands'. The journalists viewed the Act as a possible instrument for accessing interesting material for their pages and screens. Under a protocol of the year 1946 the United Nations had declared freedom of information a democratic human right. In conformity with Article 19 of the Constitution of India, the RTI Act premised that freedom of speech must include the right to know. With the RTI Act, India became the 55th country in the world to assure information freedom by legislation. The press and other media looked expectantly at the unravelling of secrecy that had shrouded decisions of the government. The RTI Act explicitly superseded many provisions of the oppressive Official Secrets Act, 1923, which was employed by the colonial government to debar the public from knowledge on sensitive matters in the interest of security. Surprisingly the provisions had remained intact on the statute books long after democracy had dawned on the country. It was no wonder that when, on 18 October 2005 General S.F. Rodrigues, the Governor of Punjab, administered the oath of office to me, the media gave that routine event more than usual coverage. The oath ceremony in Punjab Raj Bhawan was a two minute affair, which was witnessed by my father, then 88 years old, Meena's mother, 83, and some other proud members of the family.

By the very nature of his job, an information commissioner is subject to scrutiny by the media that judges do not face. Wajahat Habibullah, my counterpart in the Central Commission, agreed that CICs would need to meet the members of the fourth estate occasionally. The press considered itself as a champion of free speech, and dissemination of information. After all, press freedom formed a bulwark for the constitution of the United States of America, where libertarians like James Madison and Thomas Jefferson had battled against the British colonial weapon of sedition to curb free speech. During our first interaction, a journalist sought to confound me with a loaded, potentially embarrassing question, 'Don't you think you are an unsuitable person for this assignment?' Continuing the missive further, he observed, 'All your life you have maintained a veil of secrecy within the government. How can we trust you to suddenly uphold transparency?' On the spur of the moment, I responded, 'The previous law enjoined some form of secrecy. The Commission would ensure that the public authorities divulge information, as enjoined in the new enactment.' For good measure I added that experience of government functioning should prove an advantage for any regulator.

Setting up a new institution was an opportunity, and also a challenge. For some months, I was the sole Commissioner. Later, as the workload increased, additional members joined, taking the number to 10. The first decision was to locate the office in a place easily accessible to the public. Since the CIC was to sit in judgment over certain government activity, he must not be seen as a part of government machinery. Two floors of a building in the heart of the city shopping centre were hired. Two functionaries deemed essential were a legal adviser and a systems administrator. General Rodrigues, the Governor of Punjab and Wajahat Habibullah, central CIC, inaugurated the office by clicking a button that activated the computer programme for monitoring court work.

During my tenure as CIC, I was often to meet General Rodrigues, who was also Administrator of the Union Territory of Chandigarh. Since he was the final administrative authority for the city of Chandigarh, it was to him I turned for allotting a suitable piece of land to establish a permanent office of the Commission, which could not continue to function from makeshift hired buildings. Seemingly a small matter, it required intervention at that high level to find a local habitation for the institution. Having himself inaugurated the office in the market area, General Rodrigues was aware of the work of the Commission. The Governor is President of the State Red Cross Society. In the year 2007, General Rodrigues decided to allow the Commission to set up its office in the premises of the Red Cross Society at a prime location in Chandigarh. It is another matter that it took 10 years for that decision to be implemented.

The world knew General Rodrigues as a highly decorated soldier, who had distinguished himself as a brilliant Chief of the Army Staff. I came to see another side of his personality, that of a compassionate humanist who, with his equally dedicated wife Jean, supported numerous social causes in the state of Punjab and in the city of Chandigarh. The General injected life into the state Red Cross Society, as he helped numerous volunteers from districts with their activities. Both General and Mrs Rodrigues were delighted to observe the work of our blood bank. While inaugurating a blood donation camp, Jean Rodrigues insisted on being the first to donate, despite the doctors' reluctance to allow her to do so.

Years after he had left Punjab, Meena and I, along with the families of our son and daughter, received the gracious hospitality of General and Mrs Rodrigues in their modest home in Goa. The General personally showed his prize trophies to our very young wide-eyed grandchildren, even as Jean fussed over the adults in our group. The children were dumbstruck that an Army General was personally attending to them and apparently enjoying it.

A commissioner does not wear the robes that judges are required to. I suggested that during public hearings, the CIC and other presiding officers should be attired formally. This entailed the discomfort of wearing a coat and tie in hot and humid weather. Sadly, the dress code of the CIC was not adopted by my colleagues, who considered it an idiosyncrasy. What all the State Information Commissioners did follow rigorously was a practice of prompt disposal of matters before them and announcing decisions in open court on every stipulated date. The Commission discouraged the practice of adjourning hearings, which caused delay. In proceedings under the RTI Act, the litigants were free to make their submissions in person.

The Act lays down a simple procedure for seekers of information from the appointed public information office (PIO). If denied, the seeker can appeal to the next higher authority appointed in the government office. The final appeal against refusal is heard by the Commission. In case it is found that delivery of information has been delayed, the Commission can impose a fine on the PIO concerned. Every even-handed decision in litigation is bound to displease one party or the other. The litigant would plead for a hefty fine to be imposed on the official functionaries for wilfully delaying or denying the supply. The PIO's defence usually was that the official records are not sufficiently organized to collate the material demanded, and that he or she (the PIO) should not be penalized for deficiencies beyond their control. In regard to imposition of fines on officials, the orders of the Commission could not please both parties.

The Information Commission is the premier authority for ensuring transparency in all offices. While at the helm, I had an unusual experience of the conduct of my own commission being challenged in court. Some RTI activists, as they were called, dragged the Commission to the High Court, claiming that the Commission had not adequately replied to some strange questions, such as the floor area of the office, the staff deployed and the like. According to the Act, every authority funded substantially by government is subject to public scrutiny. Thus, the Commission itself was administratively a public authority. The frivolous petition was, of course, dismissed, since records showed that the Commission had been transparent and forthcoming. Taking a leaf from the hospitality and aviation industry, the Commission introduced a feedback form for all litigants, where they could record their level of satisfaction with the experience before the Commission. That the litigants were free to record their opinion about the performance of the commissioners too was deemed an innovation.

Beyond the legal intricacies, how did the RTI Act impact various sections in society? To begin with, unusual demands for information began to emanate, some of these from unexpected quarters. The first off the block were members of the fourth estate. The media realized that knowledge of certain items, hitherto concealed from public view, could be procured at a cost of just 10 rupees. This material could build reputations of investigative journalists, and in some cases promote sensationalism. Next among information seekers were some civil servants. Being themselves the custodians of official record, they deluged public authorities with requests for 'inside' information that helped them in their own service disputes. Businessmen could legitimately pry into official decisions affecting them commercially. Some subordinate judges, who had been disciplined by the High Court, sought information on the reasons for their penalisation. Armed with certain facts, political leaders began to take potshots at rivals. Prisoners found they could question the reasons for solitary confinement, and also seek details about the personal wealth of jailors who might have oppressed them during their incarceration.

The functioning of such hallowed institutions as the Public Service Commissions, the Universities, and even the High Courts and the Supreme Court of India was to some extent under the scanner. One interesting demand for information by a public-spirited activist had the police department in a tizzy. The department was asked to supply a list of all the recommendations received from political leaders for posting and transfer of police officers during the previous two years. The department was compelled to disclose that around 200 political leaders had approached it. In a bizarre twist, the list of the backers of the police officers included leaders from across the political spectrum, including some from opposition parties. Salacious stories were sometimes garnered through the RTI Act. In practice, the Act was found employed to serve individual rights as well as to expose instances of corruption.

On paper, RTI Act conferred on the common man the status of master. According to Section 8 of the Act, 'the information, which cannot be denied to the Parliament or a State Legislature, shall not be denied to any person.' In a way, the power available with every Indian citizen to secure information is greater than that enjoyed by his elected legislator. The Act mandates a time limit of thirty days during which any request under RTI Act is to be served. Indeed where life and liberty are involved, information has to be supplied (by police, etc.) within 48 hours of the filing of request. No such time limit exists in respect of answers to questions in the legislative assembly or Parliament. It was noted, however, that more requests under RTI Act were for items of personal interest to individuals, than for public causes. Few seekers followed the dictum stated by a 19th century British Prime Minister, W.E. Gladstone, 'Your business is not to govern the country, but it is, if you think fit, to call in account those who govern it.' Unfortunately, the authorities were seldom questioned about such crucial public issues as utilization of funds, timely completion of projects, the problems of slums and encroachments in towns, or environmental degradation. Here was public empowerment somewhat dissipated.

All notes recorded in government files, indicating decision making at various levels, were open to disclosure. For civil servants, RTI could be a shield to resist arbitrary decisions, which eventually would become public. Similarly, under an RTI umbrella public spirited political leaders were free to take conscientious decisions fearlessly.

RTI Act expects all officials to use information technology to place all important information regarding its working on its official website. In our state this was found to be virtually impossible, since many records were in disarray. Often officials were prepared to supply, but being unable to expeditiously retrieve the material demanded, became liable for punishment. Furthermore, many Public Information Officers were ill-trained and timid in handling RTI applications. RTI was more feared than hated.

The Act envisions all public authorities in the country as electronically linked to each other. Ideally, the click of a button should bring every item demanded to information seekers, as is the practice in many advanced nations. The country is far from achieving efficiency in basic record management. India boasts of a high quality of information technology, which serves the world. India's IT skills had not been effectively employed to put its own house of data in order.

It was in respect of data management that on one occasion a number of public-spirited activists placed all institutions of the state in a quandary. The activists formally complained to the State Commission under the RTI Act that most of the institutions designated as 'public authorities' had not fulfilled their obligation to place information about their working in the public domain. The complaint listed hundreds of such 'recalcitrants', which included the offices of the Governor of Punjab, the State Legislative Assembly, the High Court of Punjab and Haryana and virtually all the departments of the state government. The complaint was that every authority had failed to fulfil its obligation to publish relevant details about its functioning. The complainants argued that the Act had prescribed a period of 120 days, from the advent of the Act, for the authorities to display the entire material for the public. A full bench, consisting of all the State Information Commissioners, directed all the named authorities to catalogue and display the reference material within a frame of time.

In the year 2006, the central government proposed some amendments that would dilute the provisions of RTI Act. Before these could be placed before Parliament a public debate ensued. The opposition of the day was vehemently against any dilution. An important public figure Anna Hazare, who had commended the Act, threatened to go on hunger strike if the government went ahead. The Government was forced to backtrack. The episode demonstrated that the democratic device was potent enough to cause some apprehension in the establishment. One credo for information stalwarts was summed up by a contemporary writer, Alan Moore in *V for Vendetta*, 'People shouldn't be afraid of their government. Governments should be afraid of their people.'

In regard to information freedom, in India, the political parties in the opposition have invariably been its enthusiastic supporters, while the ruling parties have been comparatively fearful of its impact. Eventually, it was in the year 2019 that the Central Government finally succeeded in amending the RTI Act, 2005, and that too, radically. The new provisions diminish the status and authority of the Commissions, and exempt the governments from several forms of disclosure. The English poet T.S. Eliot was perceptive when he wrote, 'Humankind cannot bear very much reality.' Just like the rest of humankind, the political elite preferred that some realities remain as secure as possible behind what was dubbed by a commentator as the 'paper curtain'.[3]

In October 2006, the first anniversary of the RTI Act was celebrated with much fanfare in a grand function in Vigyan Bhawan, New Delhi, over which the Prime Minister himself presided. Unfortunately, several members of the media and some information activists who had been invited to speak on the occasion, were found to be sulking on the day. Their grouse was that the Commissions were taking too lenient a view when government officials defaulted in parting with information. Wajahat Habibullah, the Central CIC was hard put to persuade the defiant representatives to join the proceedings. The day was saved in a most unexpected manner. Jaspal Bhatti, the noted humorist, had been invited to present a satirical skit on the foibles

3 Herbert N. Foerstel, *Freedom of Information and the Right to Know*, Greenwood Press, 1999.

of government officials, who were depicted hilariously, as they concealed official records awkwardly. Jaspal Bhatti presented the spoof on the bureaucracy with his brand of slapstick humour. The mirthful entertainment on stage kept the audience amused, until the backstage efforts succeeded in wooing back the dissenters. The comedy king had saved the day. To tell the truth, Jaspal Bhatti himself had suffered at the hands of a callous bureaucracy in the state of Punjab. As an electrical engineer, Jaspal, whom I knew well, had to waste years pleading with his employer, the state electricity board to accept his resignation, so that he could pursue his vocation as a comedian par excellence.

Information is knowledge, and as the famous essayist Francis Bacon observed, knowledge itself is power. Reviewing the experiment with the democratic device, it cannot be claimed that its promise of empowering the common man has yet been fulfilled. My days as regulator of information freedom were, however, an exciting practical lesson on the functioning of democracy.

A Tape to Measure Governance

I had retired twice, first as an IAS officer, and five years later, as state Chief Information Commissioner. In the year 2010, my association with the government was unexpectedly revived. The Government of India, followed by the state governments, introduced a form of administrative reform based on appraisal of performance of its officials. A hackneyed joke goes something like this:

'When does a government employee begin to draw pension?'

The pithy answer, 'The day he joins the service!' reflects a cynical perception that government servants in India are paid, not for delivery of results, but for merely attending office. That the quality and nature of their output is not called in question; that in their official appointments, they are not accountable for what they do, or fail to.

As an experiment for bringing greater accountability, the Government of India established a Performance Management Division within the Cabinet Secretariat for monitoring and evaluation of performance of its ministries. On the same pattern, the state governments too established a mechanism for appraisal at the state level. When the Punjab government appointed me as the Adviser for performance management and appraisal for the state, I found myself involved in a novel form of governance reform. My office being in Mahatma Gandhi State Institute for Public Administration in Chandigarh, I was also engaged in some training activities conducted by the Institute. At the national level, a reputed economist by the name of Professor Prajapati Trivedi, who had previously worked at the World Bank in Washington DC, had been named as Secretary, Performance Management for the Government of India.

The actual work of performance appraisal was entrusted to panels of experts, which included retired IAS officers, and also domain specialists in various disciplines. These teams, called Task Force, set up empirical targets for every ministry and department, and measured the results achieved. On paper though a simple arrangement, in practice several unexpected difficulties came to the fore. The biggest obstacle was the bureaucracy itself. As a management expert put it, 'Bureaucracy continues to defend the status quo long after the quo has lost its status' (Lawrence J. Peters). In the state of Punjab, the council of ministers had approved the policy, but many senior civil servants were found to be lukewarm in regard to its implementation. Some senior officers were irked at the mechanism for appraisal, especially the inbuilt system of grading of performance. Since the cabinet of ministers had laid down the ground rules, the officials had to acquiesce, however reluctantly. Many departments were loath to place the analysis on the official website, which would be open to public scrutiny, an essential component of the arrangements.

The system was based on the premise that what gets measured gets done. During the five years of its existence, the Performance Management Division presented its evaluation of all ministries and departments. It also studied the systems in other countries and also in the corporate sector. Along with other members of the national task force, I was able to visit many states. In Punjab, a framework for assessing performance at the district level was brought in place. The Cabinet Secretariat aimed to link the results achieved with the recording of Annual Confidential Reports of senior officers, which determined their career prospects. A pattern of rewarding officials for good performance was also designed. It was expected that the promise of reward and the threat of punishment would galvanise performance within the government.

As it transpired, before the ambitious incentive plan could be made operational, the elected government of Dr Manmohan Singh lost the elections of the year 2014. The new government decided to wind up the performance system, which had promised much, but had not been given time to deliver. The experiment was abandoned midway. Reform in governance is work in progress. Initiatives depend for success on a sustained political will. Every government reforms itself in its own manner. My own role in the process was that of a backseat driver, to offer a route, and to cajole those at the wheel. The experience was rewarding in itself.

EPILOGUE

Close of a Journey

The time of closure of a piece of writing is akin to a parting from a loved one, a moment tinged with sadness. Over a period of months, you have become attached to the creature you were trying to mould. At this stage, it is brought home that no further can you refine the product. A host of readers will now determine its worth.

At the time of farewell, the lover will extol the virtues of the object of his affection, even as he deprecates his own flaws. In much the same manner, I ruminate on the impulses that occasioned the writing of this book. In the process of introspection, it dawns that the years of working in government serve to develop the skills of conciseness and also logical thinking. At the same time, the official milieu stifles spontaneity. By training and experience, a civil servant develops a penchant for capping every narration with a conclusion.

On venturing into good literature, 'the realms of gold' celebrated by the poet Keats, one realises that passages of writing come alive on their own, and entice the reader to look further. Cut and dry solutions emerging in a file might be the basis of a sound administrative decision affecting society, but may not enthrall the common reader for too long.

While engaged in writing, I found myself locked in an ongoing struggle between pure lucidity and creativity in expression. The playwright George Bernard Shaw was perceptive when he averred, 'The single greatest problem in communication is the illusion that it has taken place.' I had to consciously discard several predilections of a civil servant, even as I was describing the travails of one. I have tried to avoid official verbiage, but found it imperative to mention some seemingly mundane processes. An apology is due, with the rider that certain basic issues of governance need to be elucidated for an uninitiated reader. The compelling challenge was to balance form and content. A memoir describes what happened during a lifetime. It is for the writer to adopt a form that will keep his audience engrossed.

The world over, the scourge of the Covid pandemic kept many people housebound during the years 2020 and 2021. In this country there would be hardly a family that did not lose a loved one to the affliction. My wife and I, along with many close friends and relatives, were infected too. Providentially we recovered, although Meena is somewhat the worse for wear. An activity that one could pursue during the dark period was writing. Perhaps the restrictions on movement outside home would have aided the completion of this work.

These pages describe events, sights and sounds encountered along a journey, and present some slices of experience. Since this is not a work of fiction, the author must be pardoned for not adhering to the ancient classical dictum of Aristotle that any story must have a beginning, a middle and an end. In real life, there can be no closure, nor absolute conclusions. A journey too can be enjoyed in itself, irrespective of a destination. The narrative has necessarily to close in media res.

2000, Ropar, Punjab: The author with Dr A.P.J. Abdul Kalam.
(Photo autographed by the President of India in 2003)

2003, Chandigarh: Capt. Amarinder Singh, CM, Punjab, bidding farewell to the author and his wife Meena on the author's retirement.

2013, Chandigarh: The author with Leander Paes,
India's tennis champion, at an event.

2013, Chandigarh: The author signing an agreement with Madrid Tennis
Foundation, Spain, for building young champions.

1980, Chandigarh: The author, as Managing Director at MARKFED, running a 100-m sprint.

1961, Simla, Himachal Pradesh: The author with his brothers, parents and grandparents.

1971, Ropar, Punjab: The author's three-year-old daughter greeting then PM Indira Gandhi.

1920, London: Bharpur Singh, the author's grandfather, a player at the Wimbledon Lawn Tennis Championship, from whom the author inherited his love of the sport.